Make Money Teaching Online

2nd Edition

How to Land Your First Academic Job, Build Credibility, and Earn a Six-Figure Salary

DANIELLE BABB, PhD

Published by: **Mandevilla Press**
Address: **Weston, Connecticut**
Email: **d4eo@optonline.net**

ISBN Number   ISBN-13: 978-1-62704-025-9

Visit the author's websites at: www.thebabbgroup.com
Amazon Author Page: http://www.amazon.com/Danielle-Babb/e/B001IGSS0O
LinkedIn profile: https://www.linkedin.com/in/drdanibabb
Follow her on Twitter at: https://twitter.com/danibabb
Connect with her on Google Plus at: https://plus.google.com/+DaniBabb/posts
Subscribe to her YouTube page: https://www.youtube.com/user/TheBabbGroup

TABLE OF CONTENTS

ACKNOWLEDGEMENTS

Dedication

To my darling daughter Jordy, who I do not expect will read this unless she can swipe the text on her iPad, without whose never-ending persistence and demanding, this book would have been finished about two years ago.

Acknowledgements, With No Meaning Whatsoever To The Order

Jim Mirabella, co-author of version 1 and friend
Bob Diforio, agent and publisher, and my put-his-behind-on-the-line-for-his-clients hero
Leslie Bowman, editor and contributor
Tara Ross, social media expert, author, professor and contributor
The Drunk Guy at the Eatery who's name I forgot, marketing advice extraordinaire
Sharon Jumper, contributor and forum sharer-in-chief
Sharyn Warren, vita contributor
The Anonymous Dean, friend, amazing leader, colleague, contributor who shall remain nameless
Gerad Ross, cover designer
Andrew Carpenter, leader among professors and men, contributor
Debra Touhey, friend, contributor

Dawn Boyer, book format and marketing go-to guru, author

Anyone I Forgot - I'm sorry - I don't remember being absentminded.

~~ Never get so busy making a living that you forget to make a life. -- Anonymous~~

Thanks To Our Client Services Team

Chantel Slack
Bill Nazur
Julie Patterson
Jessica Sanders
Brandi Dougherty
Jonathan Arter
Lana Scroggins

Thank you for your hard work and dedication to our company and clients, and your friendship and support.

FOREWORD

Dr. Jim Mirabella, Associate Professor of Decision Sciences, Jacksonville University

Dr. Danielle Babb is perhaps the foremost authority in the world of online teaching. I had the genuine pleasure and honor of serving as her doctoral advisor, after which she worked for me in one university and with me in several others. Yet my most memorable experience with her was when we collaborated on the best-selling Make Money Teaching Online several years ago. I got to see a side of her that few others have seen, and I was an instant fan. The amount of research for our book was intense and we were thorough and detailed; I felt like she was my doctoral advisor at times. Dani is extremely intelligent, she is a technology whiz, and she has a lot of business savvy along with a drive to succeed unlike any I have ever witnessed. I feel like a better person for having known her and worked with her in so many capacities, and to this day we are still dear friends that just live on opposite sides of the country. The only times I get to see her are when I attend an annual faculty meeting or tune in to Fox News.

I have settled in to a traditional university as a tenured professor while she has taken on new roles in the online teaching world, writing newsletters, consulting, placing faculty, researching, etc. It is only fitting that Dr. Babb take the reins alone in this book, as she has surpassed me and everyone I know in her knowledge and experience regarding online teaching. With the speed of change in this side of academics and technology, there is no one more up to speed and capable of telling the world what is hot, what is not, where to teach, where to avoid, and how to turn a graduate degree into a lucrative at-home profession. She knows what it takes to be a great teacher and she lives it every hour of every day. This book is Dani's way of sharing her knowledge with the world, and I am proud of her for doing so. When we wrote our first book, I was writing as a family man while she was writing as a young, single woman, and now she is a mommy and has transformed, making her knowledge and experience even more valuable. It is with my blessing that I officially pass on my share of the glory from our first book to her, and I am excited to see where she takes it. If she ever started her own online university, I just know she would do it better than anyone, with the best faculty, best technology, and best course designs, and I would be first in line to work for her.

God bless her in her continued journeys.

Chapter 1 - Introduction to Online Teaching

"No trend has changed the face of higher education more than the shift away from a corps of full-time, tenure-track faculty to a contingent instructional workforce. That workforce includes part-time/adjunct faculty, full-time/non-tenure-track faculty, and graduate employees. Together these employees now make up an amazing 70% of the 1.3 million employee instructional workforce in higher education."
— U.S. Department of Education

According to figures from the Survey of Online Learning conducted by Babson Survey Research Group, at least 7.1 million students are taking at least one online course. This is up from 1.6 million in 2002. The same study revealed that 90% of academic leaders believe it is likely or very likely that a majority of higher education students will take at least one online class within five years. (Babson, 2014) To keep up with this demand, most universities must work with faculty who are trained and experienced as distance educators, whether part-time or full-time. This book takes you on a journey of understanding how and why online schools have been started, deciphering the good schools from the bad, obtaining jobs as online faculty, training for the faculty positions, retaining contracts, and managing courses. It will show you how to begin earning a living teaching online and then expanding your work into full-time pay if you wish!

Make Money Teaching Online (edition 1)

Welcome to the new edition of Make Money Teaching Online! It was a long battle to be able to update this book for experienced professors and new educators looking to enter into the industry. Suffice it to say the book publishing business is not always author-friendly! I am very excited to be able to release this book with updated information to help people who want to enter the rewarding career of teaching online, or find additional jobs in the marketplace. In the first version of this book, published by Wiley in 2007, Make Money Teaching Online was co-authored by Dr. Jim Mirabella and me – both of us at that time part-time faculty, making a living teaching online as what are often classified as *full-time part-timers* – or as we have called it, being "adjunctpreneurs." It is hard to believe it's been nine years since that book was written! Every piece of advice we gave you in the first version of the book was derived from personal knowledge, interviews with college deans, and/or research. We didn't just talk or write about it; we both did it. While my company, The Babb Group, Inc., had been established as a very part-time project to help professors find jobs, during 2011 and beyond, my company started growing with a focus on education – both from the perspective of faculty but also helping universities and students. We began working with universities and department chairs to help make potential students aware of what they offer, and to provide new faculty and seasoned professors more information on opportunities with current and timely information on hunting for work. This version of the book is not just based on my own experiences. Throughout the book, I will include information and data from interviews in the past four years of consulting in the industry and helping people find work, learning what works and what doesn't, and offering counsel and advice to thousands of faculty members.

In the first version of this book, a message from both Jim and me was included in chapter one. While remaining friends and partners on projects, Jim and I have gone different directions – he has focused on his tenure position at a state college and I have continued the life as an entrepreneur adjunct, helping others reach their goals in education. In this second version of the book, Jim and I continued to focus on our own goals and while he shares enthusiasm for the book and its purpose, we are not co-authoring this version. That does not mean you won't see his great advice throughout the manuscript!

A Message from Dani

While working for a university for seven years as an information technology (IT) director and going to school during the day to earn a bachelor's degree, I decided to also pursue a master of business administration (MBA) in the evenings. Managing these three obligations was very challenging (and I didn't even have a family yet – but I learned more about that later!); I decided the payoff would be worth it, and I was able to make it all work. Along the way, one of the department chairpersons for another school at the same university asked me to teach night classes on information technology for her program. I was intimidated and had limited public speaking experience, but I said yes and made a go of it. After that, the Blackboard online system was introduced to me as a tool by which I could teach an occasional class. I would be required to teach live (although Blackboard also supports otherwise), but online instead of in a classroom. I was immediately taken with the idea; it would help ease the stress of going into a classroom one or two nights per week in addition to my own courses, and I had moved quite far away from the school months earlier. Plus, my new job was requiring more travel. By the time I finished my MBA about two years later, I was teaching a full load of courses while still serving as an IT director. I moved on to another IT job in a nearby city, but still taught night classes and online classes for the university for some time thereafter. I pushed more and more to hold my classes online because the commute to the university was easily two hours; after a long day of work, it was overwhelming.

In 2002, I decided to pursue a PhD—this time, entirely online. By this point I was tired of the endless downsizing, what I viewed as the shortsightedness of some Fortune 500 chief information officers (CIOs), and the frustration that went along with corporate America's lack of loyalty. The online degree I decided to pursue was through Capella University – it was extremely flexible, was regionally accredited, and had an excellent reputation in the online world. It was one of very few online programs with doctorates at the time.

I took classes for about 18 months at an extremely accelerated pace, since the average time to complete class work for a PhD is about seven years. I didn't have to sit in a classroom; I was able to stay at my office late (I was still working as an IT director for a Fortune 500 home builder at the time). I could and did work well into the night reading, turning in assignments, and posting messages on discussion boards that I could read at midnight, at noon, on the road, in the United States, or out of the country. The flexibility I experienced as an online learner, as millions of others know, was incredible.

By the time I got to the dissertation process, I had heard from my entire committee how they enjoyed adjunct life; one was sipping cocktails by the pool while taking calls and working! I wasn't trying to avoid working hard, but I did like the appeal of the flexibility and I had seen it first-hand years before, when I was working with Blackboard to teach students remotely. I found my committee provided incredible service, guidance, and advice despite their laptop and traveling lifestyles. I finished my doctorate and, within a couple of months, had several teaching jobs online that were paying the same amount of money as my six-figure day job. I was able to handle both careers for a few months, working from Starbucks on my lunch break and working well into the wee hours of the morning before getting up to go to my day job again. Ultimately I decided to give online teaching 100% of my effort and time, thus beginning my small business of one, me, an online teacher. I found myself able to teach from remote places like Ningbo, China while traveling endlessly (and tirelessly) and was very happy with the flexible life that online adjuncting had provided, while still being able to contribute significantly to the lives of others. There are of course downsides to everything, but we will get to them later.

I quickly realized that, as in any business, there is a strong list of do's and don'ts. While my initial list was created back in 2005 and 2006 for us to draft version one of the book, many of the same principles still apply today. There are ways to approach department chairs and university presidents with your curriculum vitae, and there are ways not to. It's a steep learning curve and can be a costly one. One of my goals in this book is to help eliminate those missteps for others and create a clearer, smoother path. I also learned the online teaching community is very tightly knit and quite cozy, despite seeming quite large, and many people you meet at one institution work for many others you are also likely to run across. Negativity about your work spreads like wildfire, but so do positive comments. Obviously, the goal is to minimize the negative and maximize the positive.

Determining what you're best at, the particular value you add, and being the absolute best at it, will ensure your success for a long time and will increase your salary considerably. I enjoy working with learners as their mentors, much as my mentor did, encouraging them to do their best and pursue their dreams. I have more opportunity to travel both within the United States and internationally now than I ever did as a senior manager in industry (although my now 4-year-old child limits that a bit!), and I enjoy the flexibility and academic freedom I used to envy in others with good teaching jobs. The difference is that I, along with other adjuncts, am an entrepreneur and I manage my online teaching as a business.

Back in 2007 when this book was first released, many of my colleagues who also teach online were skeptical about a book that revealed many so-called "secrets" of teaching online; they wanted them kept secret, limiting competition. After many conversations with these colleagues, department chairs, deans, and friends, I decided that this new field offers a great opportunity that others need to be aware of, especially those juggling many responsibilities and who still need a good income to take care of their financial obligations and/or families. The demand for online teachers is growing and existing faculty will survive the influx of new teachers (and the most recent changes in education, too). I became convinced that writing the first version of the book, along with my former comprehensive and dissertation mentor, Dr. Jim Mirabella, was the best thing to do, and our respective schools have supported the endeavor. In this new version, my goal is to give you the same strong advice, but updated for the current market with current surveys and trends.

Many of the professors who were upset we were "revealing the secret" back in 2006 and 2007 have jumped on board, and are now part of our Online Teaching Forum in Facebook and Yahoo, providing advice and counsel to other professors. My goal is to mentor you, assist you in finding online teaching positions at online universities, and help make being a teacher a sought-after job, as it should be! In turn, we'll be helping the schools we love to work for by aiding them in their search for excellent candidates. What more can we ask for?

Substantial Opportunity Awaits

The world of online education is at our fingertips, and this means that many of us have an opportunity to work as full-time or part-time faculty members in an online capacity from the comfort of our homes—and earn the college credits needed to do that job in the same manner. The enrollment growth in online education, whether at for-profit or nonprofit schools, is staggering. Some of you already have a degree in hand and some teaching experience; some of you have a degree without teaching experience; and some of you lack both. Whatever the case, before you jump in headfirst you need to know the market, what is required, and how to navigate the system. This book will teach you how to prepare for an online teaching career, where to look for jobs, how to get contracts, and how to keep them.

Can I Do This?

You may be familiar with online schools; you may even have heard of the big ones like the University of Phoenix or Laureate Education. The question you ask is, "Can I do this?" Yes, you can, if you have the degree, motivation, and determination! No matter what stage of your career you are in, there are opportunities waiting for you in the world of online teaching.

But I've Never Taught Online Before!

Have you heard the cliché "Everyone has to start somewhere"? The same holds true for online teaching. Every school you work for will require you to undergo a certain number of training hours and/or assignments. In short, the schools will train you! In fact, many even *pay* for training. Have you ever taught a group of people at work how to do something on their new computer system? Have you ever taught your children how to do their algebra problems? Have you taught your parents how to use their email? Have you run brown-bag lunches at your place of employment to help everyone with a new training program or process? Did you train counterparts or teams in the military? Have you ever given a guest lecture or created or given a presentation, or informally trained a group of people in community service? Most likely we've all taught someone at some point, and yes, this experience matters. It shows you can explain something clearly in a patient, empathetic, and detail-oriented way. It needs to be detailed in your curriculum vitae, which I will discuss later in this book.

Universities use several online teaching systems, so even with online teaching experience you probably will need some additional training for each new school you work for. Don't let this discourage you—you are also reading this book, which is a big step toward learning what to do to begin teaching online.

Who Can Teach?

To begin exploring this, I'll look a bit at the individuals who are making online teaching their careers. Many teachers have doctorates or they have master's degrees and are pursuing doctorates. About

65% of our clients at The Babb Group, Inc. started their careers with their master's and about half of those ended up pursuing their doctorates. There are also former military personnel, full-time faculty members who are looking for additional income, full-time faculty who want to leave their full-time position from fear of downsizing, corporate individuals who are degreed subject-matter experts wanting additional money and success, and degreed homemakers.

Another huge pool are individuals who are retired, need additional income, and have the experience and education to back up their new careers. Some people with bachelor's degrees are looking to tutor or teach in online high schools. The opportunities are endless and the possibilities are great. I'll explore each one throughout the book, but will now provide a brief overview of the many possibilities. You will quickly see how this relates to you.

Doctoral Degrees

The most coveted degree in academia is the doctorate. The doctorate is the highest degree you can earn, although you can further your education in a post doctorate program or in another degree program altogether. The average doctoral degree takes longer to earn than a medical degree. The average time for completion, by most estimates, is seven years past the completion of the previous degree (although you can earn it much more quickly if you have the time and determination). This is definitely a heavy undertaking, but well worth every effort. If you have a doctorate (sometimes referred to as a terminal degree) or are pursuing your doctorate, the opportunities you have available to you are endless and growing by the day. Your doctorate will give you an edge over other individuals who may be applying for the same academic position that you are, and may even give you an advantage in the corporate world. Your doctorate also paves the way for you to be able to teach at any level, from doctorate down to high school. One benefit to having a terminal degree is the fine print in many job ads for online teachers, which reads something like "or terminal degree in a similar or related discipline." This means that if you have a PhD in business but the school wants a statistics professor, having the PhD may allow you to teach the course anyway. This is a pretty big change from the time version one of this book was released.

Master's Degrees

If you have a master's degree, you have plenty of opportunity for teaching. If you decide you want to make a career for yourself in academia, you should consider pursuing a doctorate, but you can still build a solid career with a master's degree. You will be qualified to teach in some master's programs and many bachelor's program. The key is the 18 graduate hour qualification requirement. For accreditation purposes, most schools will require that you have 18 graduate hours in the area that you are teaching. This is very rigidly defined by some deans and loosely defined by others. I have clients with 18 graduate hours in marketing and finance who are teaching algebra, because the dean took the word "math" from each of the course descriptions, combined it and called it a wrap. I have clients who work for deans who are very strict about how they define the 18 graduate hour rule.

Bachelor's Degrees

If you have a bachelor's degree and wish to pursue a master's degree, teaching is great justification to do so because it will open more teaching doors for you. Some schools will even let you go from your bachelor's right to your doctorate, so check around. Although the opportunity to make a good living is not at the same level as a master's or higher, you can still earn supplemental income teaching online or tutoring with a bachelor's degree.

Many of our clients choose to become private tutors, and join groups like our 'Hire Higher Educators' to look for leads and promote themselves on sites like Craigslist. Another option is to look for associate-level programs online and certification programs for your particular area of expertise. For instance, some schools offer certificates in fields such as accounting or finance that don't lead to degrees. As such, they often don't require more than a bachelor's degree to teach in them.

Professional experience counts here, so be sure to communicate your experience effectively. Also, read the section on online high schools in chapter four to explore further teaching opportunities.

Former Military

Among the highly competent online professors I know, many are former military personnel (including

Jim Mirabella, co-author of Version 1 of this book, and former Air Force captain). We meet lots of former military in online education. Military experience is highly regarded in academia, and having this experience is often a bonus when looking for jobs. You may find that many deans who interview you want to talk about your military experience before your teaching experience.

Having served in the military, you've already displayed honor, professionalism, courage, leadership, and, no doubt, incredible persistence. Who wouldn't want someone with those credentials on their team? You will still need a degree, but often the government will help with this. Use this advantage as much as possible; after all, you deserve the opportunity and have an incredible network within academia based on your military experience, even if you don't yet realize it.

Professionals

Professionals have a leg up in teaching online. In contrast to traditional education, where some professors have never left college, many online schools actually require that faculty have professional experience, not just a long list of degrees. Your professional experience will help you bring real-life examples to an online classroom, which is vitally important. You will see this exemplified in the section of chapter six on curriculum vitae (CV) writing and cover letters.

Try to categorize your professional experience, then document it as well as you can; these are the areas you're most qualified to teach online, provided you have a degree. The combination of education and professional experience can make you a valuable asset to a university because of the current emphasis on being a scholar-practitioner as opposed to strictly a scholar as in the old days or in traditional schools.

When you are an academically oriented scholar, yet you also have experience in your field that you can apply to the real world to show students why the work they are studying matters today, this is highly valuable. You just need to know how to leverage this professional experience in writing and on an interview, because your experience counts more than you may think it does. In online teaching, experience is often required, which means your professional experience may be not only a leg up, but may also be an absolute must. Being a professional does not exclude you from teaching; some night colleges and adult learning programs actually require it.

Homemakers or Stay-at-Home Parents

In 2007, I did a Today Show spot on NBC about teaching online (you can watch that oldie on my YouTube channel at youtube.com/thebabbgroup). After that, dozens of stay-at-home parents decided to become online teachers and it is with great joy that I can say I personally know each one. They have given back many times over to the online community in our Facebook forum, and are living proof that this can and does happen (by the way, you can access this forum at facebook.com/groups/onlineprofessors).

Many homemakers or stay-at-home parents have left their careers for a while (or forever) to raise children. Many homemakers are also well-degreed, professional individuals who are outstanding online teachers. You can teach while your infants nap or while your school age child is in class. Fifteen percent of our clients who look for work using our job search tools are full-time, stay-at-home parents, and part-time professors.

Retired Individuals

Many online teachers today are retired men and women who are done with their time in corporate America, yet don't want to (or can't afford to) leave the workforce. This may be due to their need for supplemental income, a challenge, or just a chance to give back to the community and impart knowledge to the next generation. The knowledge and experience that retired individuals bring, including professional experience and education, are highly sought-after in education.

For example, in one of the schools I work for, about half of my colleagues are retired. They bring a wise view of the world, incredible experience usually from multiple organizations, and a broader vision of how things fit and why education is so important. Many tell stories of living near poverty until they worked their way to a master's or doctoral degree; what could be more motivating than to read notes from a professor with this type of insight?

Retired folks are not dismissed in online education as they often are in corporate America, quite the contrary. They are respected for the tremendous wisdom, insight, and multiple experiences they bring to teaching.

Physically Disabled

Although a person can teach in front of a class while physically disabled, doing so does have its complications with regard to travel, as well as the logistics of lecturing and grading papers. I have worked with dozens of physically disabled professors who use tools and technology to help them teach. The online teaching world puts handicapped people on an almost-level playing field. Even if your handicap is speech-related (like stuttering) and would keep you from lecturing, it would not hinder your online teaching potential. It is only in the interest of privacy for dear colleagues that I do not share more here.

Chapter 2 - Online Schools: Are They for Real?

"Teaching is not a lost art, but the
regard for it is a lost tradition."
— Jacques Barzun

Many of us were told by our parents that the most important thing we could do was get a college education. They told us to study, study, study, because the best schools would accept only the brightest students, and without a college education we would never go far. Just a couple of decades ago there was a limited number of colleges with a limited number of open slots, and most classes were held during the day when adults were working. What if you were an adult and hadn't yet completed or even begun your college education?

If you did not take this advice seriously, you probably found yourself with few options for an education beyond trade school and community college, as they have open enrollment policies without a limit on the number of students admitted. Those who decided to forgo a college education probably found themselves looking for ways to get a degree part-time while maintaining a full-time job and possibly raising a family. These personal and professional barriers often made it impossible to achieve educational goals.

Fast-forward to today and you will find that the Internet boom has taken the academic world by storm. As a result, there are countless opportunities to get a college degree without leaving home. Also, there is an entirely new career path for many: that of an online faculty member.

In 2006, many faculty and students were skeptical about the phenomenon known as online education. We heard questions like, "Is it for real? How rigorous are online schools? Can a person really learn this way? Can a person really teach this way? Is it accepted as valid and legitimate by corporate America? Would a college hire you to teach if you have an online graduate degree? Are these schools even accredited? What kinds of colleges are out there hiring online faculty? Aren't they just all a bunch of diploma mills? Why would anyone want to teach online? What kinds of faculty are they hiring? What's the catch?" These are all valid questions, and many have been addressed nearly nine years later. We will take a more thorough look.

Is Online Education for Real?

Yes, online education *is* for real. In 1995, you might have been given a strange look if you told anyone about a degree you earned online. Most likely, that strange look was one of doubt and suspicion that you merely bought a diploma. Now Internet courses are so common and so accessible that you can earn a recognized degree from a well-known university or college online, even if that school is across town, the nation, or the world.

Many state schools have online programs (and this is a growing area for enrollments and for faculty positions) and community colleges are offering courses online. Internet access and ambition are the only requirements. There are many reasons for this trend: Online learning is on each individual's schedule; less travel time makes it more convenient; many programs are self-paced; and there is a wide variety of degree programs online to fit each individual's budget.

There has been a recent trend in new flexible path programs, offering students more flexible paths to degree completion and more customized approaches to learning. Competency-based programs are also becoming more common, with students (primarily business professionals) receiving credit based on demonstrated competencies using direct assessments. According to a 2005 Sloan Consortium report, "Growing by Degrees: Online Education in the United States," over 60% of schools offering face-to-face courses also offer online courses. Forty-three percent of schools with online programs offer degrees in business; 44% offer a master's program online. Over 50% of the academic leaders in higher education now see online education as a critical long-term strategy, with the largest supporters being institutions offering associate degrees.

Now, ten years later, the publication by Allen & Seaman from the Babson Survey Research Group titled "Changing Course: Ten Years of Tracking Online Education in the United States" sheds light on some trends over the past ten years. The authors note that in every year they have reported, enrollments have increased at rates in excess of those of overall higher education (2013). The proportion of students taking at least one online course is at an all-time high in their Jan. 2013 report.

Are Online Schools Less Rigorous?

As online teachers and experts on this subject, we are often asked by those we mentor and by potential teachers whether online degree programs are as rigorous as traditional programs. The answer? In many ways, they are *more rigorous* than programs at traditional schools. Why? Because accrediting bodies, which we'll get into later in more detail, didn't buy into online schools in the beginning. As a result, online schools had to work harder to achieve the same status as traditional schools. Many of the "bad eggs" in online education have been weeded out, particularly in the last two years. Some in academia don't like online education, and many Ivy League schools, and those protecting their traditional ways, don't agree that the programs are as rigorous.

However, many of the founders of online schools came from traditional academia. Consequently, many online schools have traditional academics as their core faculty. Is there still some prejudice out there? Sure. But you won't care when you start teaching, earning a great living, and enjoying the well-deserved respect of your peers. The Babson Survey notes that in the first report in their series in 2003, 57% of academic leaders rated learning outcomes in online education as "the same or superior to those in face-to-face" (2013). They note that the number is now 77%. Interestingly, they also report that 30% of chief academic officers believe their faculty accepts the value and legitimacy of online education (which is down from 2004).

Can a Student Really Learn College-Level Material Online?

Yes, a person can really learn online. In fact, in many cases, a person can learn more efficiently online than in traditional classes. There are three different types of learning styles – visual, auditory, and kinesthetic. Visual learners, comprising 60% of the population, need to see the material to learn it, and they can accomplish this easily online. Online courses are, by and large, visual in nature, and learners are able to take their time with the material and read during days/hours that best suit their schedules and energy levels.

Auditory learners, comprising 30% of the population, need to hear the material to learn it. In a traditional classroom, they get this in abundance since lectures predominate in these classes; recently, numerous audio tools have been introduced, in which colleges put lectures that students would normally have attended in person on a website for download or online streaming to smart phones. Online courses often have an audio component in which PowerPoint slides come with a recording or in which video clips show an instructor or outside expert speaking on the subject matter. Some faculty use slideshow tools to combine audio and video. This has allowed auditory learners who may have had difficulty learning online to take an online class with success.

Kinesthetic learners, comprising 10% of the

population, need to actively learn, often by physically doing something. Whereas a visual learner can learn from watching a chemistry experiment and an auditory learner can learn from listening to the experiment being discussed, a kinesthetic learner must actually repeat the experiment to most efficiently learn from it. In online courses, technology has advanced to a point where a learner can actively participate in a lesson by using a mouse (and at some universities, participating in a live lecture). There is software that allows you to dissect a frog in simulation on your computer screen or run computer networking and security simulations with students. In most online courses, students will solve problems or write out their thoughts and then submit them, making for an active environment that is, in many respects, tailor-made for kinesthetic learners.

In a nutshell, students can definitely learn online – provided, of course, that they want to learn and are willing to do the work involved. Some students who tend to be shy in class or have issues speaking in front of others will prefer online environments because they can express themselves without feeling self-conscious. Additionally, those with serious time constraints can work during the day, take care of the family at night, and still find time for school because they are not being roped into a particular class schedule. As you might imagine, this often requires more self-discipline than traditional models, but with perseverance, online learning can be exceptionally rewarding and an incredible way to enhance one's career.

Can a Professor Really Teach This Way?

As Jim and I explained in version one of this book, and since then, thousands of professors in our forum have attested to, yes you can indeed teach online. However, the skills needed to be a good online teacher are not the same as those needed by classroom teachers. A traditional classroom will test your speaking and listening skills and your ability to manage short stints of time while engaging a class of students consistently. Online courses challenge you in a different way; they will test your writing skills, responsiveness, ability to manage a large number of students, use of technology, use of integrative assignments, retention, and day in, day out time management skills.

Also, whereas traditional classrooms generally don't have prying eyes watching your courses and your work, often online courses are reviewed by individuals responsible for making sure you are doing your job since it's easy for them to log in and view a course. Both environments test your knowledge of the subject matter and your ability to assess students.

Some people are not cut out to teach in either environment, and some thrive in both environments. Teaching in an online program does not mean you cannot teach in a traditional environment, and vice-versa. Many faculty teach both on-ground and online. In a traditional course, students can hide in the back of a classroom, but they cannot hide online – you will know who is participating and who is not. In large university on-site or on-ground classes, this may not be the case and classroom discussions can often get out of control. In an online classroom, however, you can easily maintain the control of an online discussion (although sometimes it is difficult to get the discussion started online if you have a bunch of students who just like to piggyback off each other's work). For instance, you might have a learner who copies sections of peers' work into his or her own post.

Contrary to what you may believe if you have never tried online education, a teacher can truly get to know an online student, often better than a traditional student. You can more easily gauge study habits, work ethic, personality, attitude, and desire to earn a degree; you will learn to pay attention to those you need to watch and what you need to watch them for. There are several strategies you can use when dealing with learners who are working unethically in the classroom: knowing each student's work; keeping copies of posts and documents to compare work; using plagiarism tools; and typing text into Google to see if exact matches come up. Chances are the school you work for will have its own solution and will want you to follow its procedures. You can definitely teach online despite this nuance; after all, plagiarism isn't exactly a new concept. Whenever you run into an issue that makes you question whether you can truly teach this way, keep in mind that chances are someone else has already thought of a solution.

Sometimes you may question whether your work is effective. When former students tell you of their accomplishments, thanks to what they learned from you, it becomes apparent that you can indeed teach online, and it is this feedback that keeps dedicated instructors wanting to come back for more. Such praise, and knowing you have made a difference in someone's life, is what should and does feed a teacher's soul.

Online Degree Legitimacy in Corporate America

Companies in corporate America that offer tuition reimbursement pay for accredited online education. Would any sound business pay for something that it didn't believe was legitimate? With over 80% of individuals throughout their college careers taking at least one class online, how can businesses not recognize online courses? There was a time when you might have felt uncomfortable applying for a job with your degree from the University of Phoenix, for example, but now you would be hard-pressed to find a large organization without a manager who has graduated from there or a similar degree program. Pressure to get a degree while maintaining job performance has essentially forced employees to consider alternatives, and online education has quickly become the most popular option for many. The incredible strength and growth of the Internet and the general acceptance of "online anything" in a global marketplace have only helped.

According to a survey conducted by Rasmussen College (this is a school – but there are other studies correlating this data), "Are online degrees accepted by employers? Survey results you might not expect!" the acceptance of distance degrees is rising sharply as Americans' trust in the Internet grows. Rasmussen's survey of more than 100 middle and senior management positions across all industries indicated 18% of respondents are extremely likely to hire an online degree graduate and an additional 28.5% said they are very likely to do so. About half of managers did not appear to be concerned about where the degree was earned. A survey some of us may be more apt to trust (simply because it isn't published by an institution that offers online courses) is one conducted by the Society for Human Resource Management (cited in the same Rasmussen article). This survey found that 79% of participants had hired a candidate with an online degree in the past 12 months. Fontana, regional vice president of Manpower, noted, "rarely do employers question the authority of online programs in today's world." I believe one of the reasons for this is the regional accreditation and specific discipline accreditation that many online institutions now have, and the emergence of non-profits and state schools into the online world.

Can You Get Hired to Teach with an Online Degree?

Of course! With the number of online programs growing each year, opportunities for online faculty are growing, too. Many professors teach in traditional programs with their online degrees – I am living proof of that; as are thousands of faculty with whom we work. Schools have more demand than supply in many cases, so they are less concerned about university ranking than about accreditation. Trend data from the U.S. Department of Education, available on their website, clearly indicates the move toward adjunct and part-time positions, with about half of all faculty positions being part-time. In the past year, there has been additional hiring in full-time positions also. The growth in the online environment makes holding an online degree an even stronger position. There will always be some who will question your degree (if it's anything short of Ivy League), but remember that there are thousands of places that will hire you.

According to the U.S. Department of Education, in 2003 there were about 540,000 part-time faculty members in the nation, and this number is even greater now due to the tremendous online boom since then. In 2011, there were approximately 762,000 part-time faculty employed, and this does not necessarily reflect adjunct and contract work which increases the numbers even more (National Center for Education Statistics, 2011) There are plenty of opportunities to build your career and numerous growth areas in our field. If your heart's desire is to teach at a specific school, then be proactive and ask the dean what he or she looks for in prospective faculty. Don't be afraid to network and reach out.

Are All Online Schools Accredited?

No, not all online schools are accredited. We have made the decision not to work for unaccredited schools, but that doesn't mean you can't work for them. Let me explain why, since this is often a controversial issue. Teaching jobs are sometimes like credit cards – you have to have one to get one. There are times when it makes sense in our careers to get experience. You can still offer your best to students, knowing that they have chosen that institution for a reason and it is our job to educate them. Some faculty stay with these schools, even when their workload is strong. There are also different types of accreditation, discussed later in this book. We find accreditation is one criterion that is important when reviewing schools to work for; personally, I do not work for unaccredited schools, but that is a personal choice you will make for your own personal or professional reasons. In the beginning, you may have to work for one or two to get experience under your belt and build up your resume. The same rule applies when choosing where to go to school. The goal of accreditation is to ensure that education provided by institutions of higher education meets acceptable levels of quality.

There are many accrediting bodies that are not legitimate, but that allow a school to call itself accredited; the school must be *regionally* accredited for its accreditation to have significant value. There are six regional accrediting bodies in the United States: the New England Association of Schools and Colleges (NEASC at www.neasc.org), the North Central Association of Schools and Colleges (NCA at www.ncaciche.org), the Middle States Association of Colleges and Schools (MSA at www.msache.org), the Southern Association of Colleges and Schools (SACS at www.sacs.org), the Western Association of Schools and Colleges (WASC at www.wascweb.org), and the Northwest Association of Schools and Colleges (NWCCU at www.cocnasc.org).

These bodies list their accredited schools on their websites. If you earn a degree from an online school that is regionally accredited by one of these associations, you can be assured that it will be as valid as a degree from any traditional university (although some academics may disagree with this, our research from clients suggests this is the case).

Regional accreditation provides inherent validity that no other process or measure can, and it helps to ensure that your credits are transferable (although this is never a guarantee). Most employers will definitely accept your degree, and if there is tuition assistance, the program will qualify. Schools that are not accredited may be teaching the subjects well, but employers often will not help with tuition, graduate schools won't take your credits, and no respectable school will hire an adjunct with an unaccredited degree.

The Distance Education and Training Council (DETC at www.detc.org) offers legitimately accredited degrees. Through its own research, though, it admits that DETC degrees are not accepted as widely as regionally accredited ones. The problem occurs when you want to take your DETC degree and go for another degree. Many schools will not accept your units as transfer credits.

You definitely want to earn your degree from a regionally accredited college, and then subsequently teach for one. Note that there are also forms of accreditation that are tied to specific programs, such as that of the Association to Advance Collegiate Schools of Business (AACSB), and while they are excellent to have, the regional accreditation is a core requirement first and foremost.

What Kinds of Colleges Are Offering Online Courses?

Just a generation or two ago, the only types of universities in existence were not-for-profit, traditional schools often remembered more for their sports teams than their academics. You would find tenured professors who were set in their ways and lifetime academics who believed that you weren't learning anything if you used a computer to do it and who were available only to students who happened to catch them in their offices during their limited weekly office hours. Now there are four types of universities: (1) not-for-profit, traditional universities; (2) not-for-profit, nontraditional universities; (3) for-profit, nontraditional universities; and (4) for-profit, traditional universities. The world is watching this industry intently, from the perspectives of students, teachers, and employers of alumni. There has also been increased government scrutiny on the for-profit sector, specifically.

Not-for-profit, traditional universities are still the most common educational institutions; you cannot watch a college football game without seeing two of them in action. Many of these places are just now beginning to enhance their classrooms with some distance learning, but many have yet to offer courses that are 100% online, in part due to the resistance of their faculty. These are great universities to watch for future work, and we actively do this as part of our job lead service. These universities are campus-bound, have tight entrance requirements, use traditional semester schedules (often 16 weeks long), and serve traditional students (ages 18 to 25). Some of these schools are now seeing their enrollments drop as students question their need to sit in a classroom. This was partly driven by the high-tech era in which many individuals got rich with an idea and a website, and decided school was best kept at a minimum while dreams were envisioned and goals were set and accomplished. Whatever the reason, the demand for online education is rising faster than demand for traditional methods. The only major exception to this is the typical college-age, college-bound high school senior, who follows the traditional path of going to a four-year college after high school.

Public university tuition is lower due to state funding, whereas private universities are expensive. We have seen a trend recently of significant pushback on for-profit education that charges a premium for tuition, even though this has been the case for decades in the private institution sector. In traditional academia, you might also expect to see a teaching assistant delivering the lectures on many occasions, while the assigned professor is conducting research necessary to keep his or her position and to bring in grant money to the university (and work towards tenure). Adjuncts often enjoy teaching for these traditional institutions, and if you are taking an entrepreneurial approach to your work as an educator (working for different institutions in different sectors to maintain a workload), then this is a great way to help diversify your workload.

Most, if not all, of the nontraditional and bi-traditional (i.e., a combination of traditional and nontraditional, sometimes called hybrid) universities are involved in online education, and some are 100% online. These institutions are where you can hope to build your career as an adjunct, or combine full-time, part-time, and adjunct jobs into an academic career. They have many forms of delivery methods and semester length. In 2007, we noted in version one of our book that Webster University has a traditional campus in St. Louis, Missouri, but offers courses at more than 100 sites throughout the world; at these sites, classes meet for nine-week semesters, one night per week for four hours. The traditional 36 contact hours is upheld but in fewer weeks than the traditional semester. Central Michigan University has sites throughout the United States; classes meet Friday evening and all day Saturday for three weekends, thereby also totaling 36 contact hours. Other nontraditional schools offer classes in an accelerated format, meeting for less than 36 contact hours; the University of Phoenix, for example, meets one night per week for five weeks. Still other nontraditional programs employ a hybrid format in which classes meet face-to-face for a specified number of contact hours, and online for the remaining hours.

Some institutions are beginning to use online synchronous technologies as an option for the face-to-face component. Purely online programs also fit into this nontraditional category, with semesters ranging from 5 to 16 weeks. Some online schools have a rigid schedule of weekly assignments; others allow students to work at their own pace, possibly completing a course very quickly. The point is that there are no set rules for these schools; physical contact hours have become less important since assignments are online and discussions and chats are viewed as adequate substitutes. A three-credit course is more a function of the workload than of class time hours.

Diploma Mills and Scams

Many people ask if online schools are just diploma mills (institutions that merely print out diplomas, but fail to educate anyone, essentially allowing a consumer to buy a degree). Unfortunately, some of the schools operating online truly are diploma mills. Some are not accredited, are completely unethical, and don't exactly make your vita sparkle. Others may even be regionally accredited, but they just take your money, make you endure courses with little substantive content, and give away inflated grades; those in academia know which schools these are by reputation. Accredited or not, diploma mills are the schools you don't really want to work for, be associated with, or receive a piece of paper from.

Many of you have received one of those emails offering you a PhD in two weeks—all you have to do is to send in $1,000. If you are foolish enough to send in your money, you will indeed receive a diploma in the mail from a legally created, but unaccredited school. You were sold a piece of paper, not an education. In an article in GetEducated.com, Vicky Phillips noted that next to your home, education is often the biggest investment you will ever make. An education has become vital to the workforce, so companies selling bogus degrees have proliferated. In the article "What's a Diploma Mill?" David Linkletter of the Texas Higher Education Coordinating Board, an organization that regulates degree granting by private institutions in the state, says, "Just to make people go through hoops of some sort doesn't mean they're going through the right hoops" (Bartlett & Scott, Chronicle.com, Volume 50).

College scams are closely tied, if not directly related, to diploma mills. Military.com published an article titled "Avoiding Diploma Mills" (http://www.military.com/education/finding-a-school/avoiding-diploma-mills.html) noting that some key words of diploma mills are "no hassle," "no transcript," or they use a post office box for people to send money in exchange for paper, among many other red flags. Diploma mills are generally not licensed to operate in any state, are not authorized to provide tuition assistance, the GI Bill or Federal Financial Aid, and are not accredited by education agencies. Advertisements urging us to: "Earn a college degree in 60 days!" "Get your high school diploma now!" "Get this prestigious unaccredited degree!" are some of the email headlines from diploma mills I have seen in my own inbox. Usually the focus is on quickly "earning" what you "need."

Schools often choose names that sound like legitimate universities, like Columbia State University, which sounds good until the president ended up in prison. The scam was attempting to trick people into thinking it was the real, regionally accredited Columbia University. As a teacher or a student, you do not want to be affiliated with these schools in any way whatsoever.

High school diploma mills are popping up as well. Since the mid-1990s when the Internet took off at a consumer level, the number of these bad apples has grown dramatically. If you want to know that your degree will be accepted by employers and academia, it absolutely must be from an accredited institution.

In an effort to avoid being caught as unaccredited, some diploma mills set up accreditation mills. Yes, you read that right. Before you go to work for a college, make sure its accrediting body is also legitimate. It is a sad but true tale of what we must deal with in today's marketplace. Many of these diploma mills take out expensive ads on popular Internet sites. Do not trust that these (or any) advertisements are screened and that the companies advertising are legitimate; this is not the case. The best of the online stores have made the same mistakes. Amazon and Google don't have the time or resources to check for such things. Unfortunately, many people believe that an advertisement on a trusted site must be legitimate.

Red Flags for Bad Eggs

One website we use frequently, GetEducated.com (www.geteducated.com), lists 10 red flags that indicate a school might be a diploma mill:

1. Your chosen university is not accredited.
2. Your chosen university is accredited ... but NOT by an agency recognized by the Council on Higher Education Accreditation (CHEA at http://www.chea.org). The majority of Internet degree mills are "accredited." The problem is that they are accredited by bogus agencies that institutions themselves have created. These bogus accrediting agencies often have prestigious sounding names.
3. Admission criteria consist entirely of possession of a valid Visa or MasterCard. Previous academic record, grade point average, and test scores are deemed irrelevant.
4. You are offered a college degree based on a

"review" of your faxed resume. Credit for career experience is a valid option at many universities that deal with adult learners. But the process of evaluating career experience for college credit is complex. No valid distance learning university in the USA will award a graduate degree (master's or doctorate) based solely on a review of career experience. Undergraduate programs are more flexible. Accredited undergraduate programs typically limit credit for experience to a maximum of 10 courses or 30 semester credits, which is generally the equivalent of one year of a four-year degree.

5. You are promised a diploma within 30 days of application regardless of your status upon entry. Degree mills are in the business of selling paper. Ergo, they'll get that piece of paper to you as quickly as possible.

6. You are promised a degree in exchange for a lump sum—typically $2,000 for an undergraduate degree and $3,000 for a graduate degree. Universities do not commonly charge flat fees. They typically charge per credit or per course tuition and fees.

7. Your prospective online university has multiple complaints on file with the Better Business Bureau.

8. Your online "admission counselor" assures you that online universities can't be accredited by CHEA recognized agencies. This is a lie.

9. The school's website either lists no faculty or lists faculty who have attended schools accredited by bogus agencies.
10. The university offers online degrees almost exclusively to United States citizens but is conveniently located in a foreign country, quite often a tiny nation that lacks any system of academic accreditation. Don't be fooled by online degree and diploma mills. Many maintain impressive websites. All of them advertise heavily online. Look beyond flashy graphics for the name of the school's accreditation agency. Take the time to verify accreditation by an agency that is recognized by the Council of Higher Education Accreditation.

When the first version of this book was published, we noted that "according to Vicky Phillips, the CEO of GetEducated.com, there are more than 30 online diploma mills in the United States." Now, GetEducated.com notes that in 2010, 810 diploma mills, fake colleges, or other bogus institutions were allowed to operate in the United States (http://www.geteducated.com/college-degree-mills/347-top-10-states-diploma-mill-degree-mills). They list the states that have the highest number of diploma mills, in which California tops the list, long allowing unaccredited colleges to operate and award degrees, which is why many diploma mills have their headquarters in California. Since the state "approves" schools, mills sometimes use the words "state approved" rather than "accredited school" in a more thorough attempt to trick the consumer. I would encourage you to read the GetEducated article to learn more about the fake universities and "schools" with suspicious accreditation. Even if a school has real courses and a real faculty, without accreditation you will regret the time and money you invested. As an adjunct, you should stay away from unaccredited schools, regardless of the salary offered.

Even if they are legitimate, you wouldn't want to put them on your CV. Teach for an unaccredited school (not a diploma mill!) only if you absolutely need the income or experience, but remember that your experience there can be detrimental in the eyes of other schools, so tread carefully. I recommend querying our Facebook forum members for their thoughts on schools if you have questions. With over 3,500 members, chances are someone on the forum has heard of the school you want to work for and can offer insight or information about the working conditions and accreditation standards.

According to Felix McGee, Adjunct Professor of Psychology, "The Diploma and Accreditation Integrity Protection Act of 2009 helps to define diploma mills and also bars them from use when used in hiring decisions of federal agencies." This was one attempt made by the government to help reduce their impact in the marketplace. Dr. Sharon Jumper noted, "The Higher Education Act of 2008 first defined the term diploma mill and authorized the US Department of Education to withhold federal Title IV funds for financial aid from institutions that fail to meet accreditation standards. Denial of federal funds is the death knell for most institutions, particularly those who prey on the more marginalized segments of society.

The Higher Education Act (HEA) and its subsequent amendments give the Department of Education (DOE) the authority to essentially close diploma mills by denying federal funding, but the process do to so can be protracted because of the due process rights of the institutions."

This applies more to schools operating but not meeting standards, and not so much to the fake schools that take money in exchange for a diploma. Matthew D. Harris, PhD, University of Maryland University College (UMUC) Department of Government and Politics, noted, "Between 2002-2004, the Government Accountability Office (GAO), which is the investigative arm of Congress, conducted a series of studies regarding the rising problem of diploma mills. While legislation to address the issue didn't come until a few years later, it was GAO's work that originally identified the magnitude of the problem."

Why Do People Teach Online?

People are inspired to teach online for many reasons: income, personal growth, the opportunity to give back to the community, teaching others, as a stepping-stone to full-time employment, and many other reasons. There are many different types of adjunct applicants. Many applicants are traditional educators with many years' experience in the classroom, but limited expertise in online methodologies. There are instructors who are teaching in addition to their day jobs and have significant limitations on their time and capacity to teach because of their primary career. There are deans, department chairs, and other department administrators who teach on the side for other colleges (with and without their bosses' knowledge) to earn additional income and have exposure to how other schools do things. There are completely inexperienced instructors looking for their first job, and there are teachers who have been adjuncts but want full-time positions for what they believe is stability (more on that later – the opposite may be true!) There are many K-12 educators who have finished their degrees and want to teach at the college level, and I mentioned earlier that there are a lot of retired professionals who are looking for part-time work or want to share their knowledge in retirement.

There are instructors who have made adjuncting a professional business – instructors who are employed as adjuncts, instructors, or contractors by several institutions, have a lot of teaching experience, and are very flexible with their methodology. These instructors essentially earn their income by piecing their work together from multiple institutions, which is an entrepreneurial method of teaching as a means of diversifying risk and income.

Whatever your reasons for teaching online and whatever category of faculty applicant you fit into, I hope that you will get to teach what you love, and that you will love to teach. Doing a job that you love doesn't feel like a job.

So, What's the Catch?

Shari Wilson, who writes for *The Nomad Scholar*, discusses interesting perspectives about being an adjunct in her 2006 article "The Transient

Academic." In the more traditional universities and community colleges that offer online programs, an adjunct is often considered an afterthought. No one counts on adjuncts to stick around and adjuncts don't count on schools to keep them, but they continue to hope. Often given no training and no support, adjuncts may be tempted to water down the curriculum and deliver the most student-pleasing assignments, thereby assuring themselves of better evaluations while working less. Adjuncts often get bumped from their courses in favor of full-time faculty members whose classes have been cancelled or who need to increase their load for the year. Adjunct faculty are rarely invited to faculty functions, are often considered just hired help without loyalty to an institution, and are rarely considered for full-time positions, although they might be promised to be in the running. In many ways, I believe adjunct teaching is the best long-term opportunity (perhaps coupled with a full-time job) for instructors to earn a stable income while diversifying their risk.

Rob Capriccioso, in his 2005 article "Help Wanted: Low-Cost Adjuncts," writes that there are growing opportunities for adjuncts to teach the equivalent of a full-time faculty load while earning adjunct salary. For 60% less pay and no health care benefits, pension, office space, or paid vacation, these hardworking adjuncts fill the duties of a full-time faculty member for much less than half the price. Students are essentially getting cheap labor for faculty in most of their classes while tuition continues to skyrocket. With low-cost faculty, even a small class can generate a profit for the college, and a standard-sized class is highly lucrative. Schools do not bluntly advertise this, but the message is clear.

To put the cost in perspective, a recently released College and University Personnel Association (CUPA) survey reveals that in 2013, a school of business, full-time professor at a four-year institution earns an average of $118,344 per year and a non-tenured professor earns an average of $63,831 per year (http://cupahr.org, 2013). It's important to note that private colleges paid a bit above these numbers, but not substantially so. Compare these professors to the adjunct who earns about $2,000 per course, without benefits, and you can see how a school can improve its finances by hiring more adjuncts.

The Affordable Care Act (which I will discuss in more detail, along with its impact on online teaching jobs, later in this book) has changed some of the financial dynamics. We have yet to see how it will completely play out for professors, but anecdotally I can say that more full-time positions have been hired in the past 12 months than I have seen in the past several years.

Obviously, as online teachers we have to take on more work than traditional faculty members do to earn a good wage, so there is undoubtedly a fairness issue at stake. However, I will gladly forego some of the income for fewer meetings, less administrative burdens, and the ability to work from anywhere. Adjuncts can feel as though their jobs are at risk if they complain, but even full-time faculty are reporting to me in the past 12 months that they also fear being laid off as the first way to cut expenses if enrollments dip. Adjuncts, on the outside, seem to be overused and abused for far less money and hardly any respect. Without the protection of tenure, adjuncts must constantly prove themselves to get rehired.

There is no consistency in adjuncts' paychecks; health insurance is self-funded; and vacation days are really unpaid semesters off (that we usually do not want); there are many bosses to please; colleagues are barely acquaintances; and respect is hard to earn. Yet, as you'll see, there are many benefits that are difficult to quantify, but I will do my best to explain. I mention these disadvantages because I want you to go into this profession with your eyes wide open.

The Bureau of Labor Statistics posted the following quick facts: 2012 median pay for postsecondary teachers: 68,970. The number of jobs reported in postsecondary education in 2012: 1,267,700. The 2012-2022 job outlook – 19% growth, faster than average (http://www.bls.gov/ooh/education -training-and-library/postsecondary-teachers.htm).

A 2005 article in *The Chronicle of Higher Education*, "More Faculty Jobs Go to Part-Timers," notes that new faculty jobs in higher education have gone disproportionately to adjuncts, with a surprising amount of hiring being done by the for-profit sector (these are often purely online schools that are sometimes even public companies). In 2003, the hiring increase for part-timers was 10%, while the increase for full-timers was only 2%. The statistics for 2012 to now vary a lot by source. I have seen some trend towards the use of salaried employees (not necessarily full-timers) in 2014.

The rise of online universities has given way to a new life for adjuncts where there are few or no tenured, full-time faculty – and therefore we are *it* at many colleges. Instead of being the hired help at a local traditional university and working for a pittance, an adjunct can work at limitless nontraditional universities around the globe for competitive wages, restrained only by non-compete agreements that many attorneys and professionals in our group have argued cannot be enforced (check with your own attorney!). In some colleges, adjunct faculty have even begun (or attempted) to unionize with the hope of securing better pay and possibly even health benefits, but these often come with a contractual agreement that means sacrificing some of the freedom of being an adjunct or part-time employee.

Although adjuncts don't have the benefits of full-timers (though some part-time employees do), they also don't have the same obligations for meetings, committees, ceremonies, and advisees. Adjuncts may teach anywhere and everywhere. By contrast, full-timers are typically prohibited from teaching at other institutions, so their teaching pay is limited, while adjuncts have limitless potential (if they are willing to put in the effort, find efficiencies and make the commitment). I recommend reading the book *Adjunct Faculty: How to Manage Workload, Students, and Multiple Schools* by Leslie Bowman, to help manage your time.

Adjuncts also keep up with the changing world of education out of both interest and necessity, while full-timers tend to know only the world that they are in. While an adjunct may have to teach twice as much to match the pay of a full-timer, an adjunct may also choose to teach four times as much and double a full-timer's wages without dealing with school politics.

There is no official job security in working as an

adjunct that matches that of tenure; but in a world where adjuncts are suddenly in the greatest demand, doing a good job and playing the game right can give you all the job security you need to build your future without fear. Many full-time employees are the first to be laid off due to additional overhead (benefits, shared taxes and so on) when enrollments drop. From my experience, adjuncting or being a contract instructor or part-time employee can be as stable, or even more so, than being a full-time professor for one university.

Chapter 3 - Preparing Yourself for Teaching Opportunities

"We teach what we like to learn and the reason many people go into teaching is vicariously to re-experience the primary joy experienced the first time they learned something they loved."
— Stephen Brookfield, Professor & Author

So you have decided to give online teaching a try. Congratulations! It's a rewarding career and if you work in a diligent and efficient manner and take an entrepreneurial approach, adjuncting can be very stable. If you have a graduate degree, you can begin to apply for teaching positions right away. If you don't have a graduate degree, you need to look for ways to get that degree quickly and in a way that fits your schedule while emphasizing your work in training others and teaching people. That doesn't mean you cannot teach without a graduate degree, but you would be limited mainly to online high schools and tutoring; this would give you some experience while paying poorly, plus it is not the same to teach high school teenagers who are mandated to be in school versus adults who choose to be there.

You might consider earning your degree completely online, or partially online in a hybrid model, since you will be teaching in an online setting. Sometimes this experience, and identifying what separates out good from not so good instructors, can help you land your first teaching position. Whatever you decide, you need to start looking for schools at which to teach.

There are thousands of legitimate, accredited colleges and universities in the United States where you can teach online with a master's degree. Some schools award only one or two specific degrees (e.g., business, psychology, education), but most offer a multitude of degrees, and many now offer flexible degrees where learners can choose what they take and when they go to school. The opportunities to teach with a doctorate are even greater due to the lack of qualified candidates and the accreditation requirements for terminal degreed faculty (the greater your credentials the more doors will open), but you can embark on this new career with a master's and do fine.

I recommend those who are serious about making this a full-time commitment pursue a doctorate at some point. A doctorate will substantially increase your income potential and get you through the door of most colleges. If you have a bachelor's degree alone, though, don't despair; try focusing on your qualifications. Write them down if you need to, focusing specifically on your experience training others, your professional teaching experience if you have it, and your post-bachelor's training. There are online high schools, some associate degree programs, and even some bachelor's degree programs that will let you teach or tutor, although you might have to work for some unaccredited schools.

So from here, let's look at getting your master's degree, since the focus is on making a living by teaching online rather than just subsidizing your income.

Getting Your Master's Degree

If you already have a master's degree, you're in good shape! Most of our clients started teaching with a master's and no doctorate. If you do not have a master's degree, there are many excellent opportunities to earn one in about 18 months. Since it takes a few months to be hired at most schools anyway, you can start earning a master's, and when you get near completion, then you can begin sending your CV out to schools.

There is probably a university near you that offers a master's degree. Some of these local universities offer some or all of their courses online, too, so you could choose to take some courses face-to-face and others online (giving you much needed experience online from the learner perspective, a selling point even if your degree isn't completed yet).

Sometimes getting a degree from a school with a brick and mortar campus is beneficial if you apply at a school where the hiring manager has a fondness for traditional institutions. For those concerned about earning a degree online, going through a hybrid program is an excellent way to get the best of both worlds (i.e., you get to try out online courses in subjects where you are most comfortable).

You can also search the Web for the hundreds of online programs all over the world. Some are 100% online (e.g., Capella University and Walden

University); others are from schools that also offer face-to-face classes (e.g., DeVry University and University of Phoenix). Yet others are from schools with traditional degrees whose online courses are generally taught by the same faculty (e.g., Pennsylvania State University and Boston University).

Bookstores, magazines, and the Internet can be sources of many excellent books on colleges. We also offer information about various schools and department heads through our custom job search. The 100% online and the nontraditional online schools can easily be found through a Google search, or you can visit one of the many informative websites on the subject, such as:

info.theonlinedegree.com
www.adjunctnation.com
www.chronicle.com
www.degreeinfo.com
www.educationcenteronline.org
www.elearners.com
www.findaschool.org
www.geteducated.com/index.asp
www.program-online-degree.com
www.themoderndegree.com
www.worldwidelearn.com

There are many schools to choose from, and various programs will offer different credits for previously taken courses and/or work experience. Each school has its pros and cons, such as residency requirements, length of semesters, availability of classes, requirements for entrance exams, tuition, and overall reputation. I recommend you pursue a traditional university that offers online courses for your master's degree, if at all possible. It needn't be a well-known state university; it could be a small, private university, or even a faith-based one. This is not because I think less of the other nontraditional programs, but a master's from a traditional school (or at least a nonprofit) will give you an edge (according to most surveys we conduct) as you begin your career teaching online. There are pros and cons whichever method you choose. I have a book called *The Adult Student* where this is addressed with far more detail.

If you choose the traditional route for a master's, you will have a degree from a school that is easily recognized by those in the academic world as well as the corporate world, and it is more likely to be valued in the corporate world. Saying that you went to Pennsylvania State University will earn you a lot of respect, even if you took your courses online in a hybrid format or even totally online. Many business leaders are familiar with big-name schools that have strong sports programs, but may be unfamiliar with one of the 100% online programs unless they knew someone who graduated from one.

Your corporate resume will be easier to market when you don't have to explain that your school is real. This is less of an issue today than it was a few years ago, but I do think some bias still exists. If you have a choice, I think the best option is to attend class where you face the least resistance post-graduation. This is, of course, assuming you want to stay in corporate America. If you want to devote your entire career to teaching, then where you go to school matters. I recommend selecting the best school you can afford and get admitted into, one that is regionally accredited and has the flexibility you need.

You will want your degree to help you stand out when applying to teach online. With the University of Phoenix producing more graduates than any other online university, you shouldn't be surprised to see that a significant number of applicants for teaching positions graduated from there. You will find yourself at a great advantage over the competition, in part, because you will be different. When schools recruit and hire online faculty, they aim for a diverse group from varied universities.

A school's reputation will be lessened if it is known for essentially hiring its own graduates (inbreeding in academic circles is limited by accreditation bodies), and students will be more impressed to see some faculty from traditional universities (or at least with the names of traditional universities even if you took some of your courses online). It gives the school and the teacher more credibility in students' eyes even though they are attending an online school. As a result, it will score you some bonus points in the application processes at some schools.

If you are going to choose to teach face-to-face courses, be aware that some traditional universities are hesitant to hire faculty with an online degree. Some don't respect the degree (although this is rapidly changing), others don't feel that you should deliver lectures when you weren't on the other end of them, and still others are just being difficult about wanting their faculty to come from schools just like theirs and who walked the same path. Earning a degree the traditional way, even including online courses, will give you easier entry into all realms of teaching. While I earned my doctoral degree online, I earned my master's at a traditional institution. While it wasn't a strategy at the time, in hindsight it did help my entrance into education. A purely online degree at the master's level will likely limit you to teaching only in online programs until you have proven yourself elsewhere. I am not saying it can't happen (we have hundreds of clients every year who prove the contrary), only that having a master's from a traditional school, even if you took classes online, may look better for you. And in today's competitive world, any edge you can get is worth considering.

Wherever you earn your graduate degree, there are advantages to taking some or all of your courses online if you want to teach strictly online. If you're familiar with the difficulties online learners face, you will be more likely to understand your students. If you can articulate these clearly in your CV and integrate this into your teaching philosophy statement, you can note that your experience as a student has made you a better teacher. This can be an advantage in the application process. Since online schools know their own programs are credible, they won't hesitate to hire someone with a degree from an online institution. On-ground schools, however, will be less likely to hire you than if you had a degree from a traditional school, in general.

If the only option is to go to school online, by all means do it, but from a regionally accredited institution. If you go to a purely online for-profit school, focus on the time to completion, the reputation of the school, and the degree offerings. It wouldn't be worth your while to get a degree just to say you have one. A master of library science, while a real degree, will severely limit what you will be able to teach, while a master of information systems will enable you to teach nearly any undergraduate computer science course anywhere. You should enjoy the subject you are studying, but you should also be sure that there are jobs for people who have that degree.

One great source for this information is our Facebook forum, where faculty freely share their experiences and what they teach with their degrees, as well as where they went to school. If the degree you are pursuing is hard to find, then so will the openings for faculty in that area. I have a harder time finding positions for our candidates in environmental science than I do in business. However, when there is an open position, there are so few faculty applying that the candidate's chances go up considerably. Just remember that supply and demand go hand in hand. It's no wonder that business is the most commonly offered program and often has the best pay for full-time faculty.

Whatever method you decide to pursue, make sure it fits your lifestyle. This must be a priority if you want a real career teaching online and not just a situation where you're taking one or two courses on occasion.

With regard to expert tips, here's what I have seen work and what our colleagues say: I am a proponent of schools with name recognition that also let you take courses online so you can explain that you understand the students' pain because you've been there. I also agree that if you intend to teach mostly on-ground or you want a high number of your courses to come from on-ground classes, you should opt for the more traditional route. This isn't based on statistics, but what I've seen work. Having experience with both on-ground and online courses will ultimately serve you best, as long as the school's degree is accredited and respected.

Enrollment

I discuss hunting for jobs extensively in chapter six, but here you can see which schools and programs have the highest enrollments. This will help you figure out which degree you may wish to pursue (you may want to go where the jobs are, or specialize) and may help you see where you want (or don't want) to attend. There are many lists available online, and the site you visit will largely dictate the answer you get with regard to which schools and programs have the highest enrollments. There are many ways to slice and dice the data, such as the number of students by parent company, United States alone, and so forth.

Here are some you may want to consider, compiled from a variety of sources (this is not an endorsement of the schools, just an idea of who's out there) from the National Center for Education Statistics:

- University of Phoenix, Online
- Ashford University
- Arizona State University
- Liberty University
- Miami Dade College
- Lone Star College System
- Houston Community College
- University of Central Florida

- Ohio State University
- Kaplan University, Davenport Campus

You should also check out local community colleges to see if they have online programs, as they are often a great entry into the world of online teaching because you get the benefit of local support when needed and you pay far less tuition. You will undoubtedly find in your research that business is the most common program offered online. Those with a business degree have more opportunities for teaching than those with any other degree, based on enrollment and the availability of the major; however, you should note that they also have the greatest competition for those teaching positions. The largest number of opportunities exists in the programs that are 100% online and hybrid, but there are numerous schools that offer a choice of programs that may be good options where you can attend or teach. Also, don't assume you are locked into teaching within your degree field. Many of us with degrees in business teach in other disciplines, such as schools of education.

Getting Your Doctoral Degree

Let's assume you either have, or are nearing completion of a master's and you have decided to pursue a doctorate. You should know that it's a long road that will be difficult, cumbersome, and full of trials; it will eat at your ego and sometimes even your self-esteem. It is a truly humbling process. It will also make you more empathic towards others who will eventually become your mentees when your title changes to Dr. Your education often seems to be at the mercy of others who are not nearly as invested in it as you are, and this can be troubling, anxiety-producing, and worrisome. There is good reason that only 50% of people who begin a doctorate ever obtain one (Coates, 2004).

Your goal as a doctor is to help advance your discipline, to create social good, and to be a professional who is highly qualified in your field. If you were told that anything you'd pursue had a 50% rate of failure, you'd seriously reconsider doing it in the first place. Some consider it to be the fault of the educational system if students spend a great deal of money and effort only to have a 50% success rate. Remember, though, whether you reach your goal is entirely up to you, and also keep in mind that a doctorate qualifies you for jobs that no amount of experience or hiring quotas can.

Completion of Doctoral Programs

It's important to note that the number of Americans earning doctorates in the past five years has dropped more than 8%, yet again, giving you an edge. This is not true for foreign students, whose rate has risen by more than 5% in the same period of time – still a net loss result, making your degree more valuable.

Here are some more interesting facts about doctorates: More than half the people who earn them do not stay in the teaching field. This clearly shows that they're universal in their demand, and that just because you earn a doctorate doesn't mean you can't go back to industry! Many programs such as the

Doctor of Business Administration (DBA) or the Doctor of Management degree are focused a bit more on the practitioner side than the scholarly side. As committee chairs, we realize that not everyone we mentor will go on to follow in our footsteps, leave their day jobs, and pursue academia along with doing some consulting.

Many PhD programs are stepping up to the workplace challenge and are introducing programs that focus more on the practitioner than the school (called the practitioner-scholar approach as opposed to the scholar-practitioner approach). At the very least, in obtaining a doctorate you'll build an incredible network and understand research methodologies behind almost everything you see and do in modern life.

How bad can it be? As of 2013, according to the US Census Bureau, about 88% of the nation had a high school diploma, 58% some college, 41% earned an associate's or bachelor's, 31% a bachelor's, 11% a master's and/or doctorate, 3% a doctorate and/or professional degree, and about 1.6% held a doctorate. More than half of the doctorates were in science and engineering.

You can see now why a doctorate is in high demand at universities. To work as an online teacher and make a good income, the best thing you can do is set yourself apart from your competition. A doctorate will open up many worlds for you with regard to teaching opportunities. If you prefer to go the online route, you can earn an accredited doctorate just as you would from an on-ground school. Traditional schools tend to have demands that are simply that, tradition, without regard for what necessarily makes sense and why it needs to be done (read: possibly, a lot of red tape).

The point of a doctoral program is to know how to be a good researcher, understand the doctoral-level research methodologies, have a thorough review of the literature in your field, and become a subject matter expert at an in-depth level. Another goal is to be able to apply that to whatever you decide to do with hopes of making the world a better place, a more educated place to be with decisions grounded in research. Any doctorate from an accredited school will give you an advantage here. The key is to decide if you want to earn a PhD, a DBA, an EdD, or some other doctorate, and then to get it done. I'll review the most common doctorates in detail.

Doctor of Philosophy (PhD)

The Doctorate of Philosophy (PhD) can be in many subjects. The first formal PhD was instituted in 1893 in the field of education at Teachers College at Columbia University (Dill and Morrison, 1985). A PhD is a doctorate in philosophy in your area of specialization.

PhD programs usually focus on preparing a candidate to perform specialized scholarly research. The emphasis here is on the development of new theory in various topics. Most PhD graduates work as university researchers and professors or as senior researchers in government agencies or businesses.

The focus is often on being a scholar first and a practitioner second, although many programs today are emphasizing both to meet growing workplace demands.

Doctor of Business Administration (DBA)

The doctor of business administration (DBA) focuses on the application of theory rather than on the development of new theory. In many ways this exemplifies the practitioner-scholar model, while the PhD frequently exemplifies the scholar-practitioner model. By looking at it this way, you can clearly see the differences. A DBA often has more practical application for managerial settings than a PhD, but the two are very similar in other respects. They are considered academically equivalent and require difficult courses of study with a heavy research emphasis.

Students must write and defend a doctoral dissertation in addition to passing comprehensive exams at most universities or colleges. Some schools now require any tenure-track faculty member to have a terminal degree (this is a doctorate) that's either a PhD or a DBA

Take heed that, while respected by the academic world, a DBA isn't quite as recognized by corporate America where it tends to be translated as database administrator. Also, a DBA is often a part-time commitment on the part of the learner (many DBA programs want you to remain employed full-time as they are professional-based). However: Most of our clients and colleagues have lucrative and rewarding teaching careers with a DBA while still having terrific opportunity in their professional lives.

Doctor of Education (EdD)

The first Doctor of Education (EdD) program came 27 years after the first PhD. The degree was established at Harvard University Graduate School of Education. The EdD prepares professional leaders to identify and solve complex problems. The emphasis in these programs is to develop reflective and competent practitioners who are thoughtful in nature. While the PhD focuses on research and producing new knowledge, the EdD focuses on career development and being the best professional possible; although some EdD programs are more academic.

The EdD often pursues an administrative leadership role in educational institutions, whereas the PhD generally pursues scholarly practice, research, or teaching at the university level (New Mexico State University, 2005). If you want to be a credentialed psychologist, some insurance carriers won't qualify someone with an EdD, but will qualify someone with a PhD or a doctorate of psychology (Psy.D.). This makes sense given the field; so ultimately, your end goal will determine which doctorate you should choose (and there are others; these are just the most common for online teachers).

One of the newer areas in education is instructional design, and this usually falls under an EdD program. This is a highly specialized opportunity in course and curriculum design based on educational theories.

Juris Doctor (JD)

The Juris Doctor (JD) is a professional doctorate and was the first professional graduate degree in law. To earn a JD, a candidate would complete law school in the US, Canada, Australia and other common law countries. A JD is also a terminal degree, and seems to confuse a lot of attorneys who believe their degree is not a doctorate and they cannot teach. This couldn't be further from the truth! I have clients with a JD teaching history, political science, law, public policy and a host of other areas of study. A JD is a terminal graduate degree that qualifies you to teach in a host of programs and courses. Some universities will not allow you to mentor students in the dissertation process in other programs due to the professional nature of the degree, but even that isn't the case for all schools.

Regardless of what you choose, accreditation matters. You need to pay particular attention to be sure your school is accredited and note the accrediting body. The doctoral degree, whichever types you pursue, is designed to be a rigorous and a highly intellectual experience. You need to know what this feels like if you want to provide it to your own students. Most faculty members demand a lot from learners and you should be aware of this going in.

All But Dissertation: The Doctoral Candidate Status

There is a common misperception that an online teacher must have a doctoral or terminal degree to start teaching. This is simply not the case. Most of our clients and most of the professors that I know have started teaching with their master's degree. Most universities, particularly those that are regionally accredited, require 18 graduate hours in the discipline they are teaching. This is translated differently by each institution and different hiring deans may translate this differently as well.

Even job descriptions that say doctoral degree required will sometimes hire a candidate with a masters degree who is well credentialed in the area in which they need professors to teach. Some job descriptions say doctoral degree preferred, which implies it is not required. If the candidate needs to add to their workload or is just starting out, I generally recommend they apply with or without their doctoral degree to jobs, even if the position indicates a doctoral degree is required. I have had many clients successfully land jobs without the degree that the job description said was required. Other times, there are other jobs available at the institution that have not been officially announced. If the Dean wants the candidate they will hire him or her for a different position than the one being advertised.

It's important to note here, that once you make it to the dissertation phase, you are considered a doctoral candidate. At this point, your unofficial status is referred to as "all but dissertation" (ABD). As a side note: please do not use ABD on your CV or in your job applications! Many deans take offense to it and find it to be an unacceptable designation. Many universities do not allow students to use it. Doctoral Candidate is a more appropriate term with an estimated completion date on the vita. You can use doctoral candidate as a status (indicating your coursework is complete) to begin applying to jobs at this point. Many schools will see you as being almost a doctor, so they will often hire you as though you had your doctorate, but conditional on actually finishing within a specified time (this is more common for full time positions). It is important to mention your doctoral candidacy status in your opening cover letter or on your CV, as well as how far along in the process you are (noted as an estimated completion date), because most likely the dissertation will be complete by the time you're hired.

In the next chapter, I'll talk about opportunities available to you based on the highest level of education you have reached.

Chapter 4 - Types of Online Teaching Jobs

"There is an old saying that the course of civilization is a race between catastrophe and education. In a democracy such as ours, we must make sure that education wins the race."
— John F. Kennedy

There are many opportunities in the world of online teaching; the field is now stable and continuing to grow and expand, demanding quality individuals to teach at all university levels. In this chapter, we will explore many of the opportunities and requirements of the online teaching world.

Experience – Needed or Not?

"No experience needed." How we long to see those words in a job advertisement when we are fresh out of school; but alas, you must have experience to get experience. A few years ago, it seemed that the only employers willing to hire people without experience were those with jobs that no one with a college degree would want anyway. We see that changing now and the world of online teaching led the way for academics.

Just ten years ago, the world of online teaching was uncharted territory. Although a few universities had been market leaders in distance education for some time, when the first version of this book was published, most were just in their infancy. The demand for faculty to develop and teach their online courses far exceeded the supply, especially since many full-time professors have yet to teach online, and many don't want to.

Today there is more of a balance between demand and supply, with the average candidate, who is our client, applying to 80-120 jobs per interview. This is not unlike other industries, but for those who were in online education when no one knew what it was, it suddenly seems like poor odds. It certainly is not – and one of my goals in this book update is to give readers timely and relevant information to compete in the market. Keep in mind that traditional universities often expect research, grants, and such, which require a doctorate. The same requirements are not evident in the online world, particularly in the for-profit world or in community colleges with bachelor's programs.

Adjuncts are needed and universities cannot always afford the luxury of demanding experience or a doctorate. In version one of this book, it was noted that the ever-increasing cost of health care was driving the need for adjuncts. In today's climate, the Affordable Care Act has limited the number of courses some adjuncts can teach because university administrators fear reaching some threshold in which they will be fined for not providing healthcare. The ACA did two things to adjuncts: it lessened the number of courses that one can teach at a single university, and it created more opportunities as adjuncts who had stable workloads of two or three courses suddenly saw their course loads dropped to one. It also moved individuals from a part-time or contractor status to employee status at many schools. As we discuss in the pros and cons section of the chapter, most if not all adjuncts do not receive benefits, which saves universities money.

What does this mean to you? It means that you can become an online professor without already being a professor. I keep my blog updated on this topic to help professors stay current on this (and many other subjects) at www.thebabbgroup.com/blog. I would encourage you to review it often to keep current with what is happening in the marketplace.

Experience will definitely help in getting hired where the competition is fierce, especially at the more prominent universities, but there are countless opportunities to get hired without experience and ultimately get the experience needed to move up the ladder to higher-paying and more prestigious positions. The best part is that it won't take years to pay your dues; within one year you can have enough experience to compete well, provided you have the necessary academic credentials for that position.

However, just because you don't need teaching experience doesn't mean the borders are not guarded. One of the largest employers of online adjuncts is the University of Phoenix. This is an excerpt from its website (www.phoenix.edu) on "Becoming a Faculty Member": "If you are a working professional with a graduate degree, in-depth knowledge of your field, strong communication skills, computer proficiency, and a desire to help others succeed, you may have what it takes to be a University of Phoenix Online instructor."

Here you see no mention whatsoever of teaching experience. American InterContinental University Online, another major employer of online faculty, shows the following on its website (www.aiuonline.edu) with regard to "How to Apply for a Faculty Position":

Prospective faculty members must meet the following criteria to be considered:

- Documented expertise in the academic subject area as well as interpersonal, oral presentation, and written communication skills.
- Minimum of two years of industry experience with prior postsecondary teaching experience preferred.

Here teaching experience is mentioned, but not as a requirement. This is typical. "Experience required" is now "Experience preferred, but must have graduate degree." Also, note that industry training experience is often recognized as teaching experience if you were training someone in the workplace (be sure this is clearly indicated on your vita!). Chances are if you want to teach a subject, you are proficient in that subject due to either your academic qualifications or your professional experience, or both. More on each of these topics later.

Why Do Schools Want Adjuncts?

Adjuncts have long been treated as road scholars by full-time faculty in traditional universities, often getting little or no respect. Their names are not included in most college catalogs; they don't have offices, or get invited to faculty functions, and they don't sit on stage during most graduations. While full-time faculty are a small but consistent cadre of professionals who account for a large percentage of the courses taught at these traditional universities, there is usually a large group of diverse adjuncts who account for the rest.

Note that none of this is true for a fully online college like Walden University or Capella University, where there are far more adjuncts or part-time faculty than full-time faculty and they are treated with equal respect and dignity. Adjuncts are usually invited to residencies, meetings, and faculty functions; in these nontraditional universities, many of the full-time faculty began as adjuncts there and it becomes difficult for students to distinguish between adjuncts and full-time professors, with the exception of one's signature line in an email.

In any business, human resources are a big expense and often the most trying challenge to manage, so why not just hire a few more full-time instructors and eliminate the need for adjuncts?

The answers are plentiful, but the most obvious is simple economics. Adjuncts are a bargain, plain and simple. While a full-time faculty member can teach a full class and barely show a profit for the university, an adjunct can teach a small class and show a large profit. At one community college, the average full-time faculty salary is about $40,000 plus benefits per year, with a commitment to teach 10 courses. If benefits are estimated to be worth about $10,000 per year, then the salary package costs $50,000, so each course taught by a full-time professor costs the college $5,000. In this example, the tuition is $190 per yearlong course for state residents, so it takes 27 students in the class just to pay the professor's salary (and this doesn't include the building expenses or other administrative salaries).

An adjunct at this same school earns $1,650 per course without benefits, so after nine students, the college has paid the adjunct's salary. With an average class size in the low to mid 20s, the college loses money with the full-time faculty and makes a significant profit with adjuncts, so the adjuncts make it possible to afford to keep full-time faculty.

Even in a nontraditional online university, such as Capella University, adjuncts are paid a set amount per student or per course (with a drastic pay reduction if the course has low load or low enrollment). So the university is guaranteed to show a profit regardless of the class size, while full-timers earn an annual salary and need to teach full classes to help the bottom line financially. Full-timers are usually given the additional tasks of updating courses and mentoring new faculty to help offset their costs. Administrators have admitted to me they would prefer to use only adjuncts, but the accreditation agencies would hand them their heads. Adjuncts are contractors, so they aren't paid benefits, sick time, vacation time, and the like.

Besides the monetary reasons, there are logistical reasons for wanting adjuncts. With rare exceptions, traditional universities have found it necessary to expand their market to include night and weekend students as well as online students. These are not popular options for most full-time professors, who don't want to work nights and weekends and may not even want to leave the comfort of their traditional classrooms.

Since adjuncts may have full-time jobs, making it difficult for them to teach during the weekdays, they are usually open to weekends and evenings. Full-time adjuncts work during the day like other professionals, but are responsible for their own hours and maintaining their own schedules. Full-timers are left to handle daytime duties and other adjuncts are tapped for the rest. An added bonus to schools using adjuncts for their online courses is the option to hire outside of the local community; there is no geographical restriction with regard to where an adjunct lives when teaching online, so the university can hire from anywhere in the world. From your standpoint as an adjunct, you can live in California or Florida and teach anywhere in the United States or even for international colleges. From the school's viewpoint, they can pay a competitive wage to someone in a low cost-of-living state even while operating in a high cost-of-living state.

Another factor to consider is that even the best of faculty have limited strengths. No one can teach everything, so universities are often left having to fill a few odd courses. If the unfilled courses on a schedule included one physics class, two nanotechnology classes, and one Japanese class, it would be easier to hire three or four adjuncts to cover these than to find one person with the credentials for all of these.

Administratively, an adjunct can also be a dean's dream. Adjuncts are easy to hire, easy to fire, and easy to reassign. Since adjuncts are contractors who essentially work for themselves (or part-time employees in today's climate), they are more willing to do whatever is asked of them since they are paid for what they do, and they want to stay on good terms to get more future assignments.

The more enlightened university leaders in the online world have come to look at adjuncts beyond the cost savings and course scheduling advantages. Schools like Capella University (www.capella.edu) and Walden University (www.walden.edu) proudly display the names of their entire faculty on their websites, including adjuncts, which make up a large portion of faculty at those schools. Adjuncts, with academic credentials equal to those of full-time traditional faculty, provide pockets of expertise and add validity to the degree because of the well-rounded-ness of the diverse faculty.

What Types of Positions Are Available Online?

One type of position available for online teaching, as was mentioned earlier, is that of the adjunct faculty member. Adjunct faculty members teach classes on contract and are usually not employees (although it is becoming more common to make adjuncts employees as of 2014). Adjuncts (and usually part-time employee adjuncts) are free to set their own schedules within the guidelines of the university they work for; they are contractors or usually largely unmanaged (except for outcomes) by administrators.

In our first edition of this book, we had noted, "as such, they manage their time but in return they do not have the job security that the full-timers have." This has changed a bit since the first book was released. Many faculty and administrators report that when enrollments drop, the full-time faculty is the first to be cut as they offer less profit and have higher overhead. Adjuncts or contractors cannot be on a tenure track like full-time core faculty. They also do not receive benefits in most cases, but they do have flexible schedules and can make a lot of money working from home or while traveling if they so choose.

You can also take on a role as a part-time faculty member, which often sets a specific number of courses or units you will teach each term or year, and pays a salary instead of a per-course stipend. Full-time positions are also available for online faculty, which are sometimes referred to as core faculty (that can also be contract positions), or full-time teaching or mentoring positions. Many of these positions have traditional educational titles, such as Instructor, Assistant Professor, Associate Professor, or Professor. While some of these positions ask that you not work for competing institutions, many do not – and still yet, others may ask, but do not enforce it. I have run into many bosses on conference calls at other institutions where they are teaching who are deans at schools I work in. I am often asked, "Is that risky? Will I get into trouble?" The answer: it depends.

Most of us treat others the way we want to be treated and we trust everyone will maintain their own workload. When I was managing a group of faculty, I assessed them by their performance in my department, not where they may have worked in addition to the school I was managing. My point is, even if your boss is aware of it, he or she may not mind and may be doing it himself or herself – or you may have a boss who goes strictly by the rule book and asks you to step down at your other position. Do your homework and, as one of my long time colleagues and friends recommends to others, "do your job and keep your head down." Most bosses in my career have not asked or been concerned about where else I work, but that is not always the case.

I am also asked if online faculty can become department chairs or deans and work remotely. Absolutely! In fact one of the positions for which we do custom searches for our clients are online or remote administrative jobs.

Another opportunity is to become a course developer. Every university has two things that need to be done routinely – course development and course revision. Course development involves creating a brand-new course, usually with a template and a textbook, and sometimes with videos.

Developing a course can pay anywhere from one to five thousand dollars (or more), depending on the university and the level of work required. Course reviews and revisions are minor or major updates to existing courses, and can pay anywhere from a few hundred to a couple thousand dollars. This is usually an additional option adjunct faculty have; however, some universities will hire individuals just to revise courses who are an experts in that area.

When looking for job leads, these are often noted as course development positions (different from instructional design, which is a discipline in and of itself). One major benefit to developing or revising a course is that universities will often give you the right of first refusal and you will be the first they ask to teach the course.

You can also be a lead faculty member. Surprisingly to many, an adjunct/contractor can in fact become a lead faculty; this means you're responsible for updating the course regularly, and sometimes for assigning who will teach a course – often you get right of first refusal on a course as you often do as a developer. This is not always a guarantee, so be sure to ask your boss, but it can help you increase your income substantially, not to mention that it provides some level of job security.

There are even adjunct faculty members who hold higher-level positions in the hierarchy of a department. Adjuncts can oversee different majors in schools and can have responsibilities that include overseeing all of the courses in a department and the faculty assigned to those courses. Department chairs play a major role for students majoring in their subject area, as they may review some dissertations, too. The best benefit, though, is the ability to decide for yourself what your teaching schedule will be or to be given courses before other faculty members. I was responsible for a group of faculty at a non-profit faith-based institution for a couple of years and oversaw the faculty as a contractor.

Requirements of Various Programs

While each university has its own specific rules and requirements, there are some core requirements common to most of them. If you are applying to teach at a regionally accredited institution, then it will likely insist that you have your graduate degree from a regionally accredited institution. The standards are somewhat more lax at unaccredited or nationally accredited institutions, so if your degree isn't from an accredited college, you should look for these online using searches.

The degree is just the beginning, though. You must have a graduate degree with at least 18 graduate semester hours in the subject area you plan to teach, or a terminal degree in a similar area. For example, to teach finance, you wouldn't qualify with just a Masters of Business Administration (MBA) that has one or two finance courses if the dean is strictly going by the 18 graduate hour rule. But the MBA would certainly qualify you to teach general business or management. Often, with a terminal degree in business, you will academically qualify even for that same finance course, even if you do not have 18 graduate hours specifically in finance, due to the "or related discipline" requirement you will see in many job ads.

Taking all of your elective courses in a single subject area, better prepares you to teach in that subject area. It is not uncommon for graduates to go back and take a few extra courses in order to meet minimum qualifications for teaching a favorite subject. If you get a second degree, whether it is another master's or a doctorate, it is the combined graduate courses that count, so you don't have to get all of your credits from a single institution—just be sure they are accredited (preferably regionally).

Even those of you with a bachelor's degree can teach online at high schools, as well as some universities, albeit mostly college preparatory courses or noncredit courses, due to strict accreditation guidelines. You'll want to review the requirements at several schools to find out which ones would allow you to teach with a bachelor's degree. Many will take a bachelor's degree with exceptional work experience for weeknight on-ground courses or an online course here or there while you're working on your master's. However, in 2013 and 2014 I saw that become far less common than it was when the first edition of this book was published.

The traditional university setting of teaching on-campus classes in large lecture halls is often known for the "publish or perish" mentality. Faculty members are required to get published in major academic journals annually or risk losing their jobs. Having a reputation as well-published carries more weight than being the best instructor, since it is through publishing that these universities gain status. Many institutions will pay you an honorarium to list their institution as your affiliated school when you publish (that is how much they value this!)

The nontraditional university settings can be quite different for publishing, which is not a requirement, although it is very welcome and highly regarded. Most likely, you will be filling out a "what I did this year" sheet at the one-year anniversary of your hire date or end of the calendar year, which will have professional development requirements. Publishing in an academic journal weighs heavily for this evaluation. Online teaching is mostly populated by adjuncts that are contracted almost exclusively to teach classes. Thus, your history of getting published may help you get hired, but it is certainly not expected or required. Although as of late, you may be paid for doing so.

With the adult learner environment prevalent in online education, more and more universities are requesting practical experience in the field of study you would be hired to teach. The model for teaching requires that the instructor should be able to help students see real-world applicability and share lived experiences, and this requires knowledge beyond the books. Additionally, it gives a different form of credibility to the university and the instructor when the students can read an instructor bio filled with real-world accomplishments.

For a prospective teacher, probably the most critical requirement of any online educational program, whether stated or not, is the ability to communicate. In a lecture hall, a professor must be able to communicate orally to be effective, but online education requires that a professor be able to communicate in written form as well. While this seems less challenging at first glance, it is quite the opposite.

You will take courses on how to use proper tone, effect change, articulate well, and many other topics – all challenges for anyone who teaches online. Can you recall the last time someone took your email wrong? Or you miscommunicated in writing? If only we had an iPhone "un-send" button! In the online world, there are no nonverbal clues, other than perhaps emoticons, to convey expression. This is an art form with which you will need to become proficient.

There are differences in how we communicate in replying to an email, giving directions for online assignments, grading papers submitted electronically, and moderating a discussion forum. While there is no official certification for effective communication, the process of applying to teach online is an opportunity for the university administration to assess some of your skills. Unlike a face-to-face or phone interview, your written word is permanent and can be read again and again, so check your vita, cover letter, and email for typos, writing errors, and overall tone. Be sure your writing communicates what you want to communicate. I have provided some samples in chapter six and regularly update samples on my blog.

Online High Schools

For those without masters or doctoral degrees, one road worth exploring is teaching online high school. You may not have heard of such a thing, but we can assure you that they are out there. If this is of strong interest to you, I recommend networking in our Facebook forum and asking others who teach online high school where they got their experience and how they got their first jobs.

A high school diploma is a necessary step toward achieving success. The U.S. Department of Labor's Bureau of Labor Statistics indicates that the average high school graduate in 2013 earned about $179 per month more than the average person who had not completed high school. High school graduates are 68% more likely to be employed than those without a diploma.

In the past, a general equivalency diploma (GED) was the primary alternative to finishing high school. The GED is an exam comprised of five areas: writing skills, social studies, interpreting literature, science, and math. Completion does not give the student a high school diploma; they are a "GED holder." A high school graduate is of greater significance in our society than a GED holder. As a result, online schools quickly wised up and created online high schools, accredited institutions offering diplomas online.

You probably want some names – examples of online high schools. Here is a list in random order (and you will see that even the oldest of schools is embracing the idea based on their established date): Penn Foster High School (established in 1890); James Madison High School; Keystone National High School (established in 1974); Orange Lutheran High School, Advanced Academics (middle school, too!); Apex Learning; Florida Virtual High School; Brenton Academy; Brigham Young University; Christa McAuliffe Academy (regionally and nationally accredited!); Home Study International; Kentucky Virtual High School; University of Nevada Reno Independent Study; University of Texas at Austin; University of Oklahoma Independent Learning High School. You name your criteria; they are probably out there. Check out this list of online high schools too: http://www.onlineschools.com/high-school/list.

Throughout the book, I mention several great websites that will help you find online teaching jobs and available positions. Keep in mind that just because a school isn't advertising its need for faculty doesn't mean it doesn't have such a need! Follow the same steps we offer for beginning a career in online education, but adapt your resume to the high school level. The possibilities are endless and growing rapidly.

What Do You Need to Begin?

First, you need a desire to teach others. You need to want to share your experiences with others. Remember, online teachers are often referred to as facilitators—and that is what you do as an online teacher. Your students often have as much or more experience than you have, and they want respect and credit for that experience, not to be treated like typical college students who probably don't have responsibilities outside of schoolwork and play. It's essential for an online teacher to adopt the mind-set of facilitator/mentor rather than lecturer/teacher. Once you have that down and realize the differences, you can begin building your toolkit to look for online jobs.

Next, you need a degree in something from an accredited institution. If you're lucky, your degree is also in your chosen work field; if it is, matching yourself to courses and qualifying to teach will be much simpler. However, most of us are the result of several changed majors and perhaps even a career change or two. Begin to document what you want to teach in general (management, finance, economics, statistics, IT, etc.) and why you are qualified to teach it. These details need to be captured when you regularly update your CV, as well as the cover letter you use to apply for teaching positions.

You need to have the necessary technology, as we discuss in chapter 10. Finally, you must have good intentions. Teaching online or on-ground is a tremendous responsibility. If your goal is to get rich quick and put in little effort, you are in the wrong field. This is hard work, but it's rewarding and you can make a good income with tremendous flexibility.

However, your good intentions are vital to both your success and your presentation style. As dedicated professors, we tend to police ourselves, and those who don't have the right attitude about teaching will find that their colleagues won't network with them. When Jim and I wrote the first book, we had successfully helped dozens of friends and former students get jobs as online professors, but our reputations were on the line if they didn't perform, so we only recommended those who would do us proud.

Today as an educational consultant helping thousands of people get into the field of education (both traditional and online) I have come to respect the value of a personal recommendation like nothing else in the job search. If you have someone willing to give you a personal recommendation and make a connection for you, treat it like gold and do right by the person referring you. Many professors will tell you that after being in the field for a while, they have received unsolicited job offers, often as a result of referrals.

Upsides and Downsides to Adjunct Life

Adjunct life has its upsides and its downsides, as do all jobs. Many adjuncts aspire to become full-time professors, while others are content to remain adjuncts – or even "adjunctpreneurs" (trademark pending), adjuncts who work as entrepreneurs by working for multiple institutions of different types to balance their workload and diversify their risk to maintain long-term job security.

Some work full-time in their profession and use

adjunct work as a supplement to their income, whereas others choose to do it full-time. You may also choose one path and then later change mid-course. You may decide you like teaching online, or you may not.

Compensation is definitely a key issue. A full-time professor can generally expect to make at least $50,000 plus benefits annually to teach 5-10 courses per year, whereas an adjunct might earn only $1,200 to $3,000 without benefits for a single course. Mathematically, you would need to teach more than twice what a full-timer teaches to earn the same amount. This may be true on the surface, but there are hidden truths, too.

Full-time faculty must often serve on committees, attend meetings, teach courses they don't want to teach on a schedule they may not like, "publish or perish" and supervise other faculty, and sometimes develop courses for free, while adjuncts just teach (possibly attending a rare conference call) and get paid for any additional work that they take on. Over time, adjuncts can remove lower paying schools from their list of employers if they choose, replacing them with higher paying positions as they gain experience. Adjuncts are afforded more time to teach more classes.

Additionally, adjuncts get paid only for what they do, and can take a term off or lighten their load for a vacation (though read my cautions about this later in the chapter!). They get paid for most things they attend or attend to that is student related, and almost no meeting is mandatory. There is no limit to how much adjuncts can earn since they are contractors or part-time employees who get paid for what they do. An efficient adjunct professor who can stay organized can handle many classes simultaneously at multiple universities, particularly if they are in the same subject area.

Now, with the all-too-common shortened semesters in adult learning environments, it is not surprising to find adjuncts teaching more than 50 classes per year without restrictions. That puts potential earnings at well over $100,000 per year working part-time or over $200,000 per year working full-time. Adjuncts can serve on paid dissertation and comprehensive exam committees and attend paid academic residencies that learners are often required to attend. If you read our forum, you can read the stories of hundreds of faculty who freely share that they far out-earn their full-time colleagues, and sometimes they rub it in by posting a picture of their laptop at the beach while they are working and earning money.

Benefits, of course, are a major concern and healthcare can be quite costly. Many professionals are afraid to leave their employers because of losing those valuable benefits. There are two key benefits to employees that drive their job decisions above all else – vacation days and medical insurance. As an adjunct professor, your vacations are officially unpaid, but they are under your control. It is possible to take vacations while teaching, reducing workload systematically those days but still logging in, and then catching up when returning. You are essentially taking vacations while earning pay, but you are not "completely" on vacation. I think very few adjuncts ever take a real vacation. Adjuncts are automatically on unpaid vacation when classes are not in session (sometimes this is forced and not what we want), and they can choose not to teach for a semester (without pay).

Health insurance is undoubtedly the most expensive benefit to lose, but there are plans available to self-employed individuals. When one of these plans is coupled with the Health Savings Account, adjunct professors can feel secure that they are covered sufficiently and there is no need to ever feel dependent on an employer to provide group health insurance. Taking on perhaps one or two additional classes per year can pay for an entire year of health care premiums. Many online professors prefer to have one online teaching job that offers benefits as their full-time position, and then take on additional adjunct work to supplement their income. Most of our clients have this goal in mind when they come to us for educational career consulting.

Job security has also been a subject of concern for the past couple of decades. In the days of the nuclear family, a person could expect to stay with one company until retirement. Now, retirement is almost a fantasy, as most employer-funded plans are being eliminated and employees are left to maintain their own retirement plans. Universities are one of the rare places in which retirement plans are still strong, and tenured faculty are probably the only employees in the country who can feel comfortable knowing that they cannot easily be fired. Adjuncts are at the opposite end of the spectrum in that there is no true job security; there are no retirement packages, and it is easy to get fired (technically you don't get fired; you just don't get rehired).

So, why work as an adjunct? In reality, there is

an innate sense of job security that is unsurpassed. Universities need adjuncts; good ones are valued commodities. Adjuncts are often treated better than full-timers by the deans because adjuncts can easily leave, and they don't want us to. We can still supplement our income while consulting; if we aren't rehired by one university – chances are we can be hired by another to make up the lost income – although it may take some time. (This is one reason I advocate keeping job applications out there at all times, as you never know when your workload will change).

Unlike many positions, if you do your job well you can feel secure that you will get hired again, particularly if you stay in contact with your boss and if you network through attending department meetings. You probably won't be outsourced, yet you can go elsewhere at any time you choose. You can add to your workload and the universities can't ask you not to. In fact, you can teach at multiple universities at one time, thus creating a situation in which no one employer controls more than a limited percentage of your income (this is part of the adjunctpreneur method!). Try that in a full-time job! This is job security in the truest sense; it is based on your own work ethic and principles. How hard you work dictates how well you will be rewarded, and it is not at the whim of someone with less talent or education than you have. It is this principle that is the cornerstone of the plan in this book.

When you are teaching online, course setups are locked at most institutions, which means individual faculty cannot change basic structure, learning activities and resources, or assessments.

Once you design a course as you wish, you can often keep it that way forever, or until the textbook changes or, in the case of some types of IT courses, the technology changes. Typically, you can expect to invest significant time during your first run of a course, but the time drops dramatically the second time, and levels out about the third time you teach a class. If you set up your courses right, you'll even have folders of data to post with it organized by week you should post it. Leslie Bowman's book, *Online Teaching for Adjunct Faculty: How to Manage Workload, Students, and Multiple Schools* (http://amzn.to/1glLPcJ), provides strategies to help you manage workload so that each class takes no more than 2-4 hours a week (once you have gotten through the first and second times teaching a course).

Experienced professors learn to improve their courses each time after noting confusing exam questions, poor discussion questions, and repeated emails on the same topic. Sometimes schools have a process to go through for a course change and other times they don't. It doesn't take long before the course is set to your satisfaction and the course runs far more smoothly. Telling your department chairperson about the changes that need to be made in a course helps students and shows that you care about quality education. It's a win-win.

Now, here is a downside you must be aware of. Good luck ever having a real worry-free, nonworking vacation. Also, if you turn down a contract, then two things happen: (1) you don't get paid; (2) the school finds someone else to fill your shoes that term, and that person may end up filling them permanently. Turning down a contract is risky.

One solution is to never turn one down, but that means true vacations will be rare or distant memories. After ten years of teaching online, I realized "wow, I have had about 4 days off." That is no joke. With Internet access on airplanes, even air travel is no longer a place safe from the barrage of emails (great for those of us who hate going to bed with anything in the inbox; not so great if you want a break!).

Unfortunately some universities are year-round with no breaks even for major holidays, so you truly don't get a day off. Significant others will need to be aware of this time commitment. Yes, you can work from anywhere, but you will have to work at least a few hours each day. I remember walking around New York City one Friday afternoon with a significant other, hearing "I didn't know I was dating an iPhone." I was thinking, "I haven't had a half-day off in ages! This is a dream!" while he was thinking, "How could you use our time and be on your phone at all?" That was a reminder that not everyone will "get" what we do or why we do it, or how the industry works. If you have someone you care about in your life, they will be impacted. Be up front about the job and the requirements.

Another solution for a possible mini-vacation is to make some minor schedule adjustments in a course to allow yourself a lighter week than normal if the school allows, but even then, the work is not completely gone and you must still reply to emails quickly. If you get burned out easily, this job is not for you.

What Is Required of Adjuncts at Most Schools?

There is no true standard on job requirements for an online adjunct faculty member; however, there are certain requirements that are very common at most institutions. What you would have to do depends on the online platform used, the university culture, the level of the course, the type of assignments in the course, the length of the course, the size of the class, whether the course is asynchronous or synchronous, and whether you teach from a master template or are able to design your own course. The combination of requirements for a university's online program weighs heavily into determining whether the pay for teaching is truly fair.

First and foremost, you can expect to go through an orientation and online training wherever you teach. These usually take a lot of time and are designed to indoctrinate you into the school culture while teaching you the online platform. Save the homework assignments you do in training! Many of the assignments or discussion questions you are asked to complete in training are repeated, although not in the exact same words or format, at other schools. Five universities later, you will be glad to have your own previous homework to refer to. Training is usually *not paid,* so be prepared to invest time in your future.

Training is also an opportunity for the school to evaluate you before handing you a class of your own. You can expect the training to take as long as a standard course, so plan on a couple of months of training. Some schools, like Baker College (www.baker.edu), go the extra mile and have you spend a full term shadowing another instructor, too, so it takes two full terms before you can begin to earn money. Don't take these training courses lightly. You will be evaluated and judged based on your performance. A training course is not a guarantee of a contract position. Sometimes you will have someone shadowing your first class, offering a "green or red light" evaluation at the end of your course and providing hints and tips along the way. Take these very seriously; the folks who are doing this in the second phase of training hold a lot of weight with regard to who gets to keep a job and who doesn't.

Online courses can be classified as synchronous or asynchronous. Synchronous courses require that the professor be online at the same time as the students and video or chat rooms are heavily utilized. This means that during selected hours, the professor must log in and moderate a discussion actively. It is not uncommon for a school to ask the professor to schedule additional chats at different hours of the day to accommodate students in different time zones. Sometimes professors are given assigned times during which they must be online. One chat a week is often helpful if it is designed to answer everyone's questions at once, as it saves a lot of time in responding to multiple emails. But when the online chat time turns out to be just another graded discussion on top of all of the graded written discussions, it can begin to challenge your time management abilities and can quickly lessen the value of the salary earned at that school.

Asynchronous courses are far more common, especially at the graduate level, as there are no "live" chats and so each person can log in at any time, post a question or reply to a question, and wait a day for a response. Asynchronous classes offer far more flexibility for the learner and the adjunct.

Faculty meetings are not uncommon for online universities. Some will host one or two mandatory conference calls per quarter while others will host only one or two per year. Some schools will host these faculty meetings only when some major event occurs, and some never have such calls. Faculty meetings can be valuable since they keep you in touch with the school and the benefit is stronger communication among faculty and between faculty and administrators. However, excessive meetings can cut into your schedule, especially since the meeting times are not flexible. As with course chats, these additional, non-flexible hours must be factored into your decisions to work for a university because no matter how efficient you are at grading assignments, these telephone or live call hours cannot be shortened. In the beginning, don't ask and don't worry – just get the experience. Later, when you decide which universities you want to keep and which ones you don't, you can be selective based on these types of criteria. For now, just go with it.

While not common, don't be surprised if you are asked to have office hours. You must be reachable by phone and ready to reply to any student who calls during these hours. If you don't get many calls, you can get your work done during this time, but you are still committed to being at the phone. Some say "reachable," which means by email, instant messaging, or phone.

Assignments vary dramatically by course. Often a quantitative course will have many small assignments that need quick feedback, while other courses may have only a few major assignments. Grading quantitative problems is more objective and often quicker to accomplish than grading research papers, which require editing, critical evaluation, and written feedback. Faculty I work with who teach English generally teach fewer courses each term than someone teaching statistics. With quantitative problems, a solutions file can be provided so students can check their work in light of your comments. With research papers, on the other hand, your comments stand alone and must justify any grade less than an A. Whether we like it or not, some students see themselves as consumers who are paying for their grades, and can create a difficult situation for faculty who are constantly having to justify why the student didn't earn the grade he or she sought to "get." From my experience, this happens particularly in the for-profit education sector.

Sometimes it is up to the instructor to set up assignments and other times the assignments are hard-coded into the course. Requirements on grading vary by school, but you can expect to have about three to five days to grade assignments after they are submitted. In budgeting your time, you should consider that the vast majority of students submit their assignments on the day they are due, so you will find yourself grading a lot at once if you are not careful. By adjusting the deadlines in different courses or giving incentives for early submission, you can manage your time better and be more responsive in grading. This helps you meet the school's time lines and not have "grade days from hell," as they are often referred to in our forum. If you do things right, you can even schedule one day off per week for yourself.

Discussion forums can be the easiest or the hardest part of the job. In some courses, the students get so involved in the weekly discussions that your job is more of a moderator who needs only to read them and add your two cents' worth as appropriate. You want to add something each day to show you are reading and engaged with student posts, and many universities will log in to make sure you're making substantive posts based on the course time frames. Others will let you do your job and base evaluations on your performance, and manage you by exception (usually automated reports showing you didn't login for X hours or X days, breaking school guidelines).

When universities just want you to moderate the forums, the only challenges are picking good questions that will get the maximum participation and knowing how to get students to reply when they are not active. You will want to include your own experiences, add material that helps students understand the work and advance their own knowledge, and have opportunities to share their own perceptions or viewpoints.

At the opposite extreme, there are those universities that require you to comment to everyone; this means for every posting by a student, several other students must comment to that student, and you must comment to the original posting as well as the replies to that posting. Should any of them reply to you, you must reply again regardless of the status of the thread. The discussion thread grows exponentially as the class gets larger. Adjuncts are often scored (rated) by the school, based on the quantity of postings. This can be a drain on your time if not kept in check, and yet it is often the basis on which the students define whether a course is a good one or a bad one. This is one reason to start ranking your colleges by workload and pay as you acquire relationships with more of them.

Emails for online courses should ideally be kept in the course room and not in your private email, and this is required at many universities. Regardless of how communication is done at different schools, students expect quick responses and you are obligated to give them. You really need constant access to your email; a smartphone with email accessibility can make you available during office hours. Often the university will mandate that you reply to student emails within 24 hours. In more difficult courses, you can expect more emails from students crying out for help, particularly right before assignments are due, and that takes up immeasurable time.

As you go through a course, you'll learn what questions are asked most often and you may find creative solutions, like a frequently asked questions (FAQ) document that helps learners be self-directed. Another solution may be a "listen to this first" video to help students understand some of the basics of the course. Some professors build websites for specific courses with tutorials or upload YouTube videos to help students through difficult problems. Often you will see the same questions from several students, and if you reply to everyone at once in the main discussion forums, you can eliminate many repeated questions. The key here is to minimize the need for students to send emails since those communications are unplanned and urgent by definition.

In a nutshell, a university will place requirements on you in terms of responsiveness, specific hours to be available, and visible proof of your work posted in the course rooms. These vary from school to school, and often you won't get the full picture until you actually teach for the school, so be open to anything.

Time is Money: Balancing the Load and Evaluating Your Real Rate of Return

After deciding to teach online and applying everywhere, you receive an offer and the pay sounds great - but is it? Time is money, and you must consider that fact above all else. You will often find schools paying a little more than industry average but demanding a lot more than average in terms of work, making it worth less than you might think. Sometimes you will take less pay because you need the experience, or because there are some nice perks, or they treat you well or let you teach something you enjoy a lot. But you must weigh everything—above all, your time. Since the only other measurable factor in the decision-making process besides pay is one's time, let us treat that as the primary factor for our purposes.

When you get into a routine, you could potentially be in the discussion forum less than 15 minutes per day, depending on the number of discussion questions, the size of the class, how many replies you have in your database from teaching the course in the past, and the commenting requirements. In schools where the requirements are stringent, you might find yourself in the discussion forum for closer to an hour per day, possibly more. Thus, you might be committing to two to seven hours per week for just one class. Most online schools require that professors grade the discussions each week, and that adds more time to your weekly commitment.

Grading assignments can take a serious chunk of time, too. One popular online school will typically give you classes of 35 students with three assignments per week, so you would be grading 105 papers per week, each requiring detailed comments. You might find yourself spending at least 20 hours per week reading these papers. The same popular online school mandates three hours of chats per week and holds biweekly conference calls. Combined with the hours spent on discussions and assignments, a professor can expect to spend 30 hours per week on a single class. So, a salary of $2,000 per five-week course really amounts to only $13 per hour—not worth it to most of us.

A lesser-known community college that pays $1,600 for eight weeks' work is actually a better deal. A general business course there has weekly objective exams that are automatically graded, so the professor invests zero minutes per week (unless glitches occur). Discussions do not require rigorous commenting, so only about two hours per week are needed there. Learners are expected to be self-directed. The courses are asynchronous, so chats are nonexistent. Other than unplanned emails, a professor can expect to spend about three or four hours per week on the course, thus earning about $60 per hour. This is quite different from a course that appears to pay more money for a shorter semester. What's important is that you figure out what is worth your time and budget accordingly.

How Many Schools Should You Work For?

There is no limit to how many schools you can work for. One of the benefits of being a contractor or part-time employee is that you are not restricted from working anywhere. If you're good, you may at some point be offered a core faculty position. While this is an honor and a reflection of your hard work and dedication, you usually can't work for the competition; this means you may take a great pay cut.

Often a school may give you a lot of work, and you may feel that it is enough work to satisfy you, but then you are in a precarious position. In online education, we used to say that a full-time faculty member has some degree of job security; by contrast, an adjunct can be released easily without notice. While this is still generally true, some deans are reporting their full-time faculty are being let go before adjuncts because the cost of the full-time employee is higher. A talented and experienced adjunct should have no trouble finding another position, but keep in mind that it will take time to be interviewed, go through the human resources process, complete the required training, and then have classes scheduled.

Having at least three active schools means you will never feel pressured to do what you don't wish to do for fear of being unemployed. Knowing that you always have some form of income puts you in control. The more schools you are employed with, the more easily you can choose to quit some less profitable ones (or those you just don't like) and trade up in an effort to maximize your income for your invested time.

Just don't do more than you can handle, for you wouldn't want a reputation for doing substandard work – that is a death sentence in adjunct life.

Personality, Strengths, and Marketing Yourself

It's important that the job you are doing matches your personality. If you want to quit your day job because you don't like having to be there by 9 A.M. when you suffer night after night from insomnia, you won't like a synchronous class that makes you log in at 9:30 a.m. from your kitchen. If you want more set office hours and want to feel as though your job isn't just dangling in the wind requiring time throughout all hours of the night, then you may like a scheduled synchronous format better. If you like sitting in front of your computer and prefer emails to phone calls, then choose universities that don't require conference calls and that let you respond primarily, if not entirely, by email.

Determine what traits you like in a job and which ones you dislike. Ensure the online colleges you eventually work for – once your teaching portfolio is built – reflect your personality. If you don't choose carefully, say hello to burnout and a simultaneous hello to job change.

You will also need to determine what your strengths are to market yourself. While an entire section in the book is devoted to this, here is a brief overview: Marketing yourself means figuring out your best qualities and selling them to universities. Are you a fast responder? If yes, then talk about your responsiveness and demonstrate your responsiveness by replying to letters of inquiry within a couple of hours and completing and faxing back paperwork the same day it's sent to you.

If you prefer phone communications, you may ask for a voice interview to help your strengths shine through. If you are a writing expert, be sure your emails show this. If you are passionate about a topic, be sure that comes across. Understanding yourself and your personality is a key to being happy in adjunct life and to getting hired by new schools.

Chapter 5 - How Much Can I Earn?

You can pay people to teach,
but you can't pay them to care.
— Marva Collins

When I talk with people in groups, no one wants to ask this question, much less answer it (unless they can hide behind an anonymous screen name). But when I talk one-on-one with people who want to earn a living teaching online, the question almost certainly comes out in the open. "So, how much can I make teaching online?" There is nothing wrong with asking what your earning potential is. Everyone needs to earn a living and you are an educated professional. You can earn anywhere from a few hundred extra dollars monthly to a six-figure salary, depending on how much work you want to do, which schools you work for, and if you want this to be your full-time career or just extra income.

Several factors influence what you are paid to teach an online course. Remember that teaching is only one of several ways to make money working for an online school. In this chapter, I will talk about factors influencing your pay, what kind of paycheck to expect for an online course, and then additional ways to make money.

What Influences Your Pay?

This list is not all-inclusive, but reflects what my experiences have been in my own career and what clients share regarding pay. It's important to note that usually the pay is not negotiable. This means that you're made an offer; if the school really wants you, it may budget a few extra dollars, but the pay basically is what it is. Many schools are for-profit and some are public schools. They must adhere to budgets and profit and loss (P&L) projections just like the rest of corporate America. We've found less negotiating room for online courses than in our day jobs!

Negotiating a bump in salary at the end of the year is almost unheard of, although sometimes schools will do a pay adjustment across the board for all faculty at a specific time each year. If you are unhappy with the pay offered, you may suggest that with your qualifications you expected a little more. But be forewarned—this is not looked upon very highly.

Generally speaking, if you don't like the pay, you just don't take the job. We recognize that sometimes, especially in the beginning, you may have to take what you can get. Try to keep in mind that this is only until you build up your reputation.

- The school you teach for. Each and every school, and sometimes each and every program within a school, offers a different pay rate. Just like in traditional models, some schools are known for attracting top talent by paying top dollar. There are discussions in our Make a Living Teaching Online

Facebook forum about pay, where some share their pay of $10,000 per course, while others share their pay of $50 per student. Some schools set a wide net and hope they catch some excellent teachers for smaller numbers. When looking for courses to teach online, don't hesitate to ask about money once mutual interest is shown. (Don't do this, of course, within the first couple of correspondences.) Since pay rates change constantly, I won't talk specifically about which schools pay the most, but you can get current and accurate information by asking in the Facebook forum (the link is www.facebook.com/groups/onlineprofessors). Think prestigious = larger paycheck; less prestigious = smaller paycheck. Smaller schools are assumed to pay less, but this is not always the case. Sometimes the small private schools with only a handful of adjuncts pay the best.

- The level of the degree program. Generally, you are paid in order of degree hierarchy; doctoral degree programs pay the most, and then master's, then bachelor's, then associate. This is not a hard-and-fast rule, but it is the typical scenario.
- Your credentials. You don't have much negotiating room, but the initial offer may vary depending upon your own credentials. You will earn more for a more advanced degree, or for more teaching experience. If the school is recruiting you away from another university, this is even better for you and you may be able to negotiate.
- *Your role.* If you are a course lead, expect to be paid better. If you are a subject matter expert (SME), expect slightly higher pay.

- *The number of students in your course.* Some schools pay per student or will pay an overload fee (a fee for teaching above X number of students in one class). In fact, some are even "check in, check out" systems where there is no real discussion thread, only assignments you must log in, check out, and grade. These institutions usually pay per student. If you have an oversized class, expect an "over limit" fee. This also varies by university, and from a school perspective, makes financial sense. Let's say that the class size is set at 15. A school has 22 students enrolled for a course. They can pay you for two sections of 11, not quite at capacity, or they can pay you for 7 overload students. Usually the latter is cheaper for the university (and probably less work for you).
- *The course you are willing to teach.* This isn't usually advertised, but at some schools the courses that are hard to recruit for sometimes pay more. You have no way of knowing which ones these are unless you ask your colleagues with whom you are networked, and it's awkward to ask; but this is something to keep in mind.
- *Length of the term.* The longer terms typically pay more; however, it's best to document how much time you spend for each class versus the pay and determine an hourly rate so you can make decisions later on regarding which ones to continue working for and which ones to end relationships with.
- *Faculty development.* Many schools have created courses to teach faculty subjects like how to write a syllabus, how to mentor, or how to use email effectively. Some of these faculty development

courses are mandatory to complete before you are assigned a course to teach, but often a school will have several optional courses and will pay you more money for having completed the series. The pay increase may be substantial or only nominal, but often there is a greater gain in that you are seen as a serious team member and may be given more opportunities to teach. More importantly, each of these training seminars should go on your CV as educational training, furthering your appeal to other universities as you show an interest in furthering your own understanding and engaging with a group of educators.

What Can I Expect to Make for My Work?

From my experience, pay for a six-week class can range from $1,000 to $3,000. How much time one course takes you to teach will depend on whether you've taught it before, your experience teaching online, and the particular demands of that university. You will want to document this as you begin working because eventually you may have to make decisions regarding which universities are worth your while, and which ones are not.

Longer classes warrant additional pay; but keep in mind, as noted earlier, that the pay may not translate to a larger hourly wage. For 12-week courses, expect anywhere from $1,800 to $5,000, depending on your role (instructor, faculty lead, rank), your degree, and the university. You can easily see how multiple courses can begin adding up to a sizable income. Remember, though, most likely you will be a contractor or part-time employee, a status that has even less stability, technically, than employment at will. Your contract is usually for one term (6 weeks, 12 weeks, etc.) at a time. The job stability can be high if you are good, but not so high if consistently get bad student reviews or come up on "naughty lists" frequently (the auto-generated lists that go to our bosses saying who hasn't logged in, who hasn't participated, and who is late with grading).

If you are being paid per student, expect anywhere from $125 to $300 per student per course. I have seen pay as low as $50 and as high as $500. Sometimes, while the amounts seem small, being paid per student actually means you earn more money than you would in a typical online classroom setting, so don't discount these opportunities without researching them.

If you are developing a new course, you can expect to be paid $1,000 to $5,000. This can be one-time payment for the course or spread over multiple deliverables. Once you turn over the materials, the school usually owns the copyright or intellectual property rights, so read your contract before you sign. While this doesn't mean you can't use some of your own material elsewhere, it does mean you cannot copy and paste the course for another school and get paid twice for the same work—this is not acceptable practice and can get you into a lot of trouble. Remember, one major advantage to developing a course is you can often ask for right of first refusal for teaching it.

If you are revising or updating a course, expect anywhere between $500 and $2,000. Usually this is less time-intensive than developing a new course. It typically will not lead to a right of first refusal for teaching (but it can), although it does often reflect positively on your work if you turn your course in on time and work well with the course development team. Each university has a different process for this. Some let you "go develop" right into the learning management system! Others require a long process, including a course you must take, and lots of approvals each step of the way. Obviously, you will want to be paid more for the time-consuming ones, so you need to find out what is required before you accept an offer.

If you are a lead and are expected to make minor revisions, keep others apprised of your work efforts, and help recruit faculty, add anywhere from $2,000 to $10,000 per year per area you're responsible for. Usually if you are a lead for only one class, you'll be on the low side of that number; if you're responsible for multiple courses within a program, you can expect to be on the higher side.

How to Make Extra Money

There are lots of ways to make extra money teaching online. We have already mentioned several extra-pay opportunities. Another way is to make yourself an invaluable resource for the university by attending faculty events so that they know you are interested and invested. You can also publish with the university name, help the marketing team by offering to use social media to promote their efforts, offer to take on free tasks now and again – and whatever you do, don't whine about your workload! It's acceptable to make comments about oversized classes if a situation is impacting the students' learning, but avoid making comments like "you aren't paying me enough" or "why is my class so large"; that is a surefire way to get the boot next term. While doing these positive things won't directly improve your pay, they will keep you on the "top dog" list, which means that when pay raises or new opportunities come up, you're likely to be one of the people they go to first.

If you've been working for a school for years and you haven't been given any raises, it's appropriate to ask your boss if pay raises are available or "on the horizon" as some of us like to say, and if so, what can you do to be considered for one. Then explain what you've done to help the school that you are invested in the future and in it for the long haul, and proceed to ask for a modest raise. I can give you a personal example. After working for a school for four years, I asked my boss about possible pay increases for faculty who are teaching difficult courses that require synchronous sessions. My boss reviewed my pay and realized I was being paid as though I had a masters and not a doctorate! That one change increased my pay $400 per course each term.

Remember these schools operate on tight budgets, so what you perceive as a small gesture may in fact be a big deal. This is important to recognize because you don't want to get a reputation for being a complainer or ungrateful. Also, remember that if you live in California and the school is in Michigan, you may be paid Michigan wages despite your higher living costs. This means you may need to work more than your counterparts to pay your bills, but that is a decision you have to make regarding your own lifestyle.

Another way for you to make additional money

is to let your chairperson or deans know that you're willing to take on last minute classes. Sometimes, due to a family emergency, illness, crisis, or unreliability, schools have to reschedule courses or find a new instructor at the last minute. If you're willing and able to take on classes at the last minute, you may have an opportunity to make additional money. Once you begin teaching for a school, make it clear what other subjects you want to teach and are qualified to teach, and explain why, using criteria like credit hours in a subject and professional experience. Be sure to wait until you've built up a good reputation at a school before asking for more work. You want to prove yourself first.

Another option is to ask to teach faculty workshops, be a faculty trainer (be forewarned: this is a lot of work!), or be a quality auditor. Usually this requires that you spend some time going through courses and checklists to be sure faculty members are doing their jobs.

If you can write a book that would benefit the students, you might be able to sell your work through the school. When the author is seen as an expert by the school, the school may be willing to directly help with the sales. Also, since you will be in the academic world, you could contact major textbook publishers and let them know that you are available to review textbooks. They will often pay $250 to $1,000 to review a textbook, depending on the work involved. Your credentials as a professor will carry weight in being selected for this privilege, so wait until you are actually teaching before seeking these opportunities.

Chapter 6 – The Hunt: Finding Your First Job

"Anyone who stops learning is old,
whether at twenty or eighty.
Anyone who keeps learning stays young."
— Henry Ford

Finding jobs is the key to successfully beginning your online teaching career or adding jobs to your existing career. Applying for jobs and getting interviews is crucial to your career; whether it's your first online teaching job or your tenth. Throughout this chapter, I will explore several successful techniques that are new and creative, but more important, are proven strategies. As an educational consultant helping professors get jobs every single day, I have survey results and suggestions from clients in this chapter as well.

In the "old days" of online teaching, the path was to find a university and program you're both qualified for and interested in teaching, and then contact the dean and attempt to get a job. While that still works to some degree, the process is more structured, rigid, and in many ways, more "blind" than in the past. There are many resources you can use to find online universities, and there are literally thousands of online programs where you can teach.

Locating Schools

If your goal is to work at specific schools, you can ask your colleagues, friends, teachers, or anyone you know who may teach online. Join our Facebook forum and ask who is hiring in various disciplines. Find online instructors on LinkedIn who will list the schools they work for. Remember that many of you will work as online teachers who are also entrepreneurs, running a small business with one or more clients – the universities and students they serve.

One strategy is to create a top 10 list of colleges you'd like to work for and – contrary to logic – email them *last*. You want to practice – see what works and what doesn't – and you don't want to do this on your top choices. You'll be amazed at how many modifications you will make to your introductory message before you feel really good about it. Use the rejections and think through the introduction and resume several times before you send it to your top 10-school list. Still, don't wait *too* long; time is of the essence. Don't feel bad if you receive no response; that is often the case.

There are also lots of online tools you can use to find schools. Sites such as Adjunct Nation, HigherEdJobs, Indeed.com, and even Monster.com show not only schools but also lots of open online teaching jobs. These big job boards will have much more competition for each position, though, than if you contact a dean directly or you go to a specific school's career center website and apply to jobs not many people know about. Our goal with The Babb Group's job leads is to provide clients with leads that not many people know about, to increase the chance that you are one of only a few possible candidates, instead of one of hundreds or thousands.

You should apply through the mechanisms outlined in the job postings as well as the methods described in this chapter. You do not have to just follow the rules if there is a position you really want. The rules won't always get you visibility—you may be put into a database along with other people who never get looked at. Many of the jobs posted are job pools to collect CVs in case a school needs someone at any time. After all, the responses to job postings are typically filed by human resources (HR) folks and not by the well-educated deans you will be working for. So it's possible that you may be screened out because a clerk incorrectly judged you unqualified or thought your CV was poorly written. Here are some places that list more schools than you can imagine:

info.theonlinedegree.com
www.chronicle.com
www.degreeinfo.com
www.educationcenteronline.org
www.elearners.com
www.findaschool.org
www.geteducated.com
www.program-online-degree.com
www.themoderndegree.com
www.worldwidelearn.com

Finding Programs to Teach In

If your goal is to target specific schools, you may first want to ask in the forum what professors' experiences have been at various universities. Then, go to the websites of schools on your list and figure out which programs have courses you are qualified to teach and which of those courses looks interesting. We also have university lists available on our website at www.thebabbgroup.com. You will need to list the courses you feel qualified for and interested in teaching in your introductory email to a specific university. This is usually the first thing the person receiving your email asks; in addition, the fact that you are prepared and knowledgeable about the university's programs will come across in your email message. This is important, because you don't want to appear as though you are just spamming universities to find jobs. Customize your email with the dean's name, and mention specific reasons you want to work there. Remember that you aren't spamming—you are offering important services to students and you are qualified to do so. It can be tough to think of ourselves as salespeople, but we do need to sell ourselves just like small business owners need to do with their services!

The programs will list their courses and descriptions of each; be prepared to answer follow-up emails about why you are qualified to teach in the programs you indicated in your message and don't forget to attach your CV and unofficial transcripts. Often a school has a need to fill a specific course, and if your letter mentions that course, you will be more likely to stand out than someone whose CV must be read to determine if he/she is qualified to teach that course. Don't just use course names; use the school's own course numbering system. After all, wouldn't it be more impressive to state that you would like to teach STA1234—Business Statistics than to merely state that you teach statistics?

Hierarchy's Role in Finding Your Contact

Universities generally have several layers of bureaucracy, and online organizations, which are often public companies, may have even more than the norm. After you navigate to a prospective employing university's contact page, find the link for applying as an adjunct faculty member. If there isn't one, then find HR's email address; it's usually on the contact page somewhere. Send your cover letter in the body of your email and attach your CV to the very first introductory email. Later in this chapter there are examples of what your introductory letter may look like, as well as a sample CV that is available as an MS Word template on my website.

I cannot reinforce this enough – you should not be submitting a resume for a teaching job! In 2006, you could do that. Today there is far too much competition. You should be submitting a professional CV that includes a number of key sections, as a complete picture of your academic and professional career. A resume is limited to one to two pages and should be brief; a CV will often be 5-7 pages without experience and 10 or more (50 or more for long-time professors) with experience.

Human Resources

The obvious answer to finding jobs online is to contact the human resources department. However, just as direct contacts in the business world prove more effective in increasing your visibility than going through traditional methods, so is going directly to those hiring at online colleges. First, I'll discuss the human resources method. Some universities will require you to use this method regardless, so it's worth covering despite it being less effective for visibility within the right levels of the organization.

Even if you submit your CV directly to a contact, as outlined in the next section, you should also submit it to HR; you may be asked to do this anyway, so it will save time. It also may lead to the department chairperson receiving your CV twice within a couple of days—not a bad reminder of your interest.

Keep the introductory letter to human resources generic, beginning with "Dear Human Resources:" or something of that nature; however, be certain it has the same data as the email you will send directly to contacts. You do not want to have any lack of clarity regarding your qualifications.

Direct Contacts

Finding direct contacts is a great way to get jobs in academia, particularly in online schools – and having a referral from an existing employee or faculty member is even better. As in business, introducing yourself directly to the hiring manager is a very effective way to be seen, as well as to show the dedication, perseverance, and self-direction it takes to directly contact hiring managers. Understanding the hierarchy at these institutions is critical. Unlike businesses, though, schools often put their faculty, department chair, and school dean email addresses online. If they don't, it's relatively easy to find out what they are. We offer a custom job search solution for those of you who do not want to go through these headaches.

Usually, faculty members report either to a lead faculty for a specialization of study or directly to a department chair. This often depends on how big the institution is and whether it's serving a large student population, whether it's a public or private company, and the size of the school you want to work for. A university is comprised of numerous schools, which are areas of study like management, public health, or human services, and then areas of specialization within those schools, like information systems management, preventative care, or social work. Faculty chairs are often responsible for specializations and deans are responsible for entire schools. A business school dean has several faculty chairs reporting to him or her, and the faculty report to the chair or a lead. A typical hierarchy is shown in Figure 6.1 (in some schools, there is a chief academic officer or provost between the president and the deans).

Using Direct Contacts

From the diagram, it's easy to see where you need to look and who you need to contact. If you're used to working in industry, you could replace the department chairpersons with managers or directors;

however, you would rarely find their email addresses published. Universities generously provide contact information, which is a huge benefit if you are looking for a job. After you have found a university you want to work for, follow these steps for locating and then introducing yourself to the appropriate individuals:

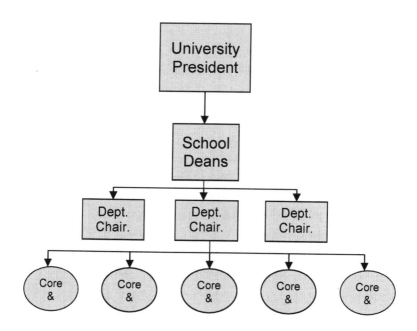

1. Look for the programs you are interested in working for and qualified to teach in.
2. Network in the online teaching forum and see what others say about the school and who to contact, what the requirements are and if possible, what the pay is.
3. Review the websites and determine who the

department chairpersons and/or the school deans are. Note their first and last names and their degrees, if posted. If degrees aren't posted, it's safest to assume that individuals have doctorates and address them formally as such. If you reach someone who doesn't have a doctorate, at worst you have called someone who isn't a doctor a doctor; this is not nearly as offensive as calling a doctor "Miss" or "Mister."

4. Compose an introductory message (see the "Sample Documents" section of this chapter) and address it to the individual you want to work for, starting off with "Dear Dr. Such and Such." Keep it a formal introductory opening, and then let your personality shine in the rest of your email.

5. The subject line needs to make it clear you are job hunting. However, if you are being referred from someone, make that clear. We recommend one of the following subjects:
    i. Adjunct Introduction: Online Teaching
    ii. Referral – Adjunct Online Position

6. Blind carbon copy (BCC) yourself. This will help you keep track of everyone you have emailed and will make it easier to follow up. Since often it takes two to three months to even get a response, you will want to follow up and keep track of who suggested you write back at a later time. An Excel spreadsheet or an email folder can easily accomplish the organization required to do this.

7. If you are sending the email to a department chairperson, carbon copy (CC) the dean. If the chair has changed positions, cc'ing the dean saves time and reduces the potential for error, but also shows that you respect the hierarchy and

know you'd be working for the chairperson.

What if the email address of the person you need to contact isn't listed? It is rare but does happen that the university lists the contact name but not the email address. You have a really good chance of still getting an email through if you use the following technique.

Most companies use one of several naming formats, simply because it's easier for technical support people and creates logical name directories for internal employees. The most common naming conventions are:

FirstInitialLastName@universityname.edu
(e.g., JTestUser@universityname.edu)

FirstName.LastName@universityname.edu
(e.g., Joe.TestUser@universityname.edu)

Lastname@universityname.edu
(e.g., testUser@universityname.edu)

If you don't know the individual's email address, look at other email addresses listed on the technical support page, the student recruitment page, or the HR page to ascertain the domain name. If it says @universityname.edu for these departments, chances are the same domain name is used for all individuals who work for the university. You can deduce the first part of the email address in the same way.

If the employment department has an email address of Jan.testUser@universityname.edu, then you can be quite certain the school uses the FirstName.LastName@universityname.edu format.

Now here is the key: You do not want an individual to see his or her email address in the "To" line three times. So be sure you follow these instructions:

> To: Choose one of the three
> BCC: Yourself
> BCC: The other two email addresses

Usually if you use this method, the individual you emailed doesn't know you have sent it to three addresses in hopes of finding one that works. The failed addresses will simply bounce back and the individual you are sending the email to won't be any the wiser. In the body of the email message, leave no indication that you weren't certain of the address.

Preparing Documents for Fast Submission

Sometimes, bureaucracy won't interfere with the online process and you will be amazed at how fast a department chair or dean responds because he or she is looking for someone with your expertise to teach a class quickly. This is a great position for the online adjunct to be in and you don't want to hold up the process or be a roadblock.

Also remember that, since you will be teaching online, you will need to check your email several times per day. There is no excuse for not doing so; if you are on the road a lot, get a smartphone that allows you to check email. You'll need it once you start teaching, anyway, as you will be required to respond to students and faculty within a certain period of time. Get used to it now! Fast responses to the school official or manager show that you will also be responsive to student needs. Don't let an email sit in the in-box for more than a couple of hours when you start hearing back from individuals at the universities you apply to. Some people will respond immediately and others will take months. Be sure to follow up with those you haven't heard from within a couple of weeks and keep them on your radar screen for two years.

Have available on your computer (and any computer you travel with) the following documents for immediate emailing if needed or requested:

- Electronic copies of *all* of your transcripts.
- The address to make a formal request for official transcripts to be sent from previous universities you have attended (and graduated from).
- Your curriculum vitae – the expanded academic version, not your business version.
- Your cover letter.
- References list—three professional references with name, title, email address, and phone number, and three academic references of colleagues or professors, along with name, title, institution, email address, and phone number. (Remember to give your references a heads-up! No surprises!)
- Three letters of recommendation in PDF format
- Three teaching evaluations, if you have them
- List of the courses you want to teach at the various colleges or schools along with your

reasoning (you should note this to yourself as you're sending emails)

- Your teaching website address, if you have one. If not, a professional (personal, not work!) site will also help. Please read the chapter on social media presence for online teaching jobs to help you understand why this matters.
- Statement of your teaching philosophy. Of everything you write, this will probably be most difficult. In no more than two paragraphs, outline how and why you teach, and what you bring to the classroom. A sample is included at the end of this chapter and my blog has outlined how to put this together at www.thebabbgroup.com/blog.

Sample Documents

Introductory Email

Your introduction email, whether to HR or to a direct contact, must reflect your personality, your teaching style, and what you'll bring to the table. In academia, the old rules of business don't apply; your CV and your cover letter are expected to be lengthy. Content is the key here. It is not recommended that you directly copy the ideas below into your own introduction and fill in the blanks; chances are many others will have the same introductory message. However, you can use them as starting points and then modify them to suit your style.

Introductory Email: Less Formal with a Referral and Experience, No Specific Courses (CV attached)

+++

Hello,

Please allow me to introduce myself; my name is Joe Smith. I am an adjunct faculty specializing in technology management, technical courses, and business courses. I received an email from Dr. Test User regarding an open position with your university.

I have taught online courses using Blackboard and WebCT and have taught in the classroom for over three years. I bring a tremendous amount of technology and management experience into the classroom and enjoy knowing I have made a difference in students' knowledge and contributed to students' professional growth.

Having both taken courses online and taught them, I have a unique perspective on balancing the benefits of online learning with individual learning styles. The eleven years of professional management experience I bring to the classroom help bring real-life examples and case studies to the studies of management and technology.

I feel that my experience both in the classroom and online as well as my commitment to the education of my students would allow me to make a significant contribution to your program. I am attaching my CV for your review, and would love to discuss with you the opportunities you may have for online teaching and how my skill set and qualifications would enhance your program. I may be reached at (999) 555-1212 anytime, or by email at joesmith@myemail.com.

Thank you for your consideration and your time.

Sincerely,

Joe Smith, PhD, MBA, BS
[Signature]
Joe Smith, PhD, MBA
Adjunct Faculty
Email: joesmith@myemailaddress.com
Alternative email: joesmith@hotmail.com
Website: http://www.mywebsite.com
Voice messages (leave email address): 949 555-1212
Cell: (999) 555-1212
Instant Messenger: joesmith@hotmail.com

++

Note how the multiple contact methods in the signature show how flexible you will be with your students. You are listing a cell phone, a voice mail, a website, and even an instant messaging address.

Introductory Email: Less Formal with a Contact and Experience (CV attached)

++

Dr. Department Chair:

Please allow me to introduce myself; my name is Joe Smith. I am an adjunct faculty specializing in technology management, technical courses, and business courses. I have taught online using Blackboard, WebCT, and numerous other systems, and have taught in the classroom for over three years. I bring a tremendous amount of technology and management experience into the classroom and enjoy knowing I have made a difference in students' knowledge and contributed to students' professional growth.

I was reviewing your website, which noted the request for IT faculty for the Master's program. Not only did this appear like an exceptional fit, but I have colleagues working at your university who speak very highly of your programs, including Dr. NewJob and Dr. Online, who would provide you with the highest of recommendations regarding my work, work ethic, and experience.

I have a PhD in Organizational Leadership and Technology Management and an MBA in Business Administration with a Technology emphasis. My prior experience with both in-class and online courses has taught me to be understanding and respectful of student needs unique in the online environment, encourage personal and professional growth and responsibility, foster a sense of community, and focus on students' education. Having both taken courses online and taught them, I have a unique perspective on balancing the benefits of online learning with individual learning styles. The years of professional management experience I bring to the classroom help bring real-life examples and case studies to the studies of management and technology. I have also been an IT professional for thirteen years, holding positions such as a Senior IT Director and currently an IT consultant running my own business.

I feel that my experience both in the classroom and online as well as my commitment to the education of my students would allow me to make a significant contribution to your program. I am attaching my resume for your review, and would love to discuss with you the opportunities you may have for online teaching and how my skill set and qualifications would enhance your program. I also have a website at the address listed below so you may get to know me a bit better. I may be reached at (999) 555-1212 anytime, or by email at joesmith@myemailaddress.com.

Thank you for your consideration and your time.

Sincerely,
Joe Smith, PhD, MBA, BS
[Signature]
Joe Smith, PhD, MBA
Adjunct Faculty
Email: joesmith@myemailaddress.com
Alternative email: joesmith@hotmail.com
Website: http://www.mywebsite.com
Voice messages (leave email address): (949) 555-1212

Cell: (999) 555-1212
Instant Messenger: joesmith@hotmail.com

+++

Address the person you want to work for as "Dear Dr." Use "Dear Human Resources" in your generic HR emails. However, when you CC the human resources department, you should address your emails to the person you'd be working for along with CC-ing the school dean.

Introductory Email: On-Ground Experience, Responding to a Request (Attach CV)

+++

Dear Dr. XYZ:

This is in reply to your job posting for Professor of Business Administration/Economics in the *Chronicle of Higher Education*. I meet your requirements, including my doctorate in business administration, 10 years of course room experience, strong understanding of statistical software, and expertise in business systems analysis.

My adjunct teaching experience includes 24 semesters of statistics, 5 semesters of operations management, 1 semester of marketing research, and an upcoming semester of management science.

My graduate-level education includes over 21 semester hours of statistics/research courses, over 10 hours of economics, and over 11 hours of marketing.

I have enclosed my CV, unofficial transcripts, statement of teaching philosophy, three letters of reference, and student evaluations from several courses I have taught. If you need further information, please call me at (999) 555-1212. I look forward to meeting you.

Yours sincerely,

Joe Smith

++

Introductory Email: Experience, Blind Introductory Letter, with Specific Courses

++

Dear Human Resources,

I am interested in pursuing an adjunct teaching opportunity with the [University] School of [Insert School]. I have a Doctorate in Business Administration from [University]. I also have over 17 years' teaching experience, including dozens of online courses in the past five years. My courses have been at all levels from Associate to Doctorate. Additionally, I have developed numerous courses and served as course director for many.

I would be most interested in teaching [Course Number and Name], [Course Number and Name], [Course Number and Name], and [Course Number and Name]. As you can see from my attached resume, I have significant teaching experience in each of these subjects and have sufficient graduate credits to qualify for teaching them. I even have work experience in these subject areas, which contributes greatly to my ability to teach effectively with adult learners.

I have also attached copies of my transcript so you can preview my qualifications (I will send official transcripts upon request). I am confident I can be a valued asset to your program. I look forward to your reply.

Sincerely,

[Insert graphic of your signature if you have one]

Dr. Joe Smith

++

Introductory Email: Limited Experience, Blind Introductory Letter, No Specific Courses

+++

To Whom It May Concern,

I would like to express my interest in joining [University] as a member of your esteemed faculty. As you will note from my resume, I am currently working on my doctoral degree in [Subject] at [University], an online institution, with a planned completion date of June 2006. I received my graduate degree in Management Information Systems and my undergraduate degree in International Business, both from [University].

I have over 17 years of professional experience, much of which was acquired at Fortune 1000 companies. I have always been directly involved with the business lines of the organizations I have worked for, allowing me to gain a thorough understanding of their primary functional areas. As a project manager, I have either led or been instrumental in seeing many business initiatives come to fruition and have trained dozens of employees in a professional setting. [Note how the writer here doesn't have much teaching experience, so he talks about his professional experience and how this will help him in the classroom. This is a very effective method!]

Although my entry into the field of instruction occurred relatively recently, I have already espoused the values and practices that I believe are necessary to provide learners with the proper framework to increase their self-worth and their value as members of the greater workforce. As an instructor, I place the student, never the material, at the center of my instructional model. I try not to "teach" in the traditional sense of the word, but to facilitate learning, which I believe is a process that begins and ends with the student.

I am a strong believer in the student-centered instructional model. The importance that I place on substantive critical feedback, especially within the online environment, has allowed me to achieve success as an instructor early on, which I always measure in my ability to bring students closer to their individual academic and professional goals, whatever they may be.

I believe that my education and extensive work experience, both as a practitioner and an educator, make me an ideal candidate to join a prestigious institution like [University]. Please contact me at your earliest convenience so that we may discuss my qualifications in greater detail, as well as the opportunity for me to become an integral part of [University].

Kind regards,

Joe Smith

++

Curriculum Vitae

I have mentioned the CV many times throughout this book. You need to spend considerable time on your CV, with or without professional help. The CV is essentially a resume that is targeted for academic positions. A CV will thoroughly detail your education, professional qualifications, and related activities. Effective CVs provide the depth necessary to showcase your qualifications without providing so much information that it overloads the reader; with enough information to make the interview more about what you bring to the table than if you are qualified. In general, CVs are longer than resumes, and are often five pages or more in length for a beginning instructor.

On my website, I have a CV template, a CV Writing Service, a CV review service and many other CV options. If you are a do-it-yourselfer, check out my blog at www.thebabbgroup.com/blog for 21 items to include in your CV. There is an infographic to help you along.

Even if you lack formal experience as an instructor, there are highly transferable skills that you can emphasize, such as training colleagues on new material, presenting at a conference, developing training materials in your job, or providing tutoring or mentoring as a volunteer. You may wish to list this in the Educator section, noted as professional trainer experience. Think hard about professional opportunities where you have given a seminar to professionals in a brown bag lunch or in a more formal setting. If this doesn't apply to you, you will need to be sure your introductory email or cover letter reflects how you are starting out in teaching but are bringing your professional experience to the classroom, and that you are looking to change careers for a reason you state. This doesn't eliminate you; we have all started somewhere with no teaching experience. Once you get one or two teaching jobs under your belt, you will have the experience to list, and you need to update your resume every single time something changes, including dates, programs, classes, or professional training.

Unlike a resume, which has rather standard sections, a CV allows the significant freedom for you to choose headings that work best for you. The most common sections used are: Education, Certifications, Honors/Awards, Grants/Fellowships Received, Publications, Institutional Service/Committee Work, Languages, Computer/Technical Skills, Subject Matter Expertise, Learning Management Systems, Teaching and Training Experience, Related Professional Experience, Internships/Assistantships, Professional Memberships/Associations, Presentations Given, Community Involvement/Volunteer Activities, Specialized Training Received, and Professional Development. Please keep a watch on my blog and our Facebook forum for the latest information about what is working out there in the field.

Remember in many of the online job application systems, you are being evaluated against keywords. Even if you do not get a job you applied for, your CV will stay in the system. That is why I advocate using the entire course description for each class, to improve keyword searching on your CV. Using a straightforward format without headers and simple lists improves the chance of the HR system correctly parsing your CV.

From personal experience and the experience of our clients, I can say that you need to consider what to list and what not to list if you work for a significant number of schools. I am not recommending that you be dishonest, just know that listing everything you do and everywhere you work may appear as though you do not have time for a new university. Deans do not automatically assume that you are only teaching a class one time per year, so be sure to note that. If you rarely teach at a school, you can use words like 'occasionally teach online' or 'teach approximately two times per year' – something that shows you are, in fact, not overworked. Some faculty remove some schools that don't take up much time but clutter up the CV. Experience is important, but the university that is hiring you also wants some degree of commitment and may not appreciate your being a professional adjunct, even if you are excellent at what you do for every university.

CV Examples

If you get a moment to thank the kind individuals who agreed to have their CVs included here, please do! These are examples of what has worked for faculty. You can always use our template and our blog, too.

Sample CV: With Teaching Experience, Professional Experience and Degrees

Dr. Andrew Carpenter allowed us to use his CV as an example of a professor with a thoroughly written and well-documented CV, with experience (both professional and academic) and graduate degrees. You will see how clear, comprehensive and thorough his CV is, and how he emphasizes his social media accounts (more on that later!) and his website. He has numerous ways for deans or HR professionals to contact him, showing his support for many types of technology and outreach. Note that in the CV examples I had to abbreviate some of the months to get them to fit with format in tact into the book, though they are spelled out in the original versions.

+++

CURRICULUM VITAE

Andrew N. Carpenter
Address…
Address…
Phone: …

Email: andy@andrewcarpenter.net
Homepage: http://www.andrewcarpenter.net/home.html
LinkedIn: http://www.linkedin.com/in/philosophyandrew/
Facebook: http://www.facebook.com/ProfAndyCarp
Twitter: http://www.twitter.com/ProfAndyCarp
Google+: http://gplus.to/ProfAndyCarp

Statement of Teaching Philosophy

As an educator, I affirm the ideals of honesty, integrity, and the human potential for moral and intellectual growth. I abhor the tyranny of low expectations and embrace the power of combining high expectations with correspondingly high levels of academic support.

In the classroom, I am relentlessly positive with my students: I assume that each student can achieve sophisticated learning and can undergo significant intellectual growth, and I work hard encouraging my students in ways designed to inspire them to work harder and to learn a LOT in their classes.

I believe that the combination of high academic expectations and a high degree of individualized academic support is extremely powerful for adult learners; my thirteen years of teaching adult students online convince me that this represents the single most powerful strategy for helping adult learners to achieve significant learning.

In sum, I understand the needs of adult learners and understand how to inspire these individuals to secure sophisticated, high-quality learning and intellectual growth.

Personal Attributes

Award-winning educator, active researcher, expert in online education. Over twenty years post-secondary teaching experience; recipient of five teaching awards from four institutions of higher learning.

Significant expertise in learning assessment, curriculum development, student retention, faculty development, faculty governance, program assessment, institutional assessment, and accreditation. Strong knowledge of academia and academic processes and systems.

Peer reviewer for Higher Learning Commission and Distance Education Training Council. Master Course Reviewer within the Quality Matters Online Course Design Quality Certification project. Vice President/President-Elect of the American Association of Philosophy Teachers.

Sustained publishing record in disciplinary scholarship and in the scholarship of teaching and learning.

Highly-organized professional with excellent communication skills who excels at critical thinking, strategic planning, and continuous improvement.

Skilled practitioner of research-based best practices for identifying, writing, assessing, and helping students to achieve learning objectives and competencies.

Possesses a clear vision of academic excellence and an uncompromised commitment to academic integrity.

Passionate educator who regularly inspires students to achieve more than they thought was possible.

Teaching Experience

Contributing Part-Time Faculty Member Feb. 2014 – present
Walden University, Minneapolis, MN

CRJS 6420 – Organizational Management and Leadership [taught online]

Public and nonprofit leaders in all areas of public administration require a thorough understanding of the expectations of their roles as leaders and managers of diverse and complex organizations. Students use theoretical and applied perspectives from which they study the intricacies of these roles, including the distinction between leadership and management, organizational culture, change management, systems theories, and organizational development. Students gain a practical understanding of these topics through the application of principles and concepts to public and nonprofit organizational settings.

HUMN 8701 - Culture and Psychology [taught online]

Culture often has a profound influence on individual beliefs, personality development, and social behavior. Therefore, mental health professionals must have a fundamental understanding of the impact and psychological implications of culture. In this course, students focus on core themes of cross-cultural psychology—specifically, cultures representing different parts of the world and cultural influences on human psychology. Students explore the cultural components, research, and theory of cross-cultural psychology, and they assess the overall impact of culture on the field of psychology around the world. Additionally, they engage in readings and practical assignments to gain a better understanding of human development and the interactions between culture and social behaviors, health, mental health, and mental illnesses.

HUMN 9001 - Dissertation [taught online]

This course offers doctoral students the opportunity to integrate their program of study into an in-depth exploration of an interest area that includes the completion of a research study. Students complete the dissertation independently, with the guidance of a dissertation supervisory committee chair and committee members. Students complete a prospectus, proposal, Institutional Review Board application, and dissertation.

RSCH 8350 - Advanced Qualitative Reasoning and Analysis [taught online]

Students in this research course build upon their established qualitative research proficiencies and provides them with practical experience in application. Students are also provided with the opportunity to develop specialized knowledge and skills within each of the common qualitative traditions for designing qualitative research at the doctoral level. Students explore more complex qualitative research designs and analyses; multiple approaches to coding and organizing data; core components of a qualitative write up; the importance of quality assurance; and the ethical considerations and social change implications of conducting qualitative research and producing knowledge. They apply their knowledge and skills by developing a qualitative research plan.

Dissertation Chair   Jan. 2014 – present
Grand Canyon University, Phoenix, AZ

DIS 955 though DIS 965 - Dissertation I through III [taught online]

These courses course provide learners with individualized support in their dissertation journey. Learners work directly with their dissertation chair and committee members to continue their research endeavors as aligned with their individual progress plan.

DIS 966 through DIS 970 - Research Continuation I through V [taught online]

These courses emphasize the finalization of the dissertation and provide learners with individualized support for completing their dissertation journey. Learners continue to work directly with their dissertation chair and committee members based on their individual progress plan for completing their dissertation.

DIS 975 - Dissertation Research Continuation [taught online]

This course emphasizes the finalization of the dissertation

and provides learners guidance for finding the appropriate venues and approaches in publishing their research findings. This will include the final steps necessary in pulling together what might have been earlier versions of chapters one, two, and three, as well as the proofing and dissertation editing strategies that are required and the steps scholars can take to make sure their results are, in fact, shared with other scholars. This includes an exploration of writing research articles, preparing to present scholarly papers, as well as other publication venues.

RES 871 - Developing the Formal Proposal [taught online]

The best researchers know how to strategically define their research agenda with the necessary clarity to inform the scholarly community and to establish a blueprint for analysis and replication. In this course, learners focus on these issues by exploring development of chapter one of their dissertation proposal. Learners are asked to create a problem statement; identify research questions and/or hypotheses; identify the data required to answer those questions; summarize the methodology they will use to investigate the problem; and provide a discussion of the study's significance and purpose, limitations/delimitations and assumptions, operational definitions, and an introduction to the problem as well as a summary of the chapter in order to demonstrate their understanding of effective research application. The development of this knowledge will result in the formation of the learner's dissertation proposal.

Adjunct Professor   Jan. 2014 – present
Boise State University, Boise, ID

HLTHST 280 - Statistical Methods for the Health Sciences [taught online]

Introduction to the application and use of statistical principles and methods in health sciences. General computer skills (Excel) required to statistically analyze quantitative and qualitative data.

Adjunct Professor   Oct. 2013 – present
Strayer University, Herndon, VA

PHI 210 - Critical Thinking [taught online]

The course develops the ability to identify, analyze, and evaluate reasoning in everyday discourse. It examines the elements of good reasoning from both a formal and informal perspective and introduces some formal techniques of the basic concepts of deductive and inductive reasoning. It also promotes reasoning skills through examining arguments from literature, politics, business, and the media. This course enables students to identify common fallacies, to reflect on the use of language for the purpose of persuasion, and to think critically about the courses and biases of the vast quantity of information that confronts us in the "Information Age."

Dissertation Chair   July 2013 – present
Northcentral University, Prescott Valley, AZ

Doctoral Dissertation Research I, II, III, and IV [taught online]

In these courses, learners progress through the final stages of their work toward the doctoral degree. These stages include committee and University approval of a dissertation proposal, application to and approval by the Institutional Review Board, the collection and analysis of research data, the preparation and approval of the final dissertation manuscript, and the successful completion of the Oral Presentation.

Adjunct Professor   Aug. 2012 – present
Saint Leo University, Saint Leo FL

PHI 101 - The Quest for Wisdom [taught online]

The course examines human beings as present to themselves, as having a narrative self-understanding, and as being on a quest for meaning and orientation in life. Some of the topics are the mystery of existence; thinking and prejudice; the good, conscience, and the power of choice; the state and the dignity of the person; the problem of materialism and scientism; and the place of imagination in articulating life's meaning.

PHI 110RS - Faith and Philosophical Enquiry [taught online]

This course examines definitions, assumptions, and arguments central to religious existence via the lens of several key classical and contemporary philosophers. Students will develop and refine their ability to think impartially and objectively about personal religious commitments, understand alternative religious points of view, and formulate and defend informed arguments and objections with respect to the subject matter. Topics include faith and reason, arguments for the existence of God, the problem of evil, and responses to religious diversity.

PHI 309 – History of Philosophy I: Ancient to Medieval [taught online]

A survey of the Western philosophical tradition from its beginnings in Greek thought to the Middle Ages; it includes the reading and analysis of fundamental texts by main figures of the period such as Plato, Aristotle, Aug.ine, Anselm, Aquinas.

PHI 310 – History of Philosophy II: The Modern World [taught online]

A survey of Western philosophical thought from the sixteenth to the nineteenth centuries; includes the reading and analysis of fundamental texts by significant figures of the period, such as Descartes, Hobbes, Locke, Hume, Kant, Hegel, Kierkegaard, and Nietzsche.

Part-Time Faculty   Feb. 2011 - present
Capella University, Minneapolis, MN

ED5006 - Survey of Research Methodology [taught online]

This course is an overview of graduate research methodology. Learners examine fundamental research methodologies and their respective quantitative and qualitative approaches to rigorous scholarly inquiry.

ED8117 – Advanced Qualitative Research Methods [taught online]

In this course, learners evaluate qualitative research methods and designs. Learners focus on developing the skills used to synthesize information related to qualitative research methodology and examine ethical issues associated with the qualitative research process.

ED8119 – Advanced Research Design [taught online]

In this course, learners identify and research an education-related idea using a competent research design that can be further developed into a dissertation prospectus. Learners demonstrate appropriate application of research methods and data collection and analysis tools and exemplify the critical-thinking skills needed to analyze a significant professional issue and synthesize it into a researchable form.

ED8123 - Statistics for Educational Research 2 [taught online]

Learners in this course apply statistical analyses appropriate to different research contexts using SPSS, a statistical software package. Learners examine statistical concepts, including analysis of variance (ANOVA), analysis of covariance (ANCOVA), correlation, regression, chi square, factor analysis, and post hoc and demonstrate different hypothesis testing techniques.

ED-R8921 - PhD Colloquium Track 1 [hybrid course]

The Track 1 colloquium includes an online courseroom, a residency experience, and a final assessment. Learners interact with peers and faculty as they participate in online courseroom and residency activities that emphasize assessment and practice of academic and intellectual skill sets essential to progressing through doctoral program course work. Learners also engage in self-reflection exercises and participate in learning experiences that address the doctoral research, critical-thinking, and professional communication competencies associated with becoming a scholar-practitioner. Following the residency experience, learners complete a final assessment that demonstrates Track 1 learning outcomes..

ED-R8922 - PhD Colloquium Track 2 [hybrid course]
The Track 2 colloquium includes an online course-room, a residency experience, and a final assessment. Learners interact with peers and faculty as they participate in online course-room and residency activities that emphasize applying the research process to their chosen discipline. Learners also expand their intellectual applications and analysis skills and the doctoral research, critical-thinking, and professional communication competencies associated with becoming a scholar-practitioner. Following the residency experience, learners complete a final assessment that demonstrates Track 2 learning outcomes.

ED-R8923 - PhD Colloquium Track 3 [hybrid course]
The Track 3 colloquium includes an online course-room, a residency experience, and a final assessment. Learners interact with peers and faculty as they participate in online course-room and residency activities that emphasize expanding and applying doctoral competencies to the independent research phase of the program in preparation for the comprehensive examination and dissertation. Learners also continue to strengthen the doctoral research, critical-thinking, and professional communication competencies associated with becoming a scholar-practitioner and focus on using intellectual and academic skill sets to synthesize and analyze theory and research as leaders in the discipline. Following the residency experience, learners complete a final assessment that demonstrates Track 3 learning outcomes.

I also serve as a **Research Proposal Reviewer** responsible for reviewing the research methodological quality and scientific merit of doctoral learners' dissertation proposals and as a **Research Consultant** assisting learners in addressing methodological issues in their dissertation planning.

Adjunct Professor & Subject Matter Expert Jan. 2011 – Aug. 2014
Grantham University, Lenexa, KS

PL201 – Introduction to Philosophy [also SME designer of this course] [taught online]

This course provides an introduction to philosophy, emphasizing content coverage and development of critical reasoning skills. It pays serious attention to the personal and practical relevance of philosophy by focusing on its experiential, therapeutic, and social applications. Topics include the definition of philosophy, philosophical argument, epistemology and metaphysics, ethics and moral decision making, and political philosophy.

PL301 – Practical Philosophy [also SME designer of this course] [taught online]

This course uses a multidisciplinary approach to explore original essays combined with classical and contemporary readings from philosophy, science, and literature. Both structure and content emphasize the relevance of philosophy to other disciplines. Topics include the meaning of life, existentialism, ethics, social and political philosophy, and the philosophy of science, metaphysics, and the existence of God.

PL401 – Philosophy of Science and Technology [also SME designer of this course] [taught online]

This course provides an introduction to philosophy and its relationship to technology. An anthology of scholarly and popular articles explores the positive, negative, ethical and unethical issues faced by society as technology changes the world that we live in – on a personal, national, and international level. Interactive activities encourage the student to think critically, analytically, and creatively, and challenge him/her to develop new ideas and map solutions to current technological and sociological issues. Topics include ethics and technology, history of technology, energy, ecology, population, health and technology, technology and the Third World, and technology of the future.

Adjunct Professor Oct. 2010 - Mar. 2014
Westwood College, Westminster, CO

CJ201 – Criminal Justice Ethics [taught online]

This course examines ethical issues within criminal justice. Topics include ethical reasoning, the influence of personal and moral beliefs on the administration of justice, and the frequent tension between social justice and criminal justice. Upon successful completion of this course, students will be able to analyze the effect of personal and moral beliefs on the criminal justice system and articulate the process of . ethical reasoning.

HUM180 – Ethical and Critical Thinking [taught online]

This course covers the principles and applications of ethical and critical thinking. Topics include argument construction and analysis, inductive and deductive reasoning, logical fallacies, perception, moral approaches, and social responsibility. Upon successful completion of this course, students will be able to analyze ethical issues, evaluate and clarify their own thinking, create sound and valid arguments, and effectively weigh the arguments of others.

Core Faculty & Subject Matter Expert June 2007 – Mar. 2012
Ellis University, Chicago, IL

ETH 513 – Business Ethics [taught online]

This course is intended to help students make ethical choices in a business context. Students analyze case studies dealing with such topics as employee rights and responsibilities, consumer issues and product liability, community and environmental issues and ethical norms in different cultures. In each area, an analytic framework is used to identify stakeholder rights and interests, and relevant moral duties and virtues.

PHI 110 – Problems in Philosophy [taught online]

An introduction to philosophy by way of selected problems from various areas of philosophy. Topics include: the nature of a priori knowledge and of scientific explanation, the existence of God, whether or not there can be moral knowledge, and the problem of free will. The course objective is to acquaint students with these philosophical issues, and through detailed discussion, to teach them how to analyze ideas critically.

PHI 220 – Ethics and Social Philosophy [taught online]

An examination of some of the most critical issues of moral and social philosophy. These include subjects such as the linguistic analysis of terms such as "good," "evil," "duty," "right" and others. The basis of different moral systems will be studied and the selections from ethical and social philosophers will be read.

PHI 230 – Technology, Science, and Values [also SME designer of this course] [taught online]

An examination of models and case studies concerned with the impact of machines on man, of technological systems on social structure, and modes of production on value systems. Special attention is paid to the ethical problems connected with newly emerging technologies.

QANT 737 – Research Methodology [taught online]

Students explore selected forms of quantitative and qualitative research, considering the strengths and weaknesses of each. Specific topics include: establishing the problem and the hypothesis; locating and reviewing relevant research literature; selecting a subject, research design, and appropriate statistical measures; and interpreting research results.

Core Faculty & Subject Matter Expert May 2001 – May 2007
Kaplan University, Ft. Lauderdale, FL

CJ 502 - Research Methodology [taught online]

This course is designed to provide students with an understanding of the research process and the ethical context within which research should be conducted. Further, it will provide the basic skills needed to conduct and evaluate research on topics relevant to the criminal justice field.

CJ 504 - Data Analysis [taught online]

This course presents statistical methods commonly used in scientific research, annual reports, and other real-life applications. Topics include descriptive statistics, basic concepts of probability, statistical inference, analysis of variance, correlation, regression, and nonparametric statistical techniques. Emphasis is on understanding and applying statistical concepts and techniques to research empirical data in the field of criminal justice.

CJ 600 - Research and Thesis I [taught online]

This course requires students to develop a formal proposal for research in criminal justice and submit it in writing to their chosen thesis committee, made up of a chairperson and two additional members, all of whom must be terminally degreed criminal justice faculty members from Kaplan University. It is acceptable to have one committee member from the faculty of another school at Kaplan University or from an outside, regionally accredited institution of higher learning with the approval of the Dean. This course is best suited for students wishing to add to the body of professional knowledge in the field of criminal justice Thesis and Research.

CJ601 - Research and Thesis II [taught online]

During this phase of the research process, students submit the final draft of their research project to their committee members for review and orally present their results during a scheduled thesis defense hearing. The research report shall be prepared according to Kaplan University guidelines and the final, approved product shall be submitted to appropriate personnel for binding and acquisition. This course is best suited for students wishing to add to the body of professional knowledge in the field of criminal justice.

GB507 - Business Ethics [taught online]

This course analyzes theories of ethics and practices that relate to such theories, for example corporate codes of conduct. Students explore their personal ethics related to their roles and behaviors within business organizations. The concept of corporate responsibility within a global context is analyzed.

HU201 - Humanities Seminar [also SME designer of this course] [taught online]

This course explores the human experience as expressed through literature, painting, sculpture, music, theater, architecture, and philosophy. Students study the major historical developments and learn how to critically read the classic texts of Western political, moral, and religious thought; students will also discuss the practical relevance of these texts to their own lives.

HU245 - Ethics [also SME designer of this course] [taught online]

In this course, students develop sound ethical reasoning and judgment through the study of practical applications of ethical theories. Topics studied include ethics as it relates to business, health care, society, and the environment. Emphasis is on practical applications of ethical principles and analytical methods.

HU280 - Bioethics [also SME designer of this course] [taught online]

In this course, students develop and apply sound ethical reasoning and judgment to important issues in health care. Topics studied include access to health care, medical privacy, end-of-life care, genetic screening, and emerging genetic technologies. Emphasis is on practical applications of ethical principles and analytic methods.

HU345 - Critical Thinking [also SME designer of this course] [taught online]

This course helps students apply tools of informal logic and critical thinking to practical situations they encounter in everyday life. Students will learn how to use methods of critical thinking to evaluate arguments, claims, and strategies for constructing sound arguments. They will also learn how to identify and respond to faulty or manipulative reasoning in their own thinking and arguments and in the thinking and arguments of others. In addition, students will assess the reasoning found in mass media (such as websites, advertisements, and newspapers). Finally, students will apply the concepts they study to real-world issues of personal and professional significance.

SS325 - Aesthetics, Democracy, and Technology [also SME designer of this course] [taught online]
This course critically explores the relationship between democratic and technological values and their contributions to either increasing or diminishing cultural phenomena such as art, morality, science, and ethics.

Adjunct Professor   Jan. 2001 – Dec. 2005
Saint Leo University, Saint Leo, FL

PHI 324 - Bio Ethics [taught online]
Examines moral problems that arise in the practice of medicine. Various theories about what is good and what is right are considered and related to bio-ethical and socio-ethical issues.

PHI 328 - Business Ethics [taught online]
A study of general moral principles and their application to ethical issues and problems pertaining to business activities and the nature of the corporation in contemporary society.

Assistant Professor   Aug. 1998 – May 2001
Antioch College, Yellow Springs, OH

PHIL 107 - History of Western Philosophy
In this class, students study four important philosophical works in their entireties: Plato's Republic, Aristotle's Politics, Descartes' Meditations, and Hume's Enquiry Concerning Human Understanding. The course also pays close attention to philosophers and philosophical questions lying outside the traditional philosophical canon, including the history of women in philosophy and an analysis of race in enlightenment thought. The course focuses on three fundamental questions: Can virtue be taught? What is community? What are the limits and nature of human knowledge?

PHIL 260 - Philosophy of Science
Students in this course read a large sample of contemporary work in the philosophy of science. The topics covered include social constructivism and the sociology of science, rationality, objectivity, and values in science, the Duhem-Quine thesis and under-determination, induction, prediction and evidence, explanation, and laws of nature. The course is designed to provide intermediate- and upper-level philosophy or science students with a thorough grounding in the methodologies and concerns of contemporary philosophy of science.

PHIL 265 - Feminist Philosophy
In this course, students study a large sample of Western philosophical thought plus additional readings (including non-Western perspectives) of the students' own choice. The course is designed to provide beginning- and intermediate-level students with a comprehensive background for further exploration of feminist philosophy, feminist literary and psychoanalytical theory, and feminist social, cultural, and political critique.

PHIL 271 - Animal Minds
Do animals think? What do they think about? Do they think in language? Are they conscious? What is their emotional life like? What do these questions even mean, and how exactly might we set out to answer them? This course engages in an interdisciplinary investigation of these and related questions. The course's primary emphasis is on contemporary scientific and philosophical perspectives. Consequently, students will be much concerned with understanding and critiquing ways that philosophers and scientists have tried to integrate thought, consciousness, and emotionality into their disciplines.

PHIL 272 - Philosophy and Psychology
An intensive interdisciplinary exploration of psychoanalytic theory, contemporary philosophy of mind, and evolutionary psychology, an emerging multidisciplinary field that uses insights from evolutionary biology, cognitive psychology,

anthropology, primatology, and archeology. This course is built on the assumption that there is a compelling intellectual need to replace the rather simplistic and flawed model of the human mind beloved in much of the social sciences. We will read, discuss, contrast, and synthesize ideas from four humanistic traditions that present vastly more complicated models of the mind: (1) philosophy of mind as developed by some current analytic philosophers, (2) postmodern views of the mind as developed by Foucault and Lacan, (3) psychoanalytic views of the mind as developed by Freud, and (4) the multidisciplinary model emerging from work in evolutionary psychology. The primary goal is to help students create their own sophisticated "working model" of the human mind.

PHIL 273 - Philosophy, Technology, and Democracy
Student in this class engage an intensive, discussion-based multidisciplinary investigation of philosophy of technology, technology studies, and technologically-informed discussions of democracy. Class members read several seminal works in their entireties and write a substantial term paper on a topic of their own choosing.

PHIL 308 - Contemporary Philosophy
An intensive study of the two central traditions of contemporary Western philosophy, analytic (or Anglo-American) philosophy and continental philosophy. This is an upper-level course that will fully verse philosophy majors in both traditions. Although anyone who has successfully completed one philosophy course may take this course, non-majors will be expected to keep up with the intense pace and with the challenging reading and writing assignments. The topics discussed include existentialism, phenomenology, hermeneutics, Marxism, critical theory, structuralism, psychoanalytic philosophy, feminist philosophy, deconstructionism, postmodernism, logical atomism, logical positivism, the private language argument, ordinary language philosophy, contemporary empiricism, linguistic theories of truth, ontological relativity, radical translation, radical interpretation, direct reference, and causal theories of meaning.

PHIL 320 - African Philosophy
An intensive study of the canonical texts of contemporary sub-Saharan African philosophy. This is an upper-level course that is designed to give majors and non-majors a solid grounding in four philosophical traditions: Contemporary ethnophilosophy, Sagacity philosophy, Rationality debates, and Nationalist-ideological philosophy. Although the course's main focus will be on gaining a critical mastery of key philosophical texts, students also read contemporary novels by Chinua Achebe and Tsitsi Dangarembga.

RELS 112 - Western Religions and their Philosophies
In this course, students study the most holy primary texts in the three dominant Western religions, Islam, Judaism, and Christianity. The course is designed to provide beginning students with a comprehensive background for further exploration of the manifold historical, cultural, theological, ethical, and political legacies of these three inextricably-linked complex spiritual traditions.

Adjunct Professor   Aug. 1995 – May 1998
McDaniel College, Westminster, MD

LIT 119/PHI 119 - Philosophy and the Twentieth-Century American Novel
The aim of this multi-disciplinary, team-taught course is to study the connections between existentialist philosophy and existentialist-inspired American Novels of the middle twentieth century.

PHI 107 - Philosophy in Film
The aim of this course is to study philosophical ideas as portrayed in contemporary and classic films. It concentrates on learning how to identify and assess the use of philosophical ideas in film.

PHI 110 - Ethics
The aim of this course is to introduce leading views in a central branch of philosophy, ethics. It concentrates on

three types of ethical theories: Consequentialist, deontological, and virtue ethics.

PHI 201- Ancient and Medieval Philosophy
The aim of this course is to study the central texts and issues of ancient and medieval philosophy. It concentrates on the thought of the two dominant figures of Greek philosophy, Plato and Aristotle and surveys much of medieval philosophical thought.

PHI 202 - Early Modern Philosophy
The aim of this course is to study central texts and issues of early modern philosophy. It concentrates on the thought of Rene Descartes, John Locke, Gottfried Wilhelm Leibniz, David Hume, and Immanuel Kant.

PHI 210 - Epistemology and Metaphysics
The aim of this course is to introduce some leading views in two central branches of philosophy, epistemology and metaphysics. The course considers a broad range of topics.

PHI 217 - Minds, Bodies, and Persons
The aim of this course is to study central texts and issues related to philosophical investigations of identity, personhood, and will.

Graduate Student Instructor   Aug. 1991 – May 1995
University of California, Berkeley, CA

PHIL 25A - Ancient Philosophy
In this course you will be introduced to philosophy by engaging with the ideas and arguments of the three most important ancient Greek philosophers: Socrates, Plato, and Aristotle. They will help us consider how we should be living our lives, what justice is, how we can acquire knowledge, what knowledge is, what one gains from asking "what is it?" questions, what change is, whether we can understand anything in the natural world, and a host of other philosophical questions that were deeply influential on the rest of western philosophy. Along the way, you'll work on the following skills: making and understanding arguments

and objections, reading difficult texts carefully, and writing clearly and precisely about philosophy. You will be learning to do philosophy by engaging with its foundational works.

PHIL 25B - Modern Philosophy
In this course we will study the philosophical views of the most important and influential thinkers in early modern philosophy (roughly, the 17th and 18th centuries). This period in western thought was nothing short of extraordinary in that it saw the overthrow of a philosophical and scientific worldview that had dominated the west for over one thousand years. Prior to the 17th century, philosophy had been a blend of church doctrine and classical philosophy, and its methodology had been quite narrowly defined. The unfortunate effect of both the church's influence on scholarly endeavors and the strictly defined methodology was that philosophical and scientific creativity was largely stifled.

PHIL 100 - Philosophical Methods
This course is restricted to Philosophy majors. It is intended to improve the student's ability to read and write philosophy. Special emphasis will be placed on developing analytic skills. There will be short written assignments each week, as well as a longer final paper, which will focus on the essays we are reading. In addition to two hours of lecture, students will meet in tutorials with a teaching assistant in order to discuss the reading, their weekly writing assignment, and the preparation for the final paper. This term, the readings will focus on problems related to free will.

PHIL 105 - Philosophy of Biology
This course studies philosophical problems in the biological sciences such as the relation between biology and the physical sciences, the status and structure of evolutionary theory, and the role of biology in the social sciences

PHIL 172 - Knowledge and Its Limits
An upper-division course on the philosophical theory of knowledge. Not a general, encyclopedic survey of the field, but an investigation and detailed discussion some of the

central problems in the subject. Knowledge of many different kinds is obviously fundamental to scientific, cultural, social, and personal life. What is it about human perception, belief, and knowledge that makes it so difficult to find a philosophically satisfying general explanation of how human knowledge is possible? And how are those obstacles to be overcome?

PHIL 178 - Kant

The course will provide an examination of Kant's critical philosophy. The first part will be devoted to the peculiarity of Kant's Copernican Revolution, understanding transcendental idealism to be a necessary condition for empirical realism. In this part we will be primarily concerned with Kant's relationship to Leibniz and Wolff, his view of philosophy's proper method, and the proof structure of the transcendental deduction. The second part of the course will deal with what is for Kant a condition for a subject to exhibit one's freedom, i.e. his understanding of autonomy and its development. In the end of the course the relationship of these two critiques will be discussed and questions will be raised about the whole system that is supposed to be the outcome of the combination of Kant's three critiques.

Professional Experience

John Hancock University   2012 – 2013
Chief Academic Officer, Oakbrook Terrace, IL

As Chief Academic Officer, I reported to the President and provided strategic vision, planning, and leadership for the University's academic advancement. I was accountable for academic quality and integrity throughout the institution and provided leadership in academic planning and budgeting and in the assessment and improvement of academic programs and services. I was also responsible for developing and implementing a wide range of near-term and long-term plans. I collaborated with the other members of the Executive Committee to maintain the University's regulatory and accreditation relationships.

Ellis University   2011 – 2012
Vice President for Academic Affairs and Chief Academic Officer,
Chicago, IL

I reported to the President and provided strategic vision,
planning, and leadership for the University's academic
advancement. I was accountable for academic quality and
integrity throughout the institution and provide leadership in
academic planning and budgeting and in the assessment and
improvement of academic programs and services. I was
responsible for developing and implementing a wide range of
near-term and long-term plans. I collaborated with the other
members of the senior management team to maintain the
University's regulatory and accreditation relationships.

Ellis University   2007 – 2012
Professor and Director of Center for Teaching and Learning,
Chicago, IL

I worked to establish a new online University serving working
adults and dedicated to academic quality and integrity. In
addition to teaching undergraduate and graduate students, I
served on the President's cabinet, directed the Center for
Teaching and Learning, serves as President of the institution's
Faculty Senate, chaired the Curriculum and Academic Standards
Committee, and co-chaired the Faculty Development Committee.
As chair of the Accreditation Writing Committee, I was the
primary author of the institution's successful self-study for
regional accreditation. I also served on numerous committees
and task forces, including the Strategic Planning Committee and
the Faculty Standards Committee.

Kaplan University   2001 – 2007
Professor and Department Chair, Ft. Lauderdale, FL

I contributed to the development of an online University whose
enrollment grew from 100 students to 30,000 during my
employment. In addition to teaching graduate and undergraduate
students and leading two academic departments, I developed
new courses, helped to develop systematic academic
assessment processes, and performed numerous faculty

leadership roles including President of the Faculty Senate and leader of the Institutional Mission Task Force.

Antioch College   1998 – 2001
Assistant Professor and Academic Department Head, Yellow Springs, OH

In addition to teaching undergraduate students and serving as the head of an academic division, I worked on academic assessment, institutional accreditation, and held several leadership roles including member of the president's Administrative Council and member of the Faculty Executive Committee.

Formal Education

PhD, Philosophy   1998
University of California, Berkeley CA
B. Phil, Philosophy   1990
University of Oxford, Oxford, UK
B.A., Philosophy   1988
Amherst College, Amherst MA

Educational Training

FERPA

Quality Matters: Helping Online Students Get Started
IRB Research Ethics
Quality Matters: Increasing Student Interactions
PCI-DSS Compliance
Quality Matters: Considering Instructional Materials
Workplace Sexual Harassment
Quality Matters: Aligning Objectives and Assessments
Copyright Law for Educators
Quality Matters: Assessment Criteria

Protection of Vulnerable Persons
Quality Matters: Applying the Quality Matters Rubric
Workplace Diversity
Effective Video Usage in the Classroom
Preventing Workplace Harassment
Ethics and Compliance Quality Assurance
FTC Identity Theft Red Flag Rules
Americans with Disabilities Act
Preventing Discrimination
Active Learning

EmbEdDing Critical Thinking
Blackboard Technical Skills
Blackboard Collaborate
Title IV Compliance
Principles of Adult Learning Theory
Veterans In Transition
Substantive Feedback
Information Security Awareness
Protecting Human Research Participants
Quality and Compliance Assurance
Advanced Security Awareness

Educational Certifications

Higher Learning Commission - Consultant-Evaluator Training, Program to Evaluate and Advance Quality
Higher Learning Commission - Consultant-Evaluator Training, Academic Quality Improvement Program
Higher Learning Commission – Action Project Reviewer Training
Distance Education Training Council - Business Standards Training
Distance Education Training Council - Peer Reviewer Training
Quality Matters Program - Peer Reviewer Certification
Quality Matters Program - Master Reviewer Certification
Quality Matters Program – Publisher Reviewer Certification

Memberships and Affiliations

Academy of Criminal Justice Sciences
American Association of Philosophy Teachers
American Philosophical Association
American Society for Eighteenth-Century Studies
Higher Education Teaching and Learning Association
North American Kant Society
Professional and Organizational Development (POD) Network
Wilfred Sellars Society

Service and Leadership

At Capella University:

School of Education Faculty Council.
At John Hancock University:
University Executive Committee; University Senior Management

Team; Convener and Leader of Academic Advisory Boards; Leader of LMS Change and Course Conversion Project (700 Courses); Supervisor of all Core and Adjunct Faculty; Supervisor of all SMEs; Hiring Manager for all Faculty Positions.

At Ellis University:

Faculty Senate President; Chair, Curriculum and Academic Standards Committee; Chair, Self-Study Writing Committee; Co-Chair, Faculty Development Committee; Director, Center for Teaching and Learning; Vice President, Academic Senate; Leader, Faculty Scholarship Task Force; Leader, Faculty Assessment of Advisory Board Recommendations; Leader, HLC Criterion 1 Self-Study Team; Co-Founder and Co-Leader, The Ellis Seminar; Faculty Visitor to the Board of Trustees; Member of Self-Study Steering Committee, Faculty Senate Executive Committee, President's Administrative Executive Committee (ex officio), Provost's Council, Academic Leadership Council, Strategic Planning Committee, Institutional Review Board, Faculty Standards Committee, Faculty Handbook Task Force.

At Kaplan University:

Faculty Senate President; Leader of Mission Statement and Purposes Redrafting Team; Leader of Ethics Team within Alternative Instructional Materials Project; Communications Department Acting Chair; Assessment Committee Interim Chair; Retreat Committee Chair; Faculty Participant in U.S. Senate Online Education Fair; Department Chair Mentor; Faculty Mentor; HLC Accreditation Self-Study Contributor; HLC Request for Institutional Change Contributor; HLC Request for Institutional Change Site Visit Interviewee; CCNE Site Visit Interviewee; elected member of Faculty Senate, Faculty Rank and Standards Committee, Institutional Review Board, Assessment Committee; appointed member of Graduate Administrative Council, Long-Range Planning Committee, Governance Committee, Faculty Workload Task Force, Faculty Rank and Standards Task Force, Characteristics of Graduate Education Task Force, Student Survey and Faculty Survey Task Force, Characteristics of Undergraduate Education Task Force, Retreat Committee; Governance Task Force.

At Antioch College:

Assistant to the Dean of Faculty for Institutional Assessment; Chair of College Assessment Committee; Co-Chair of College Accreditation and Assessment Committee; Chair of History, Philosophy, and Religious Studies Department; Chair of Philosophy Search Committee; President of College Chapter of American Association of University Professors; elected member of President's Administrative Council, Dean of Faculty's Academic Planning Council, Faculty Executive Committee; appointed member of College Budget Committee, Ad Hoc Committee on General Education, Technology Task Force, Technology Resources Multiple Search Committee.

Other:

Peer Review Corps, Higher Learning Commission of the North Central Association (Consultant-Evaluator, Program to Evaluate and Advance Quality; Systems Appraiser and Action Project Reviewer, Academic Quality Improvement Program)
Master Peer Reviewer, Quality Matters Program
Advisory Board, International Higher Education Teaching and Learning Association
Ambassador Corps (North American Ambassador), International Higher Education Teaching and Learning Association
Facilitator, American Philosophical Association/American Association of Philosophy Teachers National Seminar on Teaching and Learning in Philosophy
Vice President and President-Elect, American Association of Philosophy Teachers
Board of Directors, American Association of Philosophy Teachers
Chair, American Association of Philosophy Teachers Speaker and Award Committee
Chair, American Association of Philosophy Teachers Teaching Seminar Committee
Chair, American Association of Philosophy Teachers Lenssen Prize Committee
American Association of Philosophy Teachers Teaching Fellows Committee

Executive Board, *Contemporary Issues in Criminology and the Social Sciences*
International Editorial Board, *Studia Philosophica Wratislaviensia*
Editorial Advisory Board, *Cultural Variations and Business Performance: Contemporary Globalism* (IGI Global)
Peer review: SUNY Press, Wadsworth Publishing Company, *Kantian Review, Teaching Philosophy, Synthese,* Computers and Philosophy (CAP) conference.
Panelist, AskPhilosophers.org web project
Organizing: Summer 2006 American Association of Philosophy Teachers International Workshop-Conference on Teaching Philosophy; Summer 2005 Kaplan University Faculty Retreat; Fall 2000 meeting at Antioch of the Midwest Society of Women in Philosophy; Spring 2000 Antioch Faculty Research Symposium
Grant-funded service: Qualitative research project (with Tom Haugsby, Antioch College Professor of Cooperative Education) on preparing students for cooperative education
College Faculty Mentor for Darke County (OH) High School Career Mentorship Program
Program Co-Chair, American Association of Philosophy Teachers Sixteenth International Workshop-Conference on Teaching Philosophy
Manager, Higher Education Teaching and Learning - Learning Technology in Teaching and Learning, Linkedin.Com
Immanuel Kant topic editor of EpistemeLinks.Com web project
Course Materials editor of NOESIS: Philosophical Research Online web project
Moderator of PHILO-TEACH, an email discussion of philosophy pedagogy
Associate Editor of HIPPIAS: Limited Area Search of Philosophy on the Internet
Author of <u>Course Materials in Philosophy</u> web project.

Scholarly Publications

ARTICLES

"Administrative and Academic Structures: For-Profit and Not-for-Profit" with Craig Bach in *The Strategic Management of Higher Education Institutions* (Addison, TX: Business

Express Press, 2011), 89-108.

"The Aristotelian Heart of Marx's Condemnation of Capitalism,"
Studia Philosophica Wratislaviensia 5 (2010), 41-64.

"Social Capital and the Campus Community" with Linda
Coughlin, Susanne Morgan, and Christopher Price in *To
Improve the Academy: Resources for Faculty, Instructional,
and Organizational Development*, Vol. 29 (San Francisco:
Jossey-Bass, 2010), 201-215.

"Learning Assessment: Hyperbolic Doubts Versus Deflated
Critiques" with Craig Bach, *Analytic Teaching and
Philosophical Praxis* 30 (2010), 1-11.

"The Benefits of Philosophical Analysis for Criminological
Research, Pedagogy, and Practice" with Craig Bach in
Professional Issues in Criminal Justice 2 (2006), 3-16.

"Davidson's Transcendental Argumentation: Externalism,
Interpretation, and the Veridicality of Belief," in *From Kant to
Davidson: Philosophy and the Idea of the Transcendental*,
ed. Jeff Malpas (Routledge, 2003), 219-237.

"Kant's Earliest Solution to the Mind/Body Problem" in *Kant und
die Berliner Aufklärung*, ed. Volker Gerhardt, Rolf-Peter
Horstmann, and Ralph Shumacher (Berlin: De Gruyter,
2001), 3-12.

"Davidson's Externalism and the Unintelligibility of Massive
Error," *Disputatio* 4 (1998), 25-45.

"Kant's (Problematic) Account of Empirical Concepts,"
Proceedings of the Eighth International Kant Congress, Vol.
II (1995), 227-234.

"Truth and Reference: Some Doubts About Formal Semantics,"
Theoria et Historia Scientiarum 2 (1992), 37-53.

INTERNET AND NEW MEDIA (PEER-REVIEWED)

"Western Philosophy" (updated and revised entry), in *Microsoft
Encarta Encyclopedia and Online Reference Library*
<http://www.encarta.msn.com>, 2002.

"Kant, the Body, and Knowledge" in *The Paideia Project Online:
Proceedings of the Twentieth World Congress of Philosophy*
<http://www.bu.edu/wcp/>, edited by Stephen Dawson,
2000.

Regular reports on contemporary research and pedagogy in
"Early Modern Philosophy Update," in *Philosophy News*

Service <http://www.PhilosophyNews.com>, edited by Richard Jones, 1999 – 2000.

"Guided Tour of Kant's Philosophy of Mind," in *A Field Guide to the Philosophy of Mind* <http://www.uniroma3.it/kant/field/>, general editor Marco Nani, 1999.

Entry on "Kant's Philosophy of Mind" in *The Dictionary of the Philosophy of Mind* <http://www.artsci.wustl.edu/~philos/MindDict/>, edited by Chris Eliasmith, 1999.

PEDAGOGY

"Online Discussions and the 'Place' of Learning," *American Philosophical Association Newsletter on Teaching Philosophy* 107 (2007), 9-12.

"Using RealAudio Multimedia Content in the Philosophy Classroom," *The American Philosophical Association Newsletter on Philosophy and Computers* 100 (2000), 10-11.

"Using the Internet in the Philosophy Classroom," *The American Philosophical Association Newsletter on Philosophy and Computers* 98 (1998), 33-34.

REVIEWS AND ENCYCLOPEDIA ENTRIES

"Beccaria, Cesare: Classical School" in Frances T. Cullen and Pamela A. Wilcox, eds, *Encyclopedia of Criminological Theory*, Vol 1 (Sage Publications, 2010), 73-77.

Review of Steve Fuller's *Thomas Kuhn: A Philosophical History for Our Times. Social Epistemology* 17 (2003), 139.

Review of Martin Schönfeld's *The Philosophy of the Young Kant: The Pre-Critical Project. Kantian Review* 4 (2000), 113-116.

Review of Anthony Kenny's *Brief History of Western Philosophy. Disputatio* 7 (1999), 58-63.

Review of Susan Meld Shell's *The Embodiment of Reason: Kant on Spirit, Generation, and Community. Kantian Review* 2 (1998), 134-143.

Published in *Teaching Philosophy* 22-24 (1999-2001): Reviews of Kerry Walters and Lisa Portmess, eds., *Ethical Vegetarianism: From Pythagoras to Peter Singer;* Emmanuel Chukwudi Eze, ed., *Race and the Enlightenment: A Reader;* Robin May Schott, ed., *Feminist Interpretations of Immanuel*

Kant.

Published in *The Antioch Review* 57-60 (1999-2002): Reviews of Steve Fuller's *Thomas Kuhn: A Philosophical History for Our Times;* Alain de Botton's *The Consolations of Philosophy;* John Rawls' *The Law of Peoples;* Samuel Freeman, ed., *Collected Papers: John Rawls;* Parker J. Palmer's *The Courage to Teach: Exploring the Inner Landscape of a Teacher's Life;* and seven other books of philosophy, religion, science, history, politics, or pedagogy.

Scholarly Presentations

Sixty-three presentations including:
"Looking In the Mirror – Helping Students to Evaluate Their Own Deep-Seated Ethical Beliefs," delivered to the Central Division of the American Philosophical Association, Chicago, Feb. 2012.
Panelist on "The Value of Graduate Student Teacher Training for the Discipline of Philosophy," delivered to the Central Division of the American Philosophical Association, Chicago, Feb. 2012.
"Social Capital and Your Campus Community: Gateways to New Analysis" delivered with Linda Coughlin, Susanne Morgan, and Christopher Price to the Thirty-Fifth Annual Conference of the Professional and Organizational Development Network in Higher Education, St. Louis, Nov. 2010.
Panelist on "Philosophy as General Education: Aligning Learning Objectives with the Core Curriculum" delivered to the Eastern Division of the American Philosophical Association, New York, Dec. 2009.
"The Ethics of Globalized Criminal Justice from a Multidisciplinary Perspective," delivered with Adell V. Newman and Cloud H. Miller to the Forty-Sixth Annual Meeting of the Academy of Criminal Justice Sciences, Boston, MA, Mar. 2009.
"A Grotesque, Unintentional Parody of the Social Sciences and 'Accountability'? The Death of the Humanities at the Hands of the Social Sciences? A Philosophical Assessment of the Strongest Arguments Against Academic Assessment," delivered with Craig Bach to the American Association of Philosophy Teachers Seventeenth International Workshop-Conference on Teaching Philosophy, Guelph, Ontario, Aug. 2008.
"Teaching Philosophy to Non-Majors or: How I Came to Stop Worrying and Love 'Service Courses'," delivered to the American

Association of Philosophy Teachers Seventeenth International Workshop-Conference on Teaching Philosophy, Guelph, Ontario, Aug. 2008.

"Should Philosophy Be Taught Online?" delivered to the American Association of Philosophy Teachers Seventeenth International Workshop-Conference on Teaching Philosophy, Guelph, Ontario, Aug. 2008.

"The Benefits of Philosophical Analysis for Criminological Research, Pedagogy, and Practice," delivered with Craig Bach to the Forty-Fifth Annual Meeting of the Academy of Criminal Justice Sciences, Cincinnati, Ohio, Mar. 2008.

"Teaching Without Texts," delivered to the Pacific Division of the American Philosophical Association, San Francisco, California, Apr. 2007.

Panelist on "Criminal Justice Education in Cyberspace: Maintaining Academic Integrity in an On-Line Environment," delivered to the Forty-Forth Annual Meeting of the Academy of Criminal Justice Sciences, Seattle, Washington, Mar. 2007.

Panelist on "The Place of Teaching in Your Life as a New Faculty Member in Philosophy," delivered to the Eastern Division of the American Philosophical Association, Washington DC, Dec. 2006.

"A Shared Vision of Shared Governance," delivered with David Harpool and John LaNear to the Kaplan University Faculty Retreat, Chicago, Illinois, June 2006.

"Relating Academic Freedom to the Application of Tenure," delivered with William Weston to the Annual Meeting of the Midwest Sociological Society, Omaha, Nebraska, Mar. 2006.

"Supporting the Least Advantaged: Kaplan University's Progressive Educational Mission," delivered to the Kaplan University Faculty Retreat, Fort Lauderdale, Florida, Jan. 2006.

"Structuring Communication to Build On-line Communities," delivered with Jon Eads, Ellen Manning, Melinda Roberts, and Kara VanDam to the Eleventh Sloan-C International Conference on Asynchronous Learning Networks, Orlando, Florida, Nov. 2005.

"Faculty Life Within a Highly Centralized Curriculum: A New Conception of Faculty Freedom and Autonomy," delivered to the Kaplan University Faculty Retreat, Fort Lauderdale, Florida, Jan. 2005.

"Alternative Instructional Materials: A Case Study," delivered to the Tenth Sloan-C International Conference on Asynchronous Learning Networks, Orlando, Florida, Nov. 2004.

"A Multi-Faceted Approach to Online Faculty Training and Development," delivered with Kara VanDam and Melinda Roberts to the Tenth Sloan-C International Conference on Asynchronous Learning Networks, Orlando, Florida, Nov. 2004.

"Centralized Curricula: Faculty Autonomy, Freedom, and Satisfaction," delivered with Craig Bach to the Tenth Sloan-C International Conference on Asynchronous Learning Networks, Orlando, Florida, Nov. 2004.

"Philosophical Portfolios" delivered to the American Association of Philosophy Teachers Fifteenth International Workshop-Conference on Teaching Philosophy, University of Toledo, Aug. 2004.

"In Defense of a Centralized Curriculum," delivered to the American Association of Philosophy Teachers Fifteenth International Workshop-Conference on Teaching Philosophy, University of Toledo, Aug. 2004.

"Ethics Without Texts," delivered to the American Association of Philosophy Teachers Fifteenth International Workshop-Conference on Teaching Philosophy, University of Toledo, Aug. 2004.

"Two Advantages of On-line Interaction," delivered to the American Association of Philosophy Teachers Fifteenth International Workshop-Conference on Teaching Philosophy, University of Toledo, Aug. 2004.

"Designing and Facilitating Group Projects in Distance Education," delivered to the Kaplan University Faculty Retreat, Chicago, Illinois, July 2004.

Comments on Benjamin Yost's "On the Necessity of the Death Penalty in Kant's Moral and Political Philosophy," delivered to the Central Division of the American Philosophical Association, Cleveland, Ohio, May 2003.

"Davidson's Externalism: Neither Social Nor Perceptual," presented to the Central Division of the American Philosophical Association, Minneapolis, Minnesota, May 2001.

"Three Theses from Kant's Empirical Psychology," delivered to the Pacific Division of the American Philosophical Association, San Francisco, California, Mar. 2001.

"Send Food, Money, and Wisdom! Cooperative Education, Distance Learning, and Philosophy Pedagogy," delivered to the

Fifteenth Annual Conference on Computing and Philosophy, Carnegie Mellon University, Aug. 2000.

"Using One Paragraph Reflection Papers in Writing Intensive Courses," American Association of Philosophy Teachers Thirteenth International Workshop-Conference on Teaching Philosophy, Alverno College, Aug. 2000.

"Using RealAudio Multimedia Content in the Philosophy Classroom," American Association of Philosophy Teachers Thirteenth International Workshop-Conference on Teaching Philosophy, Alverno College, Aug. 2000.

"Online Discussions that Really Make a Difference," delivered to the American Association of Philosophy Teachers Thirteenth International Workshop-Conference on Teaching Philosophy, Alverno College, Aug. 2000.

Comments on Martin Schönfeld's "Kant's Conversion to Newtonianism," delivered to the North American Kant Society meeting at the Pacific APA, Albuquerque, New Mexico, Apr. 2000.

"Kant's Earliest Solution to the Mind/Body Problem," delivered to: The Ninth International Kant Congress, Berlin, Mar. 2000; The Eastern Division of the American Philosophical Association, Boston, Massachusetts Dec. 1999; and The Midwest Study Group of the North American Kant Society, St. Louis, Missouri Nov. 1999.

"*Vis activa* is not *Vis motrix*: Kant's critique of Wolffian Mechanics," delivered to the Eastern Division of the American Philosophical Association, Washington DC, Dec. 1998.

"Kant's Pre-Critical Account of Embodied Cognition," delivered to the Southeastern Seminar in Early Modern Philosophy, Blacksburg, Virginia, Nov. 1998.

"Kant, the Body, and Knowledge," delivered to the Twentieth World Congress of Philosophy, Boston, Massachusetts, Aug. 1998.

"Engendering Kant: Body, Soul, and Gender in Kant's Early Metaphysics," delivered to the Twenty-ninth Annual Meeting of the American Society for Eighteenth-Century Studies, South Bend, Indiana, Apr. 1998.

"Perpetual Peace or Everlasting War? Hegel's Ethical Defense of Warfare" delivered to the Tenth Annual National Conference of Concerned Philosophers for Peace, Chico, California, Sept. 1997.

"Knowing the Body as an External Object? The Strange case of Kant and Bodily Self-awareness," delivered to the Twenty-seventh Annual Meeting of the American Society for Eighteenth-Century Studies, Austin, Texas, Mar. 1996.

"The Socratic Elenchus as a Search for Truth," delivered to the Twentieth Annual Colloquium in Philosophy, Towson State University, Nov. 1995.

"Kant's (Problematic) Account of Empirical Concepts," delivered to the Eighth International Kant Congress, Memphis, Tennessee, Mar. 1995.

Awards and Honors

Engagement Challenge Award   2014
Awarded by Strayer University for teaching excellence.

Stephen Shank Recognition for Teaching Excellence 2012
Awarded by Capella University for teaching excellence.

Graduate Faculty Award   2009
Awarded by Ellis University for teaching excellence.

Independence Award   2008
Awarded by Ellis University for institutional service.

Outstanding Graduate Faculty Award   2006
Awarded by Kaplan University for teaching excellence.

Extra Mile Award   2003
Awarded by Kaplan Higher Education for teaching excellence.

Outstanding Graduate Student Instructor   1995
Awarded by the University of California at Berkeley for teaching excellence.

***Summa cum laude* Graduation Honors**   1988
Awarded by Amherst College for academic excellence.

Gail Kennedy Memorial Prize in Philosophy   1988
Awarded by Amherst College for academic excellence.

George A. Plimpton Fellowship   1988
Awarded by Amherst College for academic excellence.

Phi Beta Kappa   1987
Awarded by Amherst College for academic excellence

Highly Competent Subject Areas

Software: Adobe Acrobat, Adobe Collaborate, Adobe Connect, Elluminate, Eyejot, Genius SIS, Google Docs, GoToMeeting,

Microsoft Office, Prezi, Nvivo, Sharepoint, Skype, SPSS.

Learning Management Systems: Angel, Blackboard, Comcourse, eCollege, LoudCloud, Moodle, Pearson Learning Studio, Sakai, WebCT.

Subject Matter Expert: Biomedical Ethics, Business Ethics, Critical Thinking, Environmental Philosophy, Ethical Theories, Feminist Philosophy, History of Ancient Philosophy, History of Modern Philosophy, Medical Ethics, Philosophy of Science, Philosophy of Technology, Political Philosophy, Political Theory, Research Methodology, Statistics.

References

Dr. Dani Babb
Founder and CEO, The Babb Group
(866) 500-9101
DBabb@thebabbgroup.com

Name
Title
Phone
email

++

Sample CV: Some Teaching Experience, Professional Experience and Degrees

Sharyn Warren allowed us to show her CV as an example of a professor with a solid academic background and less instructor experience than other candidates. She clearly includes the course descriptions of courses she has taught and includes her professional profile. She makes it easy to see what she has done in her professional career, which is an important part of a CV. Also notice how she uses doctoral candidate and not ABD. This is very important! If you are a new entrant into the world of education, I recommend that you include your teaching philosophy statement, and a thorough, detailed review of each component listed in my 21 items to include in your CV article at www.thebabbgroup.com/blog

++

CURRICULUM VITAE

SHARYN L. WARREN, MSM
Address…
Address…
Phone: …
sharyn@sharynleewarren.com

PROFESSIONAL PROFILE

- Goal-oriented self-confident professional with strong organizational skills and effective written and oral communication skills.
- Information Technology (User Support).
- Several years of classroom instruction, course coordination and on-line facilitated instruction.
- Over fifteen years of experience in Human Resources Management to include: recruitment, employment law, employee relations, policy interpretation, training and development, benefits administration, budget preparation and analysis, and space planning and build out.

EDUCATION

- **EdD Doctoral Candidate - Higher Education and Adult Learning**, Walden University, Richard W. Riley College of Education and Leadership, Baltimore, MD, 2013 (Expected dissertation completion 12/15) "Factors that Contribute the Persistence of Student Success – A case study of African American Females in STEM Education"
- **MSM – Interdisciplinary Studies in Management**, University of Maryland University College, Graduate School of Management & Technology, Adelphi, MD, 2005
- **BA - Business Management/Communications**, Concordia University, Mequon, WI, 2000
- **Certificate – Project Management,** Cardinal Stritch

University, Bayshore, WI, 1995

ACADEMIC/TEACHING EXPERIENCE

Instructor - Milwaukee School of Engineering, Architectural Engineering/Construction Management Department, 2002 to 2011

- Team taught class that focuses on the foundational information of architectural engineering and construction management. Teach students in the first year of this program with class size averaging 28 students. The class focuses on learning styles, study strategies, team building skills, communications and presentation skills, time management, and college readiness.

Instructor – Milwaukee School of Engineering, General Studies Department, 2005 to 2011

- Taught freshman orientation classes. This course focused on the first year experience as it relates to the uniqueness of MSOE's programs; addressed issues such as study skills, note-taking and test-taking skills, health and wellness, credit and financial planning, team building skills and public speaking to class size averaging of 32 students. Tracked these students during their first year at MSOE with an effort towards retention.

Course Coordinator – Milwaukee School of Engineering, General Studies Department, 2005 to 2010

- Coordinated a team of 10 – 12 faculty members in the preparation of the freshman orientation course. This course is designed to meet the needs of students, whether entering college from high school or returning as an adult learner. The course provided tools, techniques, hints, ideas, illustrations, examples, methods, procedures, processes, skills, resources, and suggestions for SUCCESS! The lessons offered methods to strengthen one's academic performance based on the latest research in how people learn and succeed. Of all the classes students will take in college, this could be the one they will use most during their lifetime.

Instructor – Milwaukee School of Engineering, Rader School of Business, 2006 to 2012

- Taught Introduction to Computer Applications - this course focuses on the basic applied concepts of the software included in the Microsoft Suite. Emphasis is on the use of Word, Excel, PowerPoint, and Access. Students are taught to write research papers using Word following the APA format. Creation of data in Excel and Access to support the written research is developed. A final presentation is prepared using PowerPoint which incorporates all work from the other software applications.
- Taught Introduction to Business Management – this is a survey course on the management processes of planning, organizing, leading, and controlling. Traditional functions of management such as strategic planning and organizational design are given special emphasis to stimulate discussion on how organizations adapt to global conditions.
- Taught Nursing Informatics – this course focuses on the use of software applications in the field of Healthcare. Students are introduced to various rules and regulations of data handling using software

Instructor – Alverno College, Department of Communication and Technology, 2012 – present

- Foundations of Computing and Information Technology (CIT200) - Teach foundational course that explores the broad spectrum of computing and information technology allowing for students to demonstrate knowledge of software applications and basic computer science.

- Spreadsheet Analysis & Design (CIT 284) - The focus of this course is the mining and analysis of data for the purpose of making business decisions. The student looks at trends and patterns, makes informational calculations, and conducts other business analysis.

COURSES TAUGHT

Undergraduate
- Introduction to Computer Methods and Applications
- Principles of Business Management
- Nursing Informatics
- Introduction of Architectural Engineering
- Freshman Orientation Seminar
- Foundation of Computing & Information Technology
- Spreadsheet Analysis & Design

HIGHLIGHTS OF PROFESSIONAL EXPERIENCE

Institutional Research Manager, Milwaukee School of Engineering, Milwaukee WI, 2012 - Present
- Gather, process, coordinate, analyze, and communicate data to inform decision-making and improve effectiveness at the university.
- Manage a central data warehouse for course and faculty evaluations to support decision-making at different levels.
- Collaborate with other offices to administer institutional surveys and ensure satisfactory participation rates.
- Provide standard quarterly reports from Class Climate to Program and Department Chairs on Student Participation Rate and Faculty feedback.
- Insure the integrity of data collected.
- Specialist using Class Climate – Course Evaluation and Survey Software.

Assistant Director - Information Technology, Milwaukee

School of Engineering, Milwaukee WI, 1999 - 2012
- Responsible for strategic planning, implementation, department budget development, quality assurance and all aspects of providing support to the campus users.
- Manage a team of five FTEs and 21 student workers between two locations on campus which provide customer service and support to the MSOE user population.
- Involves ensuring the integrity of system passwords, monitoring response time to the numerous service calls received on a daily basis, tracking the follow-up resolve for user trouble tickets and continued improvement of all processes related to user support.
- Implement creative and innovative user support research to ensure that all users receive quality support, effective training, and proficiently working technology both on and off campus.
- Developed the state's first mandatory 1:1 laptop program, which affords MSOE the ability to acquire ~1,200 laptops a year that comply with industry standard capabilities for students at a discount from current market prices.
- Negotiate with vendors the selection of the mobile technology provided to the users through the Technology Program.
- Responsible for over $4 million dollars annually of portable assets and tracking of approximately 2000 laptops and the coordinated distribution of over 1200 laptops each year.
- Chair the Faculty Technology Committee.
- Member of Computer Users Committee (CUC).
- Attend Executive Education Council (EEC) meetings as department representative.
- Manage all academic and enterprise software for the campus.
- Review and approve department expenditures.
- Ensure alignment across the department towards goals and objective.
- Ensure audit compliance.

Office Manager, Meissner, Tierney, Fisher & Nichols, S.C., Milwaukee, WI, 1997 – 1999

- **Human Resources/Employee Benefits:** Recruit, hire and supervise exempt and non-exempt personnel, coordinate the placement of temporary staff, develop and implement orientation program, administer all employee benefits.
- **Training:** Train all new hires on computer applications, telecommunication system, voicemail system, and general office procedures.
- **Computer Network Administrator:** Responsible for Novell, Netware, Arc Serve networks administration and other computer software/hardware issues, provide support with email and Internet issues and successfully guide the office through a conversion from DOS operating system to Microsoft operating system.
- **Financial Management:** Prepare annual expense and operating budgets in excess of $2 million. Provide budget variance analysis to executive management committee on a monthly basis; verify and approve expenditures, generate payment for all firm and client disbursements, make weekly bank deposits in excess of $100,000 and prepare weekly cash receipts report for the shareholders.
- **Facilities Management:** Supervise maintenance of 9200 sq. ft. downtown office and supervised the renovation of an 1100 sq. ft. branch office in Hartland, Wisconsin.
- **Special Events:** Coordinate several firm marketing events including seminars, client and special guest receptions and the firm's yearly festivities.

Department Administrator, Snap-On Incorporated, Corporate Law Department, Kenosha, WI, 1994 – 1997

- Monitor and assess the workload and priorities of fifteen support staff, hire and assign permanent and temporary personnel to support special projects; facilitate monthly training and development meetings and weekly department meetings for support staff;
- Assist the General Counsel in the preparation of the department operating budget of approximately $5 million

and authorize spending against this budget.
- Plan and coordinate the conversion of the paper reference library to a computerized library system, which comprised hundreds of research books, legal volumes, and periodicals.
- Develop and implement long-range plans for staff needs; work with facilities management to coordinate space planning and utilization needs; interpret corporate policies; establish and maintain effective working relationships with other Snap-On employees, stakeholders and shareholders.
- Work with the General Counsel/Corporate Secretary and the CIO on a quarterly basis in preparation for the SEC filings and the Annual Shareholders meeting.

PROFESSIONAL AFFILIATIONS

- Tutor Supervisor, Upward Bound, Milwaukee School of Engineering
- Summer Computer Instructor, Upward Bound, Milwaukee School of Engineering
- Peer Mentor, Milwaukee School of Engineering
- Chair, Recruitment Subcommittee (Women at MSOE), Milwaukee School of Engineering
- Chair, Data Gathering Subcommittee (Women at MSOE), Milwaukee School of Engineering
- Member, Computer User Committee, Milwaukee School of Engineering
- Faculty/Staff Advisor, National Society of Black Engineers (NSBE), Milwaukee School of Engineering
- CSI Advisor – Noelle Levitz, Milwaukee School of Engineering
- Coordinator for First Year Freshman Seminar, Milwaukee School of Engineering
- Summer Instructor, Focus on Business Program, Milwaukee School of Engineering
- Customer Advisory Council, Hewlett Packard (HP)
- Higher Education Advisory Council, Hewlett Packard (HP)
- Board Member, Association of Legal Administrators

- Member, American Management Association
- Member, Association of Professional Women
- Board Director, Human Resource Management Association
- Member, American Society for Training & Development
- Member, International Black Doctoral Network Association, Inc.
- Member, American Association of University Women (AAUW)
- Member, Association of Institutional Research (AIR)

PROFESSIONAL DEVELOPMENT

- **Certificate,** Project Management, Milwaukee School of Engineering, Milwaukee, WI, 1999
- **Certificate,** Human Resource Management, Cardinal Stritch, Milwaukee, WI, 1997
- **Certified, ITIL Foundation,** Global Knowledge, 2013
- **Certified, ITIL Service Lifecycle: Service Transition,** Global Knowledge, 2014
- **Certified, ITIL Service Lifecycle: Service Strategy,** Global Knowledge, 2014

SCHOLARY PROJECTS

- Warren, Sharyn L. (2013), "Doctoral Project Study"
- Warren, Sharyn L. (2013), "Scholarly Position Paper."
- Warren, Sharyn L. (2013), "Collaborative Learning Project." Walden University
- Warren, Sharyn L. (2012), "Research Knowledge Assessment." Walden University
- Warren, Sharyn L. (2012), "Applying Knowledge of Qualitative Design & Analysis." Walden University
- Warren, Sharyn L. (2012), "Applying Knowledge of Quantitative Design & Analysis." Walden University
- Warren, Sharyn L. (2011), "Intelligence and Education." Walden University
- Warren, Sharyn L. (2011), "Andragogy or Pedagogy." Walden University

- Warren, Sharyn L. (2011), "Adult Learning Theory and Research." Walden University
- Warren, Sharyn L. (2011), "Adult Learning and Development Theories: Blended Learning." Walden University

COMMUNITY SERVICE

- Service-Leader Cameroon Project – Support Social Justice through Education, Mambu-Bafut, Cameroon, Nov. 2012 and July 2014
- Vice-President, Board of Directors, Rivers Edge Condominium Association, Brown Deer, WI, 2012 - present
- Secretary, Building Planning Committee, St. Matthew CME Church, 2011 – 2014
- President, Board of Directors, Rivers Edge Condominium Association, Brown Deer, WI, 2010 - 2012
- Secretary, Board of Directors, Rivers Edge Condominium Association, Brown Deer, WI, 2005 - 2010
- President, Assemblies of Christ Music Ministry, St. Matthew CME Church, 2008 – 2009
- Parent Member of Children's Choir, St. Matthew CME Church, Milwaukee, WI, 2003 - 2005
- Board of Directors, Hansberry Sands Theatre Company, Inc., Milwaukee, WI, 1995

+++

Before and After CV: With Teaching Experience,
Professional Experience, and Degrees

Dr. Sharon Jumper offered her "before and after 2012" CV for professors to see the difference and what worked for her when the job application systems appeared to shift and she had a more difficult time picking up new positions. You can see in this first CV that it was not as comprehensive or well documented. That worked before 2011-2012, when there was far less competition and fewer keyword searches in CVs.

In her second CV, she included her teaching philosophy statement, which I recommend doing. She also listed her highly competent subject areas, which helps you be picked up by HR robots. She includes her personal attributes and qualifications in the second version. She includes full course descriptions from catalogs, which is very important in helping your work be picked up by systems or deans doing keyword searching (or even LinkedIn HR folks looking for new hires!) She also included her references, which I omit for privacy reasons. See her before and after CV below! Months were also abbreviated to keep format in tact.

+++

Sharon D. Jumper
Address…
Address…
Phone: …
SKYPE ID: Sharon Jumper
Email: sharonjumper@hotmail.com

EDUCATION:

Walden University, Minneapolis, MN
- Completed all coursework (115 hours) for PhD in Public Policy & Public Administration, currently writing dissertation.
- Title of Dissertation: *A Capacities and Vulnerabilities Analysis of*
- *Microfinance Initiatives in Afghanistan*
- Member of Global Exchange delegation to Afghanistan
- Member of Pi Alpha Alpha Honor Society for Public Affairs & Administration

Wake Forest University School of Law, Winston-Salem, NC
- *Juris Doctor* in Law, 1992
- University Faculty Scholar, 1989-92
- Vice-President, Student Trial Bar
- Member, *Inns of Court*

Wofford College, Spartanburg, SC
- *Bachelor of Arts, Summa Cum Laude,* 1989
- Major: Government
- Minor: History
- Honors Thesis: *Divide and occupy: A comparison of French and British imperial practices and outcomes*
- *Phi Beta Kappa*
- Government Department Honors Graduate
- Intern, U.S. Senate, Hon. Ernest F. Hollings (D-SC)

CURRENT FACULTY APPOINTMENTS:

St Thomas University, Miami Gardens, FL Oct. 2012 – Present

Online Adjunct Faculty, Educational Leadership and Management Programs
Currently teaching *Public Policy for Educational Leaders* online in the EdD program.

University of Maryland   **Apr. 2011 – Present**
Online Adjunct Instructor and Faculty Mentor, Master of Science in Cybersecurity program
In addition to teaching, I also serve as a mentor for new faculty. Graduate Courses taught: *Human Aspects in Cybersecurity: Ethics, Legal Issues and Psychology; National Cybersecurity Policy and Law*
Training completed: Webtycho, WIMBA SimTray

University of the Rockies
            Apr. 2011 – Present
Online Adjunct Instructor, Doctoral and Master of Arts in Organizational Management & Leadership Programs; Doctoral and Master of Arts in Psychology and Human Services Programs
Graduate Courses taught: *Professional Ethics, Standards of Practice & Law; International Business I: Survey of Cross-Cultural Issues; International Business II: International Political Economy; International Business Ethics & the Law; Global Business Practices I: Europe, the Middle East & Africa.*

Baker College - Flint, MI   **Mar. 2004 – Present**
Online Adjunct Instructor, School of Business and Management.
Undergraduate Courses developed and/or taught: *Management Seminar; International Human Resources Management; Health Care Law and Regulation; Service Management; Business Law; Small Business Management; Human Resources and Employment Law; Emergency Medical Services Law and Ethics; Emergency Services Operations and Management.*
Training completed: Blackboard 6.0, Blackboard 7.3, Blackboard 8.0, Blackboard Content System, Baker College New Faculty Orientation. In addition to teaching courses online, I have developed new courses and updated existing courses, and have been a new faculty mentor.

Ashford University　　　　　July 2011 – Present
Online Adjunct Instructor, Criminal Justice and Business Programs
Undergraduate Courses taught: *Business Law I, International Business Law, Labor Relations, Business Law II, Introduction to Logic.*

ADDITIONAL EMPLOYMENT IN EDUCATION, COURSE DESIGN, AND CURRICULA DEVELOPMENT:

Keuka College – China Program, **Sept. 2007 – June 2012**
Undergraduate Courses developed and taught: *Strategic Management, Managerial Marketing, Human Resources Management, Business Law, Organizational Behavior.*
I was the lead instructor for Strategic Management, the capstone course of the program. Also assisted the Program Director with curriculum improvement, course mapping, and preparation for the regional accreditation review process.

Education Testing Service - Princeton, NJ, **June 2009 – June 2012**
Appointed as a Reader for the 2009, 2010, 2011, 2012 AP Exams in US Government and Politics.

Ellis University - Chicago, IL　　　Mar. 2011 – Sept. 2011
Chair, Legal Studies and Political Science
Responsible for supervising the Bachelor of Arts programs in Paralegal Studies and Political Science. In my position as Chair, I monitored classes to ensure compliance with academic requirements and regulations; conducted faculty training and development seminars; evaluated faculty performance; reviewed the academic progress of students; engage in student counseling; served on the Faculty Senate, Academic Leadership, Strategic Planning, Curriculum Development, Academic Standards, and Faculty Development Committees; and worked closely with faculty and administration to improve student persistence and academic rigor. I was assigned to a task force charged with developing and implementing a new program for faculty evaluations. I also taught and/or developed five courses per year.

Ellis University - Chicago, IL
Subject Matter Expert, Course Developer,
Online Faculty June 2005 – Mar. 2011
Graduate Courses developed and taught: *Ethics; Labor Law and Policies; Legal Issues for Non-Profit Organizations; Fair Employment Policies and Practices; Public Sector Labor Relations.*
Undergraduate Courses developed and/or taught: *Introduction to Public Administration; American Government and Politics; American Foreign Policy; History of Political Thought; International Relations; Selected Topics in Comparative Government; Selected Topics in Public Administration; Selected Topics in Political Science; Basic Legal Concepts and Administration of Justice; Business Organizations; American Society and Judicial Behavior; Criminal Procedure; Products Liability; Introduction to Paralegal Studies; Introduction to Law for Paralegals; Family Law; Real Estate Law; Law Office Management; Criminal Law; Civil Litigation; Contract Law; Torts; Civil Litigation; International Law and Organizations; Cyber Law & Ethics; Contract Law; Insurance Law; Medical Malpractice Law; Employment Law; Business Law I and II; Constitutional Law; Employment Law; Intellectual Property Law; Independent Study; Contemporary Political Thought; Rules of Evidence; Civil Litigation; and Ethics for Managers.*
In addition to my teaching and course development work, I served on the Academic Standards and Curriculum Committee.

The Saylor Foundation – Washington, DC, Jan. 2011 – Sept. 2011
Consultant and course developer for this open-access, non-profit higher education project. Developed undergraduate online courses in Political Science and National Security.
Undergraduate courses developed: *Contemporary Political Thought, Intelligence and National Security, Asia-Pacific Politics, International Law, Ethics and Public Policy.*

Norwich University – Northfield, VT Nov. 2006 – July 2010
Senior Instructor, Master of Arts in Diplomacy Program, Conflict Management Specialization. In addition to instructional duties, I have served as an advisor and committee member for Masters' theses, as well as a grader for the Masters' Comprehensive

Examinations and facilitator during graduate residency programs.

Graduate course taught: *International Law*

Senior Instructor, Bachelor of Science in National Security and Strategic Studies.

Undergraduate course developed and taught: *National Security Policy.*

Pfeiffer University, Charlotte, NC   **1996 – 1997**

Adjunct Instructor, MBA Program.

Course taught: *The Legal Environment of Business*

Developed syllabus, lecture notes, assignments, and student learning materials, and overall course structure for this course in the M.B.A program; lectured in class; graded and provided detailed feedback on student coursework; and administered all grade

VISITING FACULTY APPOINTMENTS IN CHINA AND THE UNITED ARAB EMIRATES:

Tianjin University of Finance and Economics – Tianjin, China   **Sept. – Nov. 2010, Aug. – Oct. 2011, Feb-Mar. 2012**

Visiting Faculty, Business Administration Program, in partnership with Keuka College.

Undergraduate Courses taught: *Strategic Management*

Al Ain Women's College – Al Ain, United Arab Emirates, Jan **2010 – May 2010**

Adjunct Faculty, School of Business

Undergraduate Courses taught: *Commercial Law in the UAE; Fundamentals of Business; Management Capstone Course.*

Yunnan University of Finance and Economics – Kunming, China   **Oct. – Dec. 2009, Oct. –Dec. 2011**

Visiting Faculty, Business Administration Program, in partnership with Keuka College.

Undergraduate Course taught: *Managerial Marketing, Strategic Management.*

Jimei University – Xiamen, Fujian, China
Aug. – Nov. 2007, Dec. 2011 - Jan. 2012, Apr.-June 2012

Visiting Faculty, Business Administration Program, in partnership with Keuka College.
Undergraduate Course taught: *Human Resources Management.*

PUBLICATIONS, PRESENTATIONS, AND REPORTED CASES:

- *Political, social, and economic empowerment of women in the Muslim world.* Paper and presentation at the Norwich University School of Graduate Studies Residency, Northfield, VT, June 2010.

- Session Chair, *Pedagogical innovations in education: Learning and teaching methodologies,* International Conference on Education and New Learning Technologies, in Barcelona, Spain, July 2009.

- *Using Socratic techniques to increase learning outcomes in online education,* Paper delivered at the International Conference on Education and New Learning Technologies, in Barcelona, Spain, July 2009.

- *Afghans helping Afghans: A study of Afghan-led NGO initiatives,* published in the Winter 2007 issue of the *Journal of the Society of Afghan Engineers.*

- *Is history repeating itself? A comparison of the post-Ottoman and post-Saddam occupations of Iraq,* paper and panel discussion delivered at the annual conference of the International Conference of Social Science Research, Orlando, FL, Dec. 2005.

- *Academic freedom in the post-9/11 world,* paper and panel discussion delivered at the annual conference of the Peace History Society, Nov. 2005.

- *Building a Safer World: The United Nations in the 21st Century,* Conference sponsored by UNESCO and The Atlantic Council of the U.S. Facilitator of group discussions on (1) crisis response and (2) war and conflicts. Oct., 2005.

- *Socratic teaching in the online learning environment*, paper and PowerPoint presentation delivered at the Baker College annual faculty conference, June 2005.

- *The doctoral student experience: Learning and Scholarship*, Panel participant, Walden University residency, San Diego, CA, Mar. 2005.

- *U.S. v. Wilhelm*, 4th Cir. Court of Appeals, No. 94-5764, conviction and sentence reversed.

- *U.S. v. Dean*, 4th Cir. Court of Appeals, No. 96-4446, sentence reversed and remanded.

- *Nationwide Mutual Insurance Co. v. Abernethy*, N.C. Court of Appeals, No. 9329SC507, judgment reversed and remanded, case dismissed.

OTHER PROFESSIONAL EXPERIENCE:

VP/Marketing and Business Manager   *2001-2005*
Charlotte4Sale.com

- Began this real estate brokerage venture in partnership with my husband
- Developed & implemented Internet & print media marketing plan
- Sold over $15 Million annually, 2002 - 2005
- Designed and maintained interactive websites
- Managed ongoing business, financial, and marketing operations

Attorney at Law   *1992-2001*
Charlotte, NC

- Prior to opening my own practice in 1993, employed as Associate counsel in medium-sized litigation, insurance defense, and corporate law firm.
- Drafted documents and contracts, engaged in labor negotiations for corporate clients; handled OSHA, EEOC, NLRB, IRS, ESC matters.
- Drafted pleadings, conducted depositions, handled trials and

pretrial hearings for insurance companies and other corporate and individual clients.

- Represented clients in over five thousand criminal matters, including white-collar crime and death penalty cases.
- Developed expertise in investigation, negotiation, and advocacy.
- Performed daily in a high-stress, time-sensitive environment.
- Served as volunteer Guardian *ad litem* for children who were abused, neglected, victims of crime, or subjects of highly contested custody cases.
- Frequent commentator on regional legal matters in local print media and both locally and nationally broadcasted shows.

Signals Intelligence Analyst/Enciphered Communications Analyst, U.S. Army, *1983 – 1989*

- While assigned to the National Security Agency, gathered information from various resources and gave daily intelligence briefings to National Command Authority and designates.
- While stationed in Korea, supervised the gathering of intelligence information from various collection platforms, and prepared reports for intelligence agencies for dissemination.
- Top Secret/SCI/Special Intelligence Clearance.
- Joint Services Commendation Medal; Army Achievement Medal; Good Conduct Medal; Overseas Service Medal; Army Service Ribbon; Honorable Discharge

PROFESSIONAL MEMBERSHIPS AND AFFILIATIONS:

- Life Member, National Association of Criminal Defense Lawyers
- Member, Board of Directors, Ariana Outreach
- Member, Veterans of Foreign Wars
- Member, Association of Former Intelligence Officers
- Member, American Society for Public Administration
- Member, National Contract Management Association

- Member, Academy of Political Science
- Member, American Political Science Association
- Member, Middle East Institute
- Member, International Political Science Association
- Member, People-to-People International
- Member, Southern Poverty Law Center
- Member, Peace History Society
- Member, Southern Political Science Association

++

CURRICULUM VITAE

Sharon D. Jumper

Address...
Address...
Phone: ...
SKYPE ID: Sharon Jumper
Email: sharonjumper@hotmail.com

Statement of Teaching Philosophy

Education is the gateway to opportunity. It can be life's great equalizer, allowing people to rise, despite the circumstances unto which they were born. I was driven by education since the age of 4, when I decided that I was going to "be someone important" and break the cycle of poverty in my family. I joined the Army at age 17 in order to be able to attend college. Like many of my students, I had to work and care for my family while I attended school full-time. I understand the difficulties that can arise due to competing requirements for one's time. In order to succeed in today's competitive and global workforce, students must be able to multi-task, deal effectively with contingencies, and produce high quality work in a timely manner. I share my experiences and mentor students on time management and contingency planning so that they can accomplish their tasks, prepare high quality work, and meet stated deadlines. I've also lived and worked in Europe, Asia, Africa, and the Middle East, and integrate intercultural perspectives into course discussions; this is also important in our increasingly interconnected world.

Education

Walden University, Minneapolis, MN

- Completed all coursework for PhD in Public Policy & Public Administration and currently writing dissertation.
- Dissertation: *A capacities and vulnerabilities analysis of microfinance initiatives in Afghanistan.*
- Member of Global Exchange delegation to Afghanistan
- Member of *Pi Alpha Alpha* Honor Society for Public Affairs & Administration

Wake Forest University School of Law, Winston-Salem, NC
- *Juris Doctor* in Law, 1992
- University Faculty Scholar, 1989-92
- Vice-President, Student Trial Bar
- Member, *Inns of Court*

Wofford College, Spartanburg, SC
- *Bachelor of Arts, Summa Cum Laude,* 1989
- Major: Government
- Minor: History
- Honors Thesis: *Divide and occupy: A comparison of French and British imperial practices and outcomes*
- *Phi Beta Kappa*
- Government Department Honors Graduate
- Intern, U.S. Senate, Hon. Ernest F. Hollings (D-SC)

Highly Competent Subject Areas in which I have experience teaching

- International Business
- International Relations
- International Law
- International Political Economy
- Law
- Political Science
- Public Policy
- National Security Strategies
- Diplomacy
- Business
- Entrepreneurship
- Asian Studies
- Middle Eastern Studies
- Political & Economic Development
- Microfinance
- Management
- Public Administration
- Ethics & Philosophy
- Criminal Justice
- Human Resources

- Distance Education
- Learner-Centered Instructional Strategies
- Cybersecurity
- Adult Education
- Socratic Teaching

Personal Attributes and Qualifications

- Dedicated educator committed to improving the lives and opportunities of my students
- Highly disciplined, able to meet time sensitive deadlines under pressure
- Credentialed and experienced in teaching multiple disciplines (National Security, Law, Criminal Justice, Business, Public Policy & Administration, Political Science, Philosophy & Ethics)
- Experienced at designing programs, courses, and lesson plans that contain expert-level content delivery, varied assessment strategies, and integrated real-world scenarios that foster Student Centered Learning
- Reliable team member who brings innovative ideas to collaborative projects
- Caring mentor and facilitator to faculty and students, helping them to improve themselves and achieve their goals
- Broad international experience that enables me to work successfully with diverse groups and impart intercultural lessons to students, peers, and administrators

Teaching Experience: Current Graduate Faculty Appointments

Adjunct Professor, University of Saint Mary, Leavenworth, KS   Oct. 2013-Present
I have developed and taught the following Master's level courses:

HCMGT 795 Strategic Management and Ethics
>   This course is an integrated examination of business management focusing on the application, analysis, and synthesis of business and management problems and

issues at the executive level. Students will develop a perspective of the organization as a whole and explore the means by which overall direction and strategy is established and implemented. Emphasis is on the responsibilities, skills, and perspectives required of executives. The course also examines ethical and corporate social responsibility issues and the trade-offs that must be assessed and made to achieve strategic objectives. Most students will submit the required final assessment during this course. This course is the capstone course of the MBA program and is recommended to be taken at the end of your program.

HCMGT 717 Business Skills for Health Care
This course introduces the student to the key concepts of business management. Topics include organizational management, basic marketing concepts, financial statements, general accounting principles, human resource administration, and the use of information technology in management.

HCMGT 718 Legal and Ethical Issues in Health Care
The course introduces the major ethical theories and principles students need to evaluate current legal and ethical issues in the field of health care. Students explore issues such as patient rights, withdrawing life support, promoting client autonomy, business ethics and the legal responsibilities of health care organizations. Students evaluate varied perspectives and develop a reasoned analysis of current topics.
Platform used: Moodle

Adjunct Professor, St Thomas University, Miami Gardens, FL **Oct. 2012-Present**
I have developed and taught the following Doctoral level course:
EDL 815 Public Policy Leadership and Management
This course examines various approaches to developing and managing and public policy. It is intended primarily for leaders who are department heads, policy developers, managers and executive officers in business, higher education, schools, school boards,

government and statutory agencies responsible for formulating or managing policies.
Platform used: Blackboard

Adjunct Professor, University of Maryland, University College, Adelphi, MD   Apr. 2011-Present
I have taught the following Master's level course:
CSEC 620 Human Aspects in Cybersecurity: Ethics, Legal Issues, and Psychology

> An examination of the human aspects in cybersecurity. Topics include ethics, relevant laws, regulations, policies, standards, psychology, and hacker culture. Emphasis is on the human element and the motivations for cyber crimes. Analysis will include examination of techniques that can be applied for enterprises to prevent such intrusions and attacks that threaten organizational data.

Platforms used: D2L, WebTycho, WIMBA, SimTray
Other Service: Mentor to new adjunct faculty, Served on Curriculum Committee, Participated in Competencies Development Project.

Assistant Professor, University of the Rockies, Colorado Springs, CO   Apr. 2011-Present
I have developed and taught the following Doctoral-level course:

ORG 7731 Global Business Practices I: Europe, the Middle East & Africa

> This course probes the major national and cultural issues encountered by leaders and organizations operating within Europe, the Middle East and Africa. Students will examine how these issues influence leaders, and how leaders and organizations deal with these issues, so that they can accommodate, if not advance solutions, to these issues in the organization's global strategies and practices. Examples of specific topics or issues that may be discussed include: the European Union, NATO, Palestinian-Israeli relations, and African tribal politics.

I have taught the following Master's level courses:

ORG 6728 Professional Ethics, Standards of Practice & Law
This course is a study of the ethical and legal issues
confronting the practicing psychologist. Topics related to
clinical methodology, standards of practice, and inter-
professional relations are explored. Students learn
principles of ethical decision making, standards for
human and animal use in research, and standards of
care specified by state and federal laws. Emphasis is
placed on exploration of the emotional impact that major
ethical and legal dilemmas have on decision making.
Students also master the current code of ethics of the
American Psychological Association and other
professional codes of ethics, such as the code of the
American Association of Marriage and Family Therapy
or the code of the American Counseling Association.

*ORG 6726 International Business I: Survey of Cross-Cultural
Issues*
This course compares and contrasts the core aspects of
national and regional cultures. The course will highlight
selected, contemporary cross-cultural issues that
prominently influence the behavior of international
leaders and organizations. Students will acquire
familiarity with diverse cultures and develop the ability to
shape their leadership or consulting to enable better
communication, more effective teamwork, and greater
contributions by individuals within the organization by
respecting and integrating their cultural and national
background.

*ORG 6728 International Business II: Organizational Practices
within Diverse Political Economies*
This course describes various political economic
environments within and across which international
leaders and organizations must function successfully,
ranging from those that have high levels of integration
and interaction among government, business, and
citizen organizations (e.g., China) to those where these
sectors are relatively more independent of each other
(e.g., the Netherlands). Students will learn the varying
leadership and organizational practices within these

diverse political economic contexts so they can analyze dynamics, external and internal to an organization, in order to enhance individual leadership and organizational performance.

ORG 6730 *International Business, Ethics & the Law*
This course reviews the application of ethics and legal considerations related to international organizations operating in different economic, legal, and cultural settings. The course discusses variances in individual ethics, organizational codes of conduct as well as governmental regulations among diverse nations and regional cultures. Students will learn about specific ethics and legal issues such as bribery, human rights, drug policies, child labor, and environmental standards so they can recognize and help resolve legal and ethical dilemmas faced by international organizations.

ORG 6600, *Principles of Human Resource Management*
This survey course explores the key roles of the human resources discipline and professionals in organizations. Topics include recruitment, selection, training, development, diversity, compensation, benefits, employment law, and employee relations. The course also explores human resources from the perspectives of preventing legal actions against an organization and leveraging human resources as a competitive advantage.

Platform used: Blackboard
Other Service: Curriculum development committees, Grade Comprehensive Exams

**Adjunct Instructor, Grand Canyon University, Phoenix, AZ
Dec. 2013-Present**
I have taught the following graduate course:
POS-530TE: *Arizona and Federal Government for Current Practitioners*
This course is a survey of Arizona history and government as well as of American government. It meets the teacher certification requirement for the study of Arizona government and American government.

I have also taught the following undergraduate course:

POS 301 Arizona and Federal Government
>This course is a survey of Arizona history and government, as well as American government. It meets the teacher certification requirement for Arizona government and American government.

Platform: Loud Cloud

Teaching Experience: Current Undergraduate Faculty Appointments

Adjunct Instructor, Baker College, Flint, MI
Mar. 2004 – Present
I have taught and developed the following courses:

MGT 222 Management Seminar
>Discusses a variety of significant issues related to business and organizational leadership in today's dynamic, customer-driven, global economy. This course focuses on the challenges of change and management's response to change, the diversity of management methods, and managing strategies for the future. As a seminar, this course uses peer teaching and learning approaches, involves group learning experiences in a team environment, requires practical application of concepts, and includes research and case studies. This course culminates the associate's degree of management.

HRM 401R Human Resources and Employment Law
>Provides an introduction to employment law and labor law for a non-legal professional in human resource management and labor relations. An emphasis will be placed on employment, labor, and social issues in the work environment. This course is exclusive to the Accelerated Bachelor of Business Leadership program.

MGT 231 Small Business Management
>Examines the role of small businesses in the economy

with emphasis on marketing, human resources, management, and financing of the small business. The role of the entrepreneur in business will be examined.

HRM 435B International Human Resources Management
Examines how global human resource management practices within a global context is distinctive from domestic human resource management. Students will analyze the challenges that multinational corporations are confronted with, which include cultural, political, social, and legal issues; the level of managerial skill and education; technological development in the host country. Issues such as expatriation versus local management, selecting and preparing for international assignments, cultural adaptation at the individual and system level, and the influence of globalization on future HRM practices are also examined.

LAW 211 Business Law
Provides students with an introduction to the legal issues inherent in dynamic business environments. Topics covered include the legal system, including an examination of constitutional law; business torts; contracts; intellectual property; criminal law; and the ethical considerations for business decision making.

HSC 312 Health Law and Regulations
Addresses legal issues, restraints, and problems arising from organization and delivery of healthcare services. Topics to be included are: tort law; hospital, physician, nurse, and other health professional's liability; informed consent; medical records; legal reporting obligations; abortion; autopsy, donation and experimentation; sterilization and artificial insemination; euthanasia; patient rights and responsibilities; labor relation; insurance; trial procedures; and restraint of trade are topics which are included.
Platform: Blackboard
Other Service: Curriculum development committees, New Faculty Mentor

Associate Faculty, Ashford University, Clinton, IA
2011-Present
I taught the following undergraduate courses:

PHI 103 Informal Logic
>This course is a study of correct and incorrect reasoning involved in everyday activities. The fundamentals of language and argument, deductive and inductive reasoning and other aspects of practical reasoning are examined.

BUS 372 Employee and Labor Relations
>The course provides students with both the common and complex issues related to human behavior in the workplace as it relates to employee relations, and an examination of relationships among unions, workers, management, laws and government regulation.

BUS 311 Business Law I
>Introduction to the legal environment of business in the United States. Examination of the Constitution, administrative law, contracts, agency, and the protection of competition, consumers, employees, investors, the environment, and international trade.

BUS 378 International Business Law
>This courses focuses on the legal environment associated with international commercial transactions, including an analysis of major Western and non-Western legal traditions and the supranational law of the European Community, a detailed analysis of the negotiation, formation, enforcement, and financing of international sales contracts, an analysis of international trade regulation, analysis of methods of regulating global competition, and of the protection of business property rights in international transactions.

RES 334 Real Estate Finance
>This course primarily examines the residential real estate finance markets and their impacts on consumers, but will also cover facets of commercial real estate.

Mortgage options and purchase costs will be highlighted with attention to theories of real estate investment.

Platform: Blackboard

Other Service: Curriculum development committees

Adjunct Faculty, Broward College, Ft. Lauderdale, FL
June 2014 –Present

I am teaching the following course:

BUL 4264 International Business Law

Students will be exposed to the legal implications of transacting business across national borders. The focus will be on transactional international business law including, the legal and ethical environment of international business, international contracting, importing-exporting, trade finance, and international intellectual property law and licensing. The student will gain an appreciation of the special risks of conducting business internationally and the legal pitfalls associated with those risks.

Teaching Experience: International Faculty Appointments

Visiting Professor, Keuka China Programs
Aug. 2007 – June 2012

This is a joint Bachelor's degree program between Keuka College in NY and several partner universities in the Peoples' Republic of China. I was the lead instructor for Strategic Management, the capstone course of the program. I also assisted the Program Director with curriculum improvement, course mapping, and preparation for the US regional accreditation review and affirmation process with the Middle States Association. I rotated among campuses in Tianjin, Xiamen, and Kunming, Peoples' Republic of China.

I developed taught the following undergraduate courses:

BUS 444 Strategic Management

This course introduces the student to the process by which strategic business decisions are made and implemented. It also incorporates prior functional course material in an integrated manner as a foundation for successful business management. Formal studies, casework, and a comprehensive term project are used to reinforce learning. This is the capstone course for all majors with the Division of Business and Management.

LAW 202 Business Law

An introduction to legal principles and their relationships to business organizations. Representative topics include the constitutional authority to regulate business, consumer law, employment and labor relations law, torts and crimes related to business, and intellectual property. A substantial part of the course covers contract law and commercial paper.

HRM 208 Human Resources Management

Aspects of the human resources function operable in business organizations; analysis of employment personnel testing, job classification, wage and salary administration, and performance evaluation; overview of labor relations in American business.

BUS 360 Managerial Marketing

An introduction to legal principles and their relationships to business organizations. Representative topics include the constitutional authority to regulate business, consumer law, employment and labor relations law, torts and crimes related to business, and intellectual property. A substantial part of the course covers contract law and commercial paper.

MGT 345 Organizational Behavior

Logical and rational design of organizations; emergent behavior in the individual and the group, including interaction and effect on the organization.

Adjunct Faculty, Higher Colleges of Technology, United Arab Emirates   **Jan – June 2010**
I taught the following undergraduate courses:

BMGN N310 Commercial Law and Practices in the United Arab

Emirates

This course introduces the study of law and the basic areas of law, in particular pertaining to commercial law in the UAE. The course builds upon a basic understanding of the law to result in the application of more specific laws to commercial enterprises and workplace situations. Students develop the ability to: recognize competing and conflicting legal interests, rights and obligations in various commercial fact situations; understand basic dispute resolution methods; analyze fact situations; and apply the appropriate law.

BUSN N1150 Business Essentials

This course encompasses a study of the world of business. It provides opportunities for students to explore businesses at a local, regional and global level. The students are introduced to the business environment and basic business functions and processes in a realistic and practical manner.

BUSN N2290 Business Technology IV

This final semester integrated course for the Diploma in Applied Business and Technology program advances students' skills and knowledge against the background of current events and trends in the UAE business environment. Students conduct independent research for projects, based on the application of ICT to authentic vocationally-focused business and career-based topics.

Teaching Experience: Previous Faculty Appointments

Program Chair, Political Science and Paralegal Studies, Ellis University, Chicago, IL

Mar.-Sept. 2011

I was responsible for supervising the Bachelor of Arts programs in Paralegal Studies and Political Science. In my position as Chair, I monitored classes to ensure compliance with academic requirements and regulations; conducted faculty training and development seminars; evaluated faculty performance; reviewed the academic progress of students; engage in student counseling; served on the Faculty Senate, Academic Leadership,

Strategic Planning, Curriculum Development, Academic Standards, and Faculty Development Committees; and worked closely with faculty and administration to improve student persistence and academic rigor. I was assigned to a task force charged with developing and implementing a new program for faculty evaluations. I also taught and/or developed five courses per year.

Subject Matter Expert, Course Developer, Online Faculty, Ellis University, Chicago, IL
June 2005 – Mar. 2011

Graduate Courses developed and taught: *Ethics; Labor Law and Policies; Legal Issues for Non-Profit Organizations; Fair Employment Policies and Practices; Public Sector Labor Relations.*

Undergraduate Courses developed and/or taught: *Introduction to Public Administration; American Government and Politics; American Foreign Policy; History of Political Thought; International Relations; Selected Topics in Comparative Government; Selected Topics in Public Administration; Selected Topics in Political Science; Basic Legal Concepts and Administration of Justice; Business Organizations; American Society and Judicial Behavior; Criminal Procedure; Products Liability; Introduction to Paralegal Studies; Introduction to Law for Paralegals; Family Law; Real Estate Law; Law Office Management; Criminal Law; Civil Litigation; Contract Law; Torts; Civil Litigation; International Law and Organizations; Cyber Law & Ethics; Contract Law; Insurance Law; Medical Malpractice Law; Employment Law; Business Law I and II; Constitutional Law; Employment Law; Intellectual Property Law; Independent Study; Contemporary Political Thought; Rules of Evidence; Civil Litigation; and Ethics for Managers.*

Platform: Proprietary
Other Service: Faculty Senate, Curriculum Development Committee, New Faculty Mentor

Senior Instructor, Master of Arts in Diplomacy Program, Conflict Management Specialization, Norwich University
Nov. 2006 – Dec. 2009

In addition to instructional duties, I have served as an advisor

and committee member for Masters' theses, as well as a grader for the Masters' Comprehensive Examinations and facilitator during graduate residency programs.
Graduate course taught:
GD 520 Law and the International System

> This course explores the structure of the international system as defined by its rules and guidelines. The course presents an introduction to international law terminology and its history and theory. Laws surrounding conflict, war, war crimes, and the rising areas of international law, environmental law, and laws concerning humanitarian intervention will be explored. Of special interest will be laws pertaining to human rights.

Undergraduate course developed and taught:
SPO 302 *National Security Policy*

> This course introduces the issues and institutions of national security policy. You will gain an appreciation of strategic thought and strategy formulation, the ability to assess national security issues and threats, and an understanding of the political and military institutions involved in the making and execution of national security policy.

Platform: Web Ct
Other Service: Curriculum development committees, Grader for Comprehensive Exams, Residency Reviewer.

Online Course Developer/Lead Faculty/Facilitator, Master of Science in Management, Master of Arts in Public Policy, and Master of Science in Criminal Justice Leadership Programs, New England College, Henniker, NH   Nov. 2006 – Dec. 2009
Graduate courses developed and taught:
PO 6110 Ethics in Government

> This course will examine the moral issues relating to governing and being governed. Topics include the philosophical nature and limits of representative government, ethical issues in formulating public policy, civil liberties issues, and corruption in government. Selected case studies will be utilized to develop understanding and skills dealing with ethical dilemmas in public service, particularly with regard to the role of ethics in leadership.

PO 7050 Environmental Politics and Policy

Are we facing an unprecedented environmental crisis or are environmental problems exaggerated? Has political discourse helped to shape sound environmental policies in the public interest or mainly served as an arena for a battle of special interests? What has been the role of environmental organizations and other institutions in environmental politics? What environmental issues are most likely to receive more attention in political debate and how might this debate unfold? This course will examine these and other issues.

PO 6300 Class, Race, and Poverty in America

A study of the persistent issues of class, poverty and race in America and how they compromise the pursuit of the American dream of equality and opportunity. The "War on Poverty," The Civil Rights movement, welfare reform and educational inequalities will be examined.

CJ 6810 Criminal Justice Policy and Program Evaluation

This course addresses the relationship between the establishment of policy and its implementation in programs within criminal justice organizations. Methods for evaluating programs and using the results to further inform policy development and maintain public accountability are reviewed and discussed. Well known criminal justice program evaluation studies will be critiqued and students will design evaluation research projects.

MG 6950 Contract Management

This course introduces the student to the contract management process from both buyer and seller perspectives, from pre-RFP planning, proposal development, and negotiation through contract administration and closeout. Using the work breakdown structure as a framework for planning, the course explains all typical major tasks, responsibilities, and customer interfaces.

Professional & Organizational Ethics from a Global Perspective.

CJ 6410 Professional and Organizational Ethics

This course explores and analyzes the relationships among stakeholders in the criminal justice system, and the expectations of ethical decision-making and behaviors among leaders within the organization and the system. Students will consider the moral implications and social effects of the administration of criminal justice in a free society, and the tension that exists between achieving desirable outcomes and the means by which they are achieved. Topics include theories of morality; analysis of ethical decision-making; interaction and conflicts among personal, professional, and organizational values; the effect of cultural diversity on individual and group values; current issues in criminal justice policy and practice; and how leaders in the field of criminal justice can maintain accountability in an atmosphere of conflicting stakeholder interests.

Platform: Moodle
Other Service: Curriculum development committees

Online Adjunct Instructor, School of Liberal Arts and Social Sciences, Department of Criminal Justice, Northwestern State University, *Natchitoches, LA*

Aug. 2005 – May 2010

Undergraduate courses developed and taught:

CJ 2400 Adjudication Process

Role and structure of prosecution, public defense, and courts; basic elements of the substantive criminal law; procedural law and relation to constitutional guarantees.

CJ 4450 Criminal Law

The legal definition of crime and defenses; purposes and functions of the substantive criminal law; historical foundations; limits of criminal law; case study approach.

CJ 3380 Criminal Justice Ethics

A comprehensive examination of theoretical and applied ethics and moral philosophy in criminal justice. It begins with a classical introduction from antiquity and continues to present day. The practical focus of ethical decision making topics will center on law enforcement ethics, correctional ethics, and probation/ parole ethics and will include scenarios.

CJ 4460 Criminal Evidence and Procedure

Constitutional and procedural considerations affecting arrest, search and seizure, post-conviction treatment;

origin, development, philosophy, constitutional basis of evidence; kinds and degrees of evidence and rules governing admissibility; judicial decisions interpreting individual rights and case studies; case study approach.

Professional Positions

The Saylor Foundation – Washington, DC
Jan. 2011 – Sept. 2011

Consultant and course developer for this open-access, non-profit higher education project. Developed undergraduate online courses in Political Science and National Security. Undergraduate courses developed: *Contemporary Political Thought, Intelligence and National Security, Asia-Pacific Politics, International Law, Ethics and Public Policy.*

Education Testing Service - Princeton, NJ
June 2009 – June 2012

Appointed as a Reader for the 2009, 2010, 2011, 2012 AP Exams in US Government and Politics.

Attorney at Law   1992 – 2001
Charlotte, NC

- Prior to opening my own practice in 1993, employed as Associate counsel in medium-sized litigation, insurance defense, and corporate law firm.
- Drafted documents and contracts, engaged in labor negotiations for corporate clients; handled OSHA, EEOC, NLRB, IRS, ESC matters.
- Drafted pleadings, conducted depositions, handled trials and pretrial hearings for insurance companies and other corporate and individual clients.
- Represented clients in over five thousand criminal matters, including white-collar crime and death penalty cases.
- Developed expertise in investigation, negotiation, and advocacy.
- Performed daily in a high-stress, time-sensitive environment.
- Served as volunteer Guardian *ad litem* for children who were

abused, neglected, victims of crime, or subjects of highly contested custody cases.
- Frequent commentator on regional legal matters in local print media and both locally and nationally broadcasted shows.

Entrepreneurial Experience

VP/Marketing and Business Manager   **2001 – 2005**
Charlotte4Sale.com
- Began this real estate brokerage venture in partnership with my husband
- Developed and implemented Internet & print media marketing plan
- Sold over $15 Million annually, 2002 - 2005
- Designed and maintained interactive websites
- Managed ongoing business, financial, and marketing operations

Articles, Presentations, and Research

- *Wilted roses in Afghanistan: A study of efforts of microfinance groups to improve rights and opportunities for Afghan women.* Paper and presentation delivered at the International Academic Conference on Law and Politics, Istanbul, Turkey, Apr. 2014.

- *Political, social, and economic empowerment of women in the Muslim world.* Paper and presentation at the Norwich University School of Graduate Studies Residency, Northfield, VT, June 2010.

- Session Chair, *Pedagogical innovations in education: Learning and teaching methodologies,* International Conference on Education and New Learning Technologies, in Barcelona, Spain, July 2009.

- *Using Socratic techniques to increase learning outcomes in online education,* Paper delivered at the International Conference on Education and New Learning Technologies, in Barcelona, Spain, July 2009.

- *Afghans helping Afghans: A study of Afghan-led NGO initiatives,* published in the Winter 2007 issue of the *Journal of the Society of Afghan Engineers.*

- *Is history repeating itself? A comparison of the post-Ottoman and post-Saddam occupations of Iraq,* paper and panel discussion delivered at the annual conference of the International Conference of Social Science Research, Orlando, FL, Dec. 2005.

- *Academic freedom in the post-9/11 world,* paper and panel discussion delivered at the annual conference of the Peace History Society, Rock Hill, South Carolina, Nov. 2005.

- *Building a Safer World: The United Nations in the 21st Century,* Conference sponsored by UNESCO and The Atlantic Council of the U.S. Facilitator of group discussions on (1) crisis response and (2) war and conflicts. Virtual Conference. Oct., 2005.

- *Socratic teaching in the online learning environment,* paper and PowerPoint presentation delivered at the Baker College annual faculty conference, June 2005.

- *The doctoral student experience: Learning and Scholarship,* Panel participant, Walden University residency, San Diego, CA, Mar. 2005.

Military Service

Signals Intelligence Analyst/Enciphered Communications Analyst, U.S. Army,   *1983 – 1989*
- While assigned to the National Security Agency, gathered information from various resources and gave daily intelligence briefings to National Command Authority and designates.
- While stationed in Korea, supervised the gathering of intelligence information from various collection platforms, and prepared reports for intelligence agencies for dissemination.

- Top Secret/SCI/Special Intelligence Clearance.
- Joint Services Commendation Medal; Army Achievement Medal; Good Conduct Medal; Overseas Service Medal; Army Service Ribbon; Honorable Discharge

Professional Affiliations

- Life Member, National Association of Criminal Defense Lawyers
- Member, Board of Directors, Ariana Outreach
- Member, Veterans of Foreign Wars
- Member, Association of Former Intelligence Officers
- Member, American Society for Public Administration
- Member, National Contract Management Association
- Member, Academy of Political Science
- Member, American Political Science Association
- Member, Middle East Institute
- Member, International Political Science Association
- Member, People-to-People International
- Member, Southern Poverty Law Center
- Member, Peace History Society
- Member, Southern Political Science Association

Platforms

Moodle, Blackboard, WebCT, Angel, WebTycho, D2L, Sakai, Several proprietary LMS

Chapter 7 - The Interview: What Universities Look For

"In a completely rational society, the best of us
would be teachers and the rest of us
would have to settle for something less."
— Lee Iacocca

So you have gotten your application to the university and you have piqued their interest. Good for you! This is a critical accomplishment and you should be proud. Now you need to prepare yourself for the more crucial step—closing the deal! As with any job interview, you have to step up and make yourself stand above the rest of the crowd vying for the same position. Sometimes you are lucky and have a niche, one for which the university is badly in need of people with your qualifications. You might find yourself competing with people who have more education and/or more experience.

Sometimes the interview process is a dreaded one, but it does not need to be. You can prepare well and find out as much information as you can about the school by talking to the 3000+ faculty members you are networked with in our forum. Relatively speaking, most of these interviews don't compare with other professional interviews in difficulty level. Very rarely is there an in-person interview or a test as there often is in business or technical jobs; sometimes there isn't even a phone call. While the process of applying for adjunct positions is similar to the business application process at first, once you get to this stage, you must take it up a notch. Suddenly the script is gone and you are left to sell yourself in a way that varies from university to university. Take solace in knowing that there are some common themes and you will get good at this very quickly, especially if you flood the market with applications as I suggest. In this chapter, I will explain the interview process, what to expect from it, and how to prepare for it.

Interview Processes of Online Schools

First, I will differentiate the interview processes by types of universities. Specifically, we will examine interview processes for traditional universities, nontraditional universities and community colleges, and faith-based schools.

Traditional universities are the bricks-and-mortar places with live classrooms, a limited enrollment, and a minimum score required on College Board exams; they usually have a real campus with dormitories and sports teams. The nontraditional universities and community colleges typically have unlimited enrollment, or what is sometimes referred to as open enrollment, often have no College Board requirements, sometimes offer online courses or are online schools, and often seem to be hiring. The faith-based schools can be partially or completely online and often have open enrollment, but have an interview process that rivals and challenges those of traditional universities and models in many ways.

Traditional Universities

The traditional university that has added an online program, has a well-established faculty, and a reputation built on selectivity of students and a more traditional view of academics and faculty. It does not have open enrollment and so can afford to be picky about who teaches there. The more elite universities utilize their full-time faculty in the online program to promote the reputation of the online program as equaling the classroom.

If you are lucky enough to be selected for an interview with one of these universities, be prepared for an interview process that mirrors what you would do if you were trying to get a full-time job there. You can expect to be sent detailed questionnaires that probe you beyond the standard application. They will want to know about your specific skills, use of Web technology, your teaching philosophy, whether you have published recently in any academic journals, what publications are on the horizon, as well as some other pertinent and time-consuming information requests. Specific questions are unique to each university, but you can expect some common themes; the questions are not too difficult to answer but may take more time than you expected. Note here that your written response is part of the interview. How you respond, how quickly you do it, and how professional and well-written it is will carry a lot of weight in whether you advance in the interview process. From the moment you receive anything from the university asking more of you, remind yourself that you are always being graded, so keep your wits about you.

Another very important element: traditional university deans often report to us that they want to see how much of a subject matter expert someone is in a very specific field of study. So, for instance, they do not want a "business professor," they want a "multinational corporations in the modern society" instructor, and they want your experience and your CV and publications to reflect that you are a subject matter expert, and not a jack-of-all-trades. This isn't always the case, but it is more often the case in traditional schools than in others.

Whether or not you do fill out an interview questionnaire, you can expect a phone interview. In fact, you can expect several phone interviews, beginning with the search committee or department chair, or possibly with human resources, and eventually leading up to the dean. Sometimes you will have several people interviewing you at one time, often including full-time tenured professors from that university.

Expect to be asked easy questions like: Tell us about your online teaching experience. What courses have you taught online? For whom have you taught online? Why do you enjoy teaching online? What have you published and what publications do you have in the works?

Other common questions you may hear are How is teaching online different from teaching on-ground? What exceptions do you make when teaching online compared with your on-ground experience? (That is assuming, of course, that you have some experience in both venues.)

After you are comfortable with the interview, expect things to be turned up a notch with: Why do you want to teach for Whatsamatta U.? What unique skills do you possess that would benefit Whatsamatta U.? What are your strengths and weaknesses as an online professor? How does your teaching philosophy fit in with the culture here at Whatsamatta U.? (and one of the favorites)… We are currently interviewing 18 candidates for this position; why should we hire you?

Imagine trying to answer these impromptu, especially when they tell you that you are allowed only three minutes to answer each question. Don't be surprised when they wrap up the call and ask if you have any questions for them. You need to have some! If you have none, they may see it as a sign that you are not interested, do not think critically, and haven't done your homework.

It is really important that you've searched the Web, networked with others, asked questions in our forum, and communicated with faculty who are familiar with the school's programs and reputation. Make a list of questions to ask that show your interest. These should be genuine questions; after all, most likely you do in fact have questions you need answers to. Consider the following as food for thought: What are the expectations of your online faculty? How much emphasis do you put on professional experience versus academic experience? How many courses do you currently offer online? (Only ask this if it isn't a fully online school!) What are your top priorities for new facilitators? What is your university's teaching philosophy? What is your enrollment/drop rate compared with other schools? How am I evaluated as a faculty member? Do you allow your faculty to teach for other schools?"

The list goes on, but just as in a traditional job or business interview, you need to engage the faculty or school representatives here. Asking questions gets them to ask more about you and learn more about you, which is a good thing.

Warning: Traditional universities may not take kindly to your being a professional adjunct, as they fully expect that beyond your professional job, their students are your only students and you are loyal to the university. This means you must be careful about how you market yourself to them. Before you think that all of this bureaucracy makes it not worth your time, think again. Your CV will look far more impressive when you are a faculty member of a major university such as Stanford, MIT, Georgia Tech, or the University of Texas. Just be prepared to address the issue of whether you intend to teach for other schools. Job experience is good, but so is loyalty, so depending on the school—toe the line.

Whew! Sounds like a lot of work, and it is, but this is the exception rather than the rule. Most of your interviews will be with nontraditional universities, such as the University of Phoenix, which has both ground-based and online courses, or Capella University, which is 100% online, or community or state colleges that offer online courses.

Nontraditional Universities, Community and State Colleges

The two don't seem to fit together, but they do

in more ways than you might think. Yes, community colleges have traditional daytime students, full-time faculty, real campuses, and standard semesters, while nontraditional universities often have limited full-time faculty, almost all adult students, hold mostly night/weekend classes, and work out of an office building.

What these institutions do have in common, though, is that they often have open enrollment, with no limit on the number of students they admit (in fact the goal is often to admit as many as possible – as one boss put it, "our policy to decide who to admit and who not to admit is if they stand in front of a mirror and it fogs up"), and all three reach out to adult learners. As such, they are almost always hiring online faculty. Sometimes this is the form of a *job pool*, where the university keeps an open "slot" on their Human Resources (HR) website for faculty to upload their CV in case they have needs in the future. As discussed in this book, you need to get your applications to the right people up front, and if they are interested in you, they may fast-track you (particularly if you apply with a recommendation).

Often the process for interviewing is quick because the school doesn't have the manpower to go through a formal process with every applicant. You will probably receive a phone call from a single person, probably the department chair or dean, and he or she will ask a few key questions about your skills, background, availability, and flexibility, and will then give you a chance to ask questions. You may be asked specifically about your online teaching experience and whether you've used the school's platform, which is its online classroom system. You can use this as an opportunity to find out more about the university, the pay, the commitment required of online professors, and how scheduling works. If you hit it off, you can expect to advance to the next round – training – rather quickly.

The big-name traditional universities seldom have this formal training because they don't hire faculty with great regularity, but these open enrollment programs tend to take hundreds of applications each week and select a small percentage for consideration. Don't take it too lightly; the training itself is part of the interview process. Your email and written correspondence as well as your verbal skills on the phone are being evaluated, but it is when you participate in the standard online training that you are truly being interviewed, albeit very subtly. This is the area where many potential faculty members are weeded out; they essentially waste many weeks of their time in training only to never be offered a position.

The training courses usually include one on the Web platform, another on general university policies, and sometimes another on the proper way to teach online (i.e., doing things the way that university wants them done). Sometimes these training modules are rolled up into one or two courses, if you are lucky.

One of the established faculty members (sometimes an adjunct) facilitates the course, and you *must* participate like a real student in a real course. This means full participation – If the school requires five days per week of participation, then you must be there five days per week. You are actually graded on your written assignments, timeliness, online courtesy or netiquette, ability to work in groups, and whether you fit into the culture of the university. Tracking tools are used to see how often you actually log in to the course and often how much time you spend in it.

The online training programs use discussion forums just like the courses that you will facilitate if you get the job. In the discussion forums, expect to see questions like How would you deal with a student who plagiarizes? Should there be a forced grade distribution?

They may also give you real-life situations to respond to – situations like this: Joe asks for three extra days for his assignment due to health reasons. Based on university policy, what would your answer to Joe be? Construct a formal letter to Joe and post it in the discussion thread.

These questions are not there just to give you practice on the platform; they are there to interview you and to see how you respond to other comments with which you may or may not agree. Remember to keep your work stored somewhere! Often the same questions are asked at other universities' training, with just slight modifications.

At the close of the course, the course facilitator will make a recommendation as to whether you should or should not teach for the university. Don't let your guard down for one minute. This doesn't mean you should worry about the training – it is not difficult and often the routine is similar throughout the nontraditional universities; but it is unpaid time that you must sacrifice with serious effort. If you save your work and discussion responses, you may find them helpful in the next course at the next university. More about training will be addressed in the next chapter.

Faith-Based Universities

If you are a person of faith and would welcome the notion of being able to discuss and mention topics that are off-limits at some schools, then you should consider applying to one of several faith-based universities that have opened their school to online learners. I recommend looking for schools that match your particular faith if you would like to teach at one of these colleges. In 2006, we wrote, "while faith-based schools often don't pay as well as secular ones, they can be more rewarding in other ways and worth the effort." In the past two years, I have found this to no longer be the case, and have found smaller faith-based institutions to pay as well or even better than for-profit education.

Indiana Wesleyan University and Liberty University are among the most traditional Christian universities in the country. You can expect such faith-based universities to hold faculty, including adjuncts, to a strict philosophical and religious standard. Liberty University automatically emails immediately those individuals you entered as references into the HR system, looking for recommendations that include your commitment to your Christian faith. You will be uploading your pastoral reference into the job application system (not uncommon at Christian schools). You must consent to a background check, provide a detailed statement of faith, provide a letter of reference from a pastor, and respond to several tough questions.

Many faith-based institutions will ask for things like:

- A biographical sketch
- An explanation on how you came to your faith
- Your subsequent spiritual growth
- Your church involvement
- How you came to your particular academic discipline
- Your personal goals both as an educator and a professional in your field.

Most of the faith-based institutions post their faculty requirements with regard to faith and religion on their websites, and you should read this before applying. Other than a small number of schools I can think of, most will require that you fully commit to their faith before they will accept your candidacy. You can expect your interview to include questions about your faith, and to demonstrate how you will integrate faith in the classroom (knowing that not all students will be of the same faith).

Here are some questions you might see: How do you integrate scriptural truth into your discipline? How would students see evidence of this? How has salvation of Christ as your Savior affected your life? Identify and explain to us any personal ministry, church involvement, or spiritual growth that has been important to you during the past year.

I have been on some interviews where I am asked specific questions about my faith, and why, for example, "there was a picture of you on Facebook from two years ago with a glass of wine." So yes – heads up! They may well be looking at your social media profiles (more on this later in the book).

Obviously, these questions require more time

and more thought-out answers than "How would you handle Joe's situation with his homework being late?" In addition, many Christian schools may ask you to sign that you are committed to making a difference, based on their philosophy, through teaching. You must state unequivocally that you agree to their truth and values (such as the Bible being the direct word of God), and that you are committed to living your life in a Christ-like way. Christian colleges will often ask you to make this statement of testament and of faith. They may include the existence of God, God as the creator of the universe, the reality of salvation through Christ, and punishment (Heaven and Hell).

Needless to say, if you do not believe in these philosophies, you will not fare well here, nor should you even apply. However, whatever your faith, chances are there is a faith-based school that is looking for faculty. Do some online searches and then the answers to the questions they ask will come naturally to you. Ask in the Facebook forum for some suggestions on schools that are built on your particular faith and I have no doubt you will get a long list of answers.

After your application packet, transcripts, and letters of reference arrive at the school, you can expect one or more phone interviews. The phone interviews can be rather intense; however, usually the people you talk with are quite pleasant. Expect to be asked more about your faith, possibly to give opening or closing prayer, to make a personal testament on the phone, and to discuss your ability and method of integrating faith with traditional learning.

What to Expect: What Do Deans Want?

What do deans really want in an adjunct? Think of it like computer dating—you want the perfect mate, but you settle for someone pretty good. After all, it is just a date. If it were marriage, you would have stricter standards. The same holds true for adjunct faculty. Adjuncts are the equivalent of a computer date, while tenured faculty members are married to the school. Since you wouldn't date someone without some form of an interview process (and these days a background check, too!), whether it is in person, on the phone, or through some online form, you shouldn't expect to get a teaching position without the same.

As with anyone you would willingly date, there are qualities you look for in such a person – "must have," "preferred," "nice to have," and "can live without." Deans, likewise, each have such a unique list for their ideal choice, although some qualities are common to most deans' lists. Let's first look at the "must haves." You can expect all schools to want you to be qualified to teach for them; this means having the required number of graduate semester hours from an accredited college, and those hours need to be in the subject you will potentially be teaching. You can also expect all schools to want you to have your own computer with Internet access, and that you have a strong command of the English language. Each of these qualifications should come out in your cover letter, CV, and phone interview.

Probably the most common "preferred" quality that deans seek is prior teaching experience. You will even see the word "preferred" in many job ads for online professors. If you are new to education, note "preferred," and also please reread the chapter on being a "newbie" in online education. We all had to start somewhere, and chances are you have trained someone or some group in your professional career or have guest-lectured at a local college, and can list this in your educational experience section.

If you don't have any of these experiences, consider creating a course on Babb Academy – you can earn money and you will have experience to list! Yes, there are those few online programs that are strict about not hiring you to teach for them without prior teaching experience; they don't want you to be cutting your teeth on their students. If they really like you, they may even tell you to go teach a couple of courses at a community college and then call them back in a few months, but most often they won't even consider you. Thankfully for many of you, experience is not a "must have" in many schools.

Depending on the school, your personality or lack of expertise may be an issue. I know that sounds terrible to "write out loud," but it is true. In a smaller or more prestigious university, you can expect the dean to look for the best fit with the faculty. This is not stated in any job description or advertisement, but administrators would like to see certain types of faculty in their school, in part to keep the peace with the tenured faculty, but mostly to protect the reputation of the school. The larger online programs and community colleges are reported to be less picky, as they have many slots to fill. The fact that you are qualified is critical; the fact that you are a pleasant conversationalist is unimportant, especially since they are not likely to talk with you after the interview, nor are your students, who will communicate with you primarily via an online forum or email.

Another "preferred" quality is that you be responsive. How quickly you respond to the dean's emails and phone calls will set part of the tone in the hiring process. You might think this should be a required trait, but if you teach a subject that is hard to fill, a lot can be overlooked. So unless you like to teach the subjects that most dread, it helps to be pleasant and responsive. It is wise to find your niche and do some research to find out how much in demand your particular qualifications are.

Topping the "nice to have" list is that you are a published author in journals, books, magazines (anywhere is better than nowhere, but journals are best). There are those few schools that are currently using publications as a tiebreaker for hiring adjuncts, although they are rare, at least for now. Getting published looks great on your application; it makes the school look better and the tenured faculty tend to accept you more easily (although you are not likely to meet them anyway if you teach online). This does not show up on job ads, but you want to include your publications and conference presentations in your CV if you have any. If you have your own website, be sure to have a presentations section; it is even better if you can record any on-ground presentations you have.

Another "nice to have" is patience. You won't get a class every semester, quarter, or whatever term system the university is on. If you are happy to sit on the bench and wait to be put in the game, never complaining, you will eventually be in the starting lineup on a regular basis. However, you must keep yourself visible without nagging. If you nag the dean about when your next class is being offered, don't expect to earn brownie points. Obviously, it is important that you stay visible, but you cannot annoy the leadership team every time your class gets canceled for low enrollment, you are asked to teach a directed study due to a small number of students for low pay, or you don't get a class for three months. This goes hand-in-hand with another "nice to have"—flexibility.

If you are willing to teach anything, anywhere, anytime, you will be on every dean's dance ticket. Their job can be quite difficult, considering that they have to find instructors, schedule classes, keep tenured or full-time faculty smiling, deal with student complaints, and evaluate faculty – and probably teach a course or two themselves every term. Most likely, they are paid less than you are when you teach for three universities and are working many more hours. I try to be very patient and kind to my bosses, not just because I want to be assigned courses, but because I know their job is truly hard. I respect it, and I hope that comes across in my messages.

In addition, many online schools strive for regional accreditation, which can be a nightmare to obtain. The less of a burden you are and the more you come across as the answer to a dean's problems, the more likely you will become a go-to faculty member.

If you can address several items on the perfect adjunct list of every dean, finding work as an adjunct will be much easier. However, if you insist on enhancing that list with other qualities about yourself, beware! Some "can live without" qualities may sound great but can actually hurt you or get you ignored. Keep your politics, religion, and even favorite sports teams out of your correspondence unless it is apparent that mention of them can help; for example, if the dean happened to attend your alma mater, you can certainly note that.

In a faith-based school, it is a sure bet that you can safely discuss religious issues, and can even delve into politics as they pertain to family issues or as they relate to the religion you subscribe to (so long as it's the same as the school's). This type of dialogue can score you points, but if you are not careful, it can instead cost you dearly. Most faith-based institutions have a lot of students who are not of that particular faith and they do not want their faculty members alienating them.

Remember that you are being hired to teach a course that the school needs to be taught; your favorite baseball team and your opinion on an issue like border patrol are not germane and should be kept in reserve until after you get the job and feel a sense of comfort with your boss and colleagues. Even then, some wouldn't recommend it.

Another heads up – the same holds true for the teaching forum! I have had over 50 deans or department heads message me in 2014 saying something like "can you believe so and so said such and such?" or "what people say in that forum blows me away sometimes." Almost always it's about politics. Remember that your current and potential bosses are reading what you write. You have that forum to be candid in, but keep it about what matters.

When it comes to what the dean wants, actions speak louder than words. You can write what you are all about, and, except for your credentials generated from your transcripts, everything else will come out in your personal correspondence. How quickly you reply, the tone of your messages, the professionalism of your documents, the openness and availability you make clear in your actions, and so forth will tell the dean whether you are a candidate worthy of that first date.

The discussion forums of the mandatory training will often set you up to show more of your personality and that is where you must curb yourself so as not to give away too much about yourself. Remember that in a class of 20, someone is bound to not agree with you, so you should restrict your opinions to class materials only. Talk about relevant issues like retention, how important communication with learners is, strategies for success, and how critical it is for adult learners to feel as though their life experience matters in class. After all, an opinionated person will often be seen as someone whom others cannot work with as well as someone who will try to bring up controversial topics in class or use the classroom as their soapbox. Once you earn the deans' trust and respect, they will be coming to you for your opinions, but show that you are willing to do things their way first.

On the Inside Track: Academic Administrator Comments

Dr. Andrew N Carpenter shared his perspective on several questions related to getting hired and keeping your position. Andrew N. Carpenter, PhD, is the former Chief Academic Officer of Ellis and John Hancock Universities. A native of Santa Fe, New Mexico, he earned degrees in philosophy from Amherst College (BA, summa cum laude), the University of Oxford (B.Phil), and the University of California at Berkeley (PhD); his academic specialty is the history of early modern philosophy.

Dr. Carpenter has served in numerous administrative and faculty leadership roles at proprietary and not-for-profit institutions of higher learning and has significant expertise in organizational development, academic governance, academic policy creation, continuous quality improvement, strategic planning, faculty development, and the assessment of institutions of higher learning, academic programs, and student learning. He is an expert in online learning, has extensive curriculum development experience, and is a member of the peer review corps of the Higher Learning Commission of the North Central Association, the Accrediting Commission of the Distance Education and Training Council, and the Quality Matters Project (Certified Master Reviewer).

He serves on the board of directors of the American Association of Philosophy Teachers and the advisory board of the International Higher Education Teaching and Learning Association; he is also active in the Professional and Organizational Development Network and serves on several academic journal editorial boards. He has an extensive publishing record in philosophy and in the scholarship of teaching and learning, including recent publications on learning assessment, developing social capital within academic communities, and administrative and academic structures in for-profit and not-for-profit institutions of higher learning. He has earned six teaching awards from five institutions of higher learning and previously served as a member of the faculty executive committee at Antioch College, as the president of the faculty senates of Kaplan University and Ellis University, and as the Chief Academic Officer of Ellis University and John Hancock University. By the way – these are the types of amazing administrators that help others in our forums and why I emphasize networking in there so avidly!

Here is the interview narrative with Dr. Carpenter:

Q: What qualities do you look for in new hires?
A: Passion about education, sophisticated understanding of the learning needs of adult learners and a clear vision of how to meet those needs, commitment to high levels of academic quality and integrity, significant teaching experience.

Q: If your best friend was interviewing for a faculty position, what would you tell him or her to look out for or be sure to address?
A: I would recommend that he or she work to construct an honest conversation with the interviewers with the aim of trying to understand whether the job, the students, and the institution's organizational and academic cultures were truly good fits for my friend's passions as an educator and career goals. Interviews are a two-way street, and interviewees need to learn from the interviewers whether the job is a good fit for their needs and interests.

Q: What is the goal of your interview? What are you looking for (or looking to *not* find?).
A: My primary goal is to see whether there is a good match between the institution's needs, the institution's students' learning needs, and the candidate's passions and career goals. I love it when I find a confident candidate committed to academic excellence with a clear vision of his or her career path, including professional growth and improvement.

Q: How much searching do you do on social media about the candidate before talking with them? Does what you see weigh in your decision to hire? Any examples you can share?
A: For a part time job, none. For a full-time job, a Google search to learn more about the candidate and see whether online information is consistent with submitted information and self-presentation during interviews.

Q: After hiring, what are some ways you evaluate instructors besides student evaluations? How seriously are student evaluations taken? Some deans tell us only the very happy or very upset students respond. Is that what you find too?
A: To me, the gold standard is a qualitative evaluation of a professor's classroom behavior combined with one or two one-on-one discussions to share assessments and identify areas of strength and weakness. Many student evaluation instruments are poorly designed, poorly implemented and poorly analyzed -- and when any of those flaws are present they won't produce useful information."

Q: What suggestions do you have for faculty who work at a lot of institutions in presenting themselves to you for hire?
A: Be honest about their capacity to handle multiple responsibilities, and be clear about the reasons why they are seeking additional responsibilities. If they are seeking more income and have time to take on more work, say so clearly and persuasively. If they are seeking to replace a job they don't like with one they think is better, explain that clearly. Never lie about your other commitments, either directly or by omission!

Next, I interviewed a dean of a college who chose to remain anonymous. The institution the dean works for is a non-profit, private institution with online degrees. The dean shares insightful information about what happens during the interviewing process:

Q: What qualities do you look for in new hires?
A: We look for genuine curiosity and active engagement: instructors who have a history of student support, self-efficacy, asking great questions, and actively engaging in the learning process with the student.
We look for lifelong learners: faculty who continually improve, invite feedback, share best practices, and engage in ongoing personal learning and growth in the topic area. We have found a strong correlation between faculty members who exhibit these behaviors and those who continually improve content, rather than simply "recycling" content.

We look for technology savvy-ness: we have an exercise in the interview process where we invite faculty to share a LINK to a 5-10 minute video presentation on a topic related to the course content. This will tell me quickly whether they have the tech-savvy-ness that we are looking for. We look for faculty who want to be a PART of the organization and who actively share ideas and participate in events when they can."

Q: What is the goal of your interview? What are you looking for (or looking to not find?)
A: We look for evidence that potential instructors are highly focused on student support and development. We look for instructors who can share their experiences with a learning-centered approach (where the instructor is learning from the students even as the students learn from him/her) rather than a expertise-centered approach ("I am here to teach you because I am the expert").
We also look for evidence of someone with a genuine spirit of wanting to give back, and not just out to make a buck (though we know that this is also important). The difference reveals itself in levels of active engagement.

Q: How much searching do you do on social media about the candidate before talking with them? Does what you see weigh in your decision to hire? Any examples you can share?
A: We do search potential candidates in public forums. We look at how potential instructors present themselves online. Professionalism is important. We know that our students are looking them up online, so

we see what we can find and consider how the student might perceive the instructor.

Q: After hiring, what are some ways you evaluate instructors besides student evaluations? How seriously are student evaluations taken? Some deans tell us only the very happy or very upset students respond. Is that what you find too?
A: We take student evaluations very seriously, but also with a grain of salt. We are aware that upset students fill out the evaluations and that happy students do too. However, evaluations also reveal patterns and we keep an eye out for these. We actively invite our students to provide constructive feedback, and we share back with students what improvements we make based on their feedback. This helps keep more students engaged with the feedback process when they know that their feedback is taken seriously, and that we do make improvements based on the feedback.

Q: What suggestions do you have for faculty who work at many institutions in presenting themselves to you for hire?
A: While we are aware that faculty members teach for other institutions, we also want to know that they will be actively engaged in ours. We want to know that they will honor our standards and expectations, hold our students to high standards, and they will not just inflate grades to get a better evaluation. We want to know that instructors that we hire have sufficient time, given the demands of their life, to provide our students with adequate attention and to be genuinely engaged. This shows up in the announcements, the

contributions to the course content, the participation in the discussion boards, and the level of feedback provided in assignment reviews. We see it in the course reviews, and our students feel it too.

Common Interview Questions

While you may feel nervous, remember that the people interviewing you more often than not report they are trying to "rule you in" not "kick you out," so come to the interview with this in mind. Some of the more common interview questions: (note this is on my blog at thebabbgroup.com/blog and is frequently updated, so check there for more insight as we learn about it from faculty and deans):

1. Share with me/us your experience with teaching adults. The interviewer wants to find out not just about your experience, but that you know there is a difference between teaching adults and teaching traditional students. I suggest making this clear in your response.

2. Share with me/us your experience teaching online. Just like the question about your experience teaching adults, the interviewer may just be checking to be sure you know that there is a difference between the methodologies and engagement level online and those used in traditional education. He or she is also looking for your experience level ("I have X years' experience teaching in XYZ platforms teaching ABC subjects" is a nice way to start this one). If you have no experience teaching online, just be candid about it. "I have experience doing ABC, but I have yet to teach

online. However, I believe an online instructor needs to…" and this is where your teaching philosophy comes in. What does an online instructor need to do? What open source platforms have you used just to learn them online (Moodle, etc.)? Did you have experience as an online student that transfers into the classroom as a professor?

3. How did you hear about this position? If you have a reference or a referral (please be sure they are in good standing with the university, to the best of your ability, before name-dropping!) then explain that. If you found it online, you can say that too. I would suggest somehow bringing in why you wanted to work here or what you found appealing in the job description as well.

4. Why do you want to work here? Simple enough. You read about them online, right? You learned about them in our forums, right? You have heard great things about how they uphold academic integrity, how they stand behind their faculty, they communicate regularly, your colleagues love working there, etc. If you are applying to a faith-based school, be sure to mention this element.

5. How do you engage students? If you have experience doing this, you know that communication, emails, announcements, thought-provoking questions, getting to know your students, and making them feel important in class matters. If you are a new instructor, you will be engaging your students by doing these very same things and you have learned from online professors you have taken courses from or have

talked with colleagues about, right?

6. Tell me about a scenario you have dealt with recently in which you had to work with a very difficult student. Explain the situation and how you handled it.

Deans tell me they are looking for candidates who know they need to (1) Follow university protocol first and foremost; (2) Communicate; (3) Try to reach the student; (4) Try to understand both sides of the issue when applicable; (5) Let the student's adviser know; (6) Re-engage the students to try to retain the learner. With these items in mind, try to tell the story. Explain what the background is with no names whatsoever (no university names and no student names), how you handled it, and what the outcome was.

Another common issue for deans is: "I see you work for quite a few universities. How are you going to fit this into your workload?"

Try not to take offense to this question. Simple answers here will do wonders. If these scenarios apply, talk about them. (1) The other universities you work for only schedule you X number of times per year and you find yourself very often with far less work than you can handle. (2) You manage your time very effectively. (3) You never take on more work than you can handle and still provide quality instruction. (4) While your CV may seem as though you work for a lot of places, this has given you a lot of experience and scheduling is all over the map, with little consistency.

Deans tell me they want candidates who address this question candidly and honestly, and that they understand an adjuncts workload can be scattered and that it is very likely the candidate does, in fact, have time for the job.

Try to turn each question into a dialogue. Answer the questions, but allow the interviewer to get to know you, too. Let them hear how personable and thorough you are (while not boring them, so don't take five minutes to answer a simple question). Honest answers are important, and remember almost everything is verifiable online. You may get asked questions about your subject matter expertise, but I find this is rare; usually it's for positions in research methodology. The interview is an important time for you to emphasize the points you would like to make.

When the interviewer asks if you have questions the answer is absolutely never "no, I do not" (unless you don't want to work there).

Some questions you may consider asking:

- How long are the terms?
- What platforms do you use?
- Do you require or allow synchronous sessions?
- I want to work for a school that upholds academic integrity. Can you tell me a little bit about your policies in this area?
- Who would I be directly working for?
- What is the course review process if I notice something could use updating?

The goal with your questions is not only to get answers, but to show the person interviewing you that you "know how the process works" and are asking questions that imply you will better the curriculum and be a thorough instructor.

Addressing Your Strengths

There are some basic rules to remember when applying to teach online for a university. (1) As with any job, you get only one chance to make a first impression. (2) Teaching what you want is not as important as teaching what the school needs. (3) Knowing your weaknesses is actually considered a positive. (4) It doesn't matter what you think you can teach—you must have the credentials to back it up. (5) It is better to be the subject matter expert in one important subject than to be just a good jack-of-all-trades (particularly at a traditional university). (6) Academic skills may get you in the door, but interpersonal skills will keep you there.

Rule 1: You Get Only One Chance to Make a First Impression as a Professor

The first course you teach at a university may be your last or your only. It is important that you start out on the right foot. You need to know what you are capable of teaching and let the school know it. You want to shine bright, and what better way to do so than by teaching something at which you excel? That said, if your niche is very specialized, like world history as it relates to nineteenth-century architecture, you might create a problem for yourself. Keep your topics broad while focusing on what you're good at. There is a fine line to walk here. When they see the added value you bring to the program, your value will rise. You are far more likely to get excellent student evaluations when you know your subject matter – and yes, it does come through online. Student evaluations may not be too important for long-time adjuncts that have proven themselves during years at a university, but rookies may be scrutinized thoroughly, depending on the institution.

Rule 2: Teaching What You Want is Not as Important as Teaching What is Needed

If you are picky and inflexible about teaching only a specific course or two, you may be in for a long wait. Different schools have different needs. You need to bend somewhat, within reason. Suppose your strength may be in compensation, but the need is for someone to teach human resource management, which is closely related. If you are willing to jump in and bail the school out, you will then be in the rotation and can request to teach compensation at a future time. The school is not seeking to find a class to suit you; it is seeking faculty to fit the courses being offered. This is very similar to job hunting in the business world.

You would rarely just send a blanket email to a CEO saying, "This is what I can do; find a job for me." Rather, you'd apply to a specific position that is open. When you introduce yourself, you also introduce your skill set. The leadership within the organization immediately begins thinking of the courses that need to be taught by adjuncts, and then attempts to potentially match you. Often they'll send a list of courses that need to be taught and ask what your comfort level is teaching them.

Rule 3: Knowing Your Weaknesses is Actually a Strength

Don't be ashamed of being weak in a subject area. It is far better to know your weaknesses and avoid them than pretend that they are not weaknesses and give an unrecoverable first impression. If the dean begs you to teach out of your comfort zone, he or she should be made aware of the risk you're taking. This happens more often than you might think when schools can't fill high-demand courses in tough subjects. You can expect incredible support as you struggle with teaching the course, and it will be to your benefit to continue.

Sometimes instructors even have to do their own research to address student questions; while this isn't ideal, it's acceptable in some circumstances. Often the dean will owe you a favor, and then you can expect to get your choice of courses and a reputation for being a team player. This only comes from being open about your weaknesses, or at least not biting off more than you can chew because of exaggerating your expertise.

Rule 4: It Doesn't Matter What You Think You Can Teach—You Must Have the Credentials to Back It Up

Some online professors might think they can teach a course in information technology just because they can use a computer and surf the Web, but without 18 graduate hours in IT, you are not academically qualified. You may know all of the bones in the human body, but you need 18 graduate hours in biology or a related science to teach anatomy and physiology. One of the reasons there is a degree of job security in being an adjunct professor with a doctorate is that anyone who thinks they can teach our courses cannot just take our jobs away. They must put in the years and earn a doctorate with 18 graduate hours in our subject areas, and then prove themselves from the ground up. What this means to you, though, is to take all of the courses you can in the areas you want to teach so that you are academically qualified.

Rule 5: It Is Better to Be the King or Queen in One Important Subject Than to Be Just a Good Jack-of-All-Trades

Think about the star quarterbacks, pitchers, goalies, and point guards you have known about. Now think about the utility players who can do it all. Whatever the sport, you can probably name the millionaire stars who play a single position, but the utility players are often on the bench, never getting invited to all-star games since they are not known for any one position, and making run-of-the-mill salaries. It is not that deans wouldn't like to have a utility player who can teach everything, but when it comes to staffing a course they want the best at each course; and if you are not among the best, you may not be high enough on any list. Yes, the deans will tell you that they appreciate having you around, but the consistent teaching opportunities go to the superstars in each course; so try to become one.

When they start calling you the subject matter expert (SME), you will know that you have found your niche there. However, that doesn't mean that if your MBA specialization was in IT you aren't qualified to teach general management courses. You still have an MBA, so try to match your skill set to courses. Now – one caveat to this. Sometimes being able to teach in an entire discipline is hugely important. Your course may not run every term, and you need classes to pay your bills. When you are credentialed to teach at a school, be sure that they do this properly and consider asking to have you included in courses that run more often than some niche courses. One hundred level courses for example will run more often than 400 level courses. Business Administration will run more often than E-Commerce for Nonprofit Companies.

Rule 6: Academic Skills May Get You in the Door, but Interpersonal Skills Will Keep You There

Once you are teaching for a university, do what you can to make yourself shine. Communicate with key personnel at the university, including clerical ones. Let them remember that you are alive, but not to the point of nagging. Don't forward jokes or any potentially controversial emails unless you have established a bond that dictates this to be acceptable behavior. If you are good at researching articles, send some links to useful ones for the dean to share with other faculty. If you have some best practices, share them. If you are published, humbly let your boss know. Participate in the school's faculty discussion forum if that is your thing. Volunteer for committees that you can comfortably handle. Agree to write an occasional article for the school newsletter. Network with your colleagues and focus on learning the ways of the current environment.

How you work with others will often dictate your status at the school. If you are someone who doesn't like to mingle or who gets opinionated and offensive unintentionally, it is better just to keep a low profile than to give anyone reason to dislike you. Of course, you should work to improve such interpersonal problems, but for now, the key is to maintain job security.

These are the key rules to keep in mind. Teaching online is not too difficult; getting hired to teach online is a bit more challenging; making a living at it requires a myriad of skills that take time to develop and master. Reading this book is but the first step.

Six Ways to Mess Up Your Chances of Getting the Job

Rightfully so, I spend a lot of time in this book on interviewing. After getting an interview, it's the next most important step in the process of being hired. But there are ways you can mess up your chances of getting a teaching job. After I posted an article about this on my blog, I had deans email, saying "thank you for being candid" and "thanks for posting this, so true!" and "you're spot on. Thanks for telling people what not to do. Most of these will cause me to flush the CV down the toilet." (I am not joking by the way). You can also see comments directly on the blog page.

Over the past months, as clients let me know what they do (and do not do) to get hired to teach, I have been querying deans and department chairs to find out what faculty are doing in job interviews (or after) that was a deal breaker for them. Also keep in mind two important things:

Not every job posted will be filled by an outside person. Sometimes schools post positions for a required number of days, already having a strong "feeling" who they will hire from inside the school. I know this is less than ideal for those of us who are outside candidates, but it happens and you should be aware of it. This is one of many reasons it's important to have job applications going all the time! We have services to help you on our website!

Try not to take the Dear John letters personally. This has been a topic of conversation on our Facebook forum. If a Dear John letter says that you are not qualified but you know you are, chances are the HR department used a form letter to respond to you. Which begs the question: "Should I email HR and tell them that I am qualified?" You can, but you run the risk of running into the #1 complaint I hear below. I personally find that it's better to just apply to something else again later and leave those HR folks alone.

Please note that this is not everything – and it also does not apply to every job and every hiring manager. These were the most common comments I have heard, the version without any sugar coating.

1. Too much follow up. We have been told since high school career counseling to follow up after a job interview. While that is generally a good rule of thumb, too much of a good thing is not always so good. A nice "Thank you for the interview, I am excited at the possibility of

joining your team" may do. One of the top responses from deans and human resource managers when asked why a candidate did not get a job (even if they interviewed well), was excessive follow up. What defined excessive? That varied, but generally more than one email in a week after the interview was considered excessive. The wheels in academia (sometimes) turn slowly. To keep from hitting the send button too fast, you could store your follow up in drafts to be sent at a later date. There is a fine line between following up and being annoying.

2. A lot of back and forth conversation immediately following the interview. You hit it off with the dean on the phone; you thank him or her for their time; they reply in kind. You then reply (again) asking if they'd like copies of your work, what you can do to expedite the process, etc. The hiring manager replies something like "we will let you know" or "we are not quite to that point yet." You reply with "okay let me know when you are, in the meantime can I send you articles I am working on?" Err – no.

3. Trying to become social media buddies right away. Yes, it happens. LinkedIn is a great tool for connecting and sharing with colleagues. Friending the hiring administrator on Facebook right after the interview is a different story. When you have been colleagues for five years, met in person a few times, and shared pictures of your children that might be another story. For now, keep it professional.

4. Demanding too much or too little money. This is a tough one. You do not want to undersell yourself, but you also do not want to ask for so much money that you are disqualified. A simple "I am open to various degrees of pay based on the work requirements and your pay scales," and then asking what their pay scales are, is appropriate (if you are to that point in the conversation). If HR does not bring this up, I recommend saving it for the dean to get past the HR department. Some institutions use HR to screen for salary and employment history before moving a candidate on.

5. Not doing your homework. A dean told me that she was interviewing a candidate for a faith-based institution and asked how the candidate integrates her personal faith into the classroom. The candidate responded with something like "Faith? Why would I do that?" Check out institutions online - at least their mission, vision, and philosophy - before the interview.

6. Not supplying information right away when asked by email. You have a great interview; HR gets back to you and asks for unofficial transcripts by email and for official transcripts to be mailed. Yes, this is a good sign. Then, you wait a week to send unofficial documents, and then have the transcript processor send official transcripts by email. First, you waited too long. Second, the HR person asked for them by mail, not by email. Don't ask questions, just send items the way the representative asks for them. Too much back

and forth falls into #2 and also makes the HR person's job much harder. The goal is to make it easy and pleasant for them to hire you.

What to Do with Limited Experience

Many of you are reading this book because you want to teach, but you don't have much experience. Surprisingly, lots of different activities can count for teaching experience by universities' standards. The key is that you can't be too picky with regard to which schools you teach for in the beginning. If you have limited experience, play up any of these activities (and anything else you can think of):

- *Experience on the job training peer*s. Write this in your CV with regard to the actual responsibility you had for their learning. If you've ever conducted a computer-based training course or taught a group of people how to do something on a computer or in any particular area, note this as experience training people.
- *Experience as a presenter of new ideas or rollouts of new company plans.* You can easily discuss the way you trained everyone on the new process, solicited feedback, shared ideas, and then communicated to others.
- *Experience making presentations to groups.* This may include professional organizations, your own business, previous courses you were involved in, or seminars.
- *Experience guest lecturing at universities.* If you don't have any, email the faculty at universities

who teach in your area of expertise and volunteer yourself. Most will jump at the opportunity and within weeks, you will have additional experience for your CV specifically in academia. Even offer to host someone's class for a field trip if your place of business would suit the course.

- *Experience hosting brown bag lunches or conducting speaking engagements at the office, if you are a professional.*
- *Create a class at Babb Academy* or one of the other tools out there, like Fedora or Udemy. You will get course development and teaching experience to list on your CV. If you would like to find out about what we offer subject matter experts, email academy@thebabbgroup.com.

The key here is that if you don't have experience teaching at a school, you will have to be creative, but under no circumstances should you blow your experience out of proportion or be dishonest. All of us started somewhere and deans respect that. Some doctoral programs (like the EdD at City University of Seattle) offer teaching assistant spots to their top students, which is almost unheard of in the industry. This is another reason to network, so you know what your options are.

Proving Responsiveness

It may feel like a fishing expedition to apply to teach online at any one school, but once in a while you get a bite – a real, human-generated, they-are-interested-in-you, email. Sometimes you will get an auto-generated response that puts you in a holding pattern, and sometimes you'll get one that instructs you to take further action. It is critical that you know what cards you have been dealt so you know how to play the hand. There are four basic kinds of emails you can expect to see from your efforts.

Response 1: Auto-Generated Rejection

If you submitted an application on the university's website, you can always expect some type of auto-generated response. A common one reads like this: "Thank you for your interest in teaching for Whatsamatta U. Unfortunately, I don't have any openings at this point, but you will definitely be considered for courses in the spring semester." Or something like this: "Dear Sir/Madam, Thank you for your application for the position of Adjunct Professor at Whatsamatta U. We did receive a large number of applications for this position, resulting in a very stringent selection procedure. Regretfully, you have not been selected to participate in the training at this time." It may also say that your resume is in a database and that you'll be contacted when there is a match, although the actual likelihood of this happening has been slim in our experience. If you get either of these responses, don't keep your hopes up. Yes, there is a chance that you can still get hired by getting in touch with the right person, but your file has already been put in the reject pile or the official HR database, and chances are that no one will be calling you. If you have a friend on the inside that can put you in touch with the right person, take a shot; otherwise, you are probably better off moving on.

It is not uncommon for an experienced, well-educated, highly qualified candidate to be rejected, while an inexperienced recent graduate gets hired. Sometimes these schools pay poorly and they know they are wasting their time to recruit highly qualified professors who are used to being paid well. Their goal is to give experience to new faculty in return for low salaries. This isn't bad for you if you have no experience; it is a way to add to your CV. Unless you are willing to work for low pay in exchange for experience, you wouldn't want to teach at these schools anyway, so don't be upset to get a rejection letter.

Another common occurrence is to be rejected because you are teaching for a major competitor, although this is not directly disclosed to you. It is up to you what goes on your CV, but with the networking that goes on in the online teaching world (if you teach more than an occasional course for a school) your name may get around. Be careful not to try to hide too much. After all, you must show that you are capable of teaching online, and that is best shown by teaching for other online schools.

Response 2: Auto-Generated Acknowledgment

Another common auto-generated response you might get after applying at the university's website might read like this: "Thank you for your interest in our opening! Our recruiters have received your resume and will be reviewing it shortly. If your skills and qualifications match our opening, we will be sure to contact you. We appreciate your interest in our organization."

If you see such a message, do not feel like you

are as good as hired, even if you are an accomplished writer, an experienced faculty member, and have a PhD. Either a computer or a clerical person will determine if you are qualified for further review, and that often is tied to whether you put specific buzzwords in your application. These are not rocket scientists with a thesaurus, but instead are typically low-paid clerks who are told to pass along potential candidates to teach a specific subject, like computer science.

If your application mentions PC, IT, and information systems, but never uses the word *computer*, you might just get overlooked. Keyword searching matters, and is one of the reasons that I recommend writing out the full course description into your CVs. Doing so improves keyword searching – both automated and human. With the hundreds or thousands of applications human resources recruiters must review, they are just looking for quick matches, not necessarily the best fits. The dean will do a more thorough review.

The lesson here is to try to use a lot of different terms to maximize your chances of success, but not to look as though you're a jack-of-all trades and a master-of-none. As far as the email goes, do not respond to it since your response wouldn't go to anyone specific.

At this stage, you should follow the advice provided in this book and seek out the deans, course directors, or faculty chairs and send personal emails indicating that you have already applied online. Mentioning this is important since they will often direct you to do this anyhow, and it shows that you are proactive. Also tell them of your specific teaching interests, and attach your CV and scanned transcripts so they don't have to go through the database to get them.

Response 3: Email from Recruiter

If you are lucky enough to have your email score a hit in the online application process, you can expect an email from a recruiter. It may go something like:

+++

Hi Jim!

Thank you for your interest in teaching opportunities with Whatsamatta U. We are interested in developing long-term relationships with superior instructors who possess high professional standards, excellent communication skills, enthusiasm, and a commitment to teaching and learning. We look for individuals who hold a minimum of a master's degree (in some areas a PhD is preferred), several years of teaching experience in higher education, as well as significant professional experience in the field in which they teach. We have a strong commitment to delivering high-quality courses. To that end, courses are developed centrally and delivered by our instructors. In addition to the minimum qualifications listed above, new online instructors are expected to:

- Provide official transcripts for each degree earned.
- Participate in a three-day asynchronous online

assessment of their facilitation skills, which can take up to six months to schedule.
- Work proactively and cooperatively with new faculty trainers during the period of course preparation and course delivery.
- Ensure compliance for online instruction.
- Participate in the New Online Faculty Training Program.

Upon successful completion of training, new online instructors are expected to:

- Spend four to five days per week online (including one day on the weekend) for a minimum of 30 minutes each day managing their course delivery. This is in addition to the grading of homework and other course deliverables.
- Work with new faculty trainers who monitor and evaluate their week-to-week activity and effectiveness in managing the delivery of their course.
- Have simultaneous access to both Internet and phone.

If, after reviewing the expectations above and making a realistic assessment of the time you have available, you are still interested in applying for an online teaching assignment, follow these steps:

1. Visit www.whattsamatta.edu and view our catalog and course descriptions.
2. Choose up to a maximum of three courses that you are interested in and feel qualified to teach.
3. Complete the attached Faculty Qualification Form

for each course you have chosen.
4. Submit the form(s) and a copy of your resume and any other information you think appropriate for us to review to recruiter@myemailaddress.com.

Again, thank you for your interest and we look forward to hearing from you!

+++

If you should get such a reply, then you are officially being eyed. At this point, you should not waste a moment. Go to the catalog and find courses you can teach. It is best if you pick courses that are sure things for you (i.e., courses that you have a lot of graduate credits in, courses that relate heavily to your work experience, and courses that match your prior teaching experience – particularly if the school has disclosed the types of instructors it is looking for). Don't worry about teaching other subjects; once you are hired, you can suggest your other strengths, but you must get in the door first, and so you must impress the recruiter as much as possible and as quickly as possible. If you are unable to do the task immediately for some reason, at least reply and thank the recruiter, ensuring him or her that you will complete the required tasks in the next week. Note: It is going to take a couple of weeks to get your transcripts, anyway, but you should at least impress the recruiter with your responsiveness; it will go a long way.

Response 4: Expression of Interest from Key

Personnel

If you made direct contact with key personnel and sparked some interest, they will likely tell HR that they want your file, and the wheels will start turning. This is the way it works best, and it is by far the most direct and expedient manner by which you can be hired. The email you will get is not standard by any means, but essentially expresses interest. For example, one email that Dr. Mirabella received and published in the first version of the book began:

+++

Dear Dr. Mirabella,

I received your very impressive resume, and I was interested in seeing if we might be a fit for a position we're seeking to fill this year. I would appreciate it if you would send me [miscellaneous documents listed here]. As soon as I hear back from you, I look forward to seeing about either a full-time or adjunct distance learning position. Finally, I was interested to see your background with the Air Force Academy. As a 26-year veteran of the U.S. Army, I spent eight of my last nine years in uniform at West Point, and I recall fondly some visits I made to Colorado Springs. Have a wonderful week, and thanks for getting back with me.

+++

You can see the personal connection made here. Writing to specific individuals should capture their attention in some unique way. It can carry a lot of weight if done correctly. This letter basically means that the teaching position is yours to lose, but don't become so overconfident that you cause yourself harm. You have made a strong first impression, but the next step is critical because they still have not seen your responsiveness. Get back to them immediately. Dr. Mirabella replied within two hours and received a further reply, which began "Thanks for your prompt reply!" This shows a genuine interest that cannot be assessed from your transcripts or resume. Consider that you have just received your first exam and earned an A+, but there are more exams to come, so don't let up. Just take solace in knowing that, even if the hiring process is objective, it doesn't hurt to give yourself a subjective edge in the eyes of the decision maker. Be sure to thoughtfully respond to each message, and do so promptly.

What you should take from this is the need to act quickly. If you have a busy week or you're about to take a cruise, then postpone submitting applications or sending emails until you can properly deal with responses to them or use your smartphone and reply right away. You may even want to spread out the applications a few days apart so as not to get hit with numerous requests at once. Candidates who use our job services often do this by default, forwarding the job leads we offer to the job application service queue. It is up to you, but be prepared to respond immediately or you may never be able to recover this lost opportunity to add to your online teaching repertoire.

Odd Requests and How to Handle Them

When you do receive a reply from a school, often the school will want more from you than you have already provided. You can expect to see requests for transcripts, letters of reference, faculty qualification forms, copies of student evaluations and the university's official online application (if you haven't already completed it). You may also receive some less common requests, such as a (very long) form with tough questions or a paper job application you must use "ink to sign and mail." The most annoying by far are the faculty new hire packets you'll receive in email with all of the information asked for all over again. Prepare to spend at least an hour filling them out, and even possibly having them notarized.

A big note here about I9s and notaries. In the early days of online education, we did not need to fill out the I9 form, an employment eligibility verification form. Essentially, it asks a notary to verify that you provided authentic documents from a list of acceptable ones, which may include your social security card, passport, driver's license, or other forms of identification. Now, I know of absolutely zero schools that do not require it, including for contract positions. However – many states have created rules whereby notaries cannot notarize these forms because they are not "trained in determining what documents are real or fake." You can see the gotcha problem here.

Four possible solutions: (1) Go to a neighborhood where the notary wants the money more than he/she cares about possibly getting into trouble for notarizing. Yes, they are everywhere. Check cashing stores, some UPS stores, you name it. (2) Get to know a notary, mobile or on-site, who will do you the favor. (3) Ask HR to use FaceTime or Skype and show them the documents "in person" so they can verify them. This works! A creative HR department in South Carolina came up with this idea and I have used it at other schools since. (4) Get a bunch of forms notarized when you are traveling. Many states aren't so strict about rules for notaries. Do not sign and date the form (or cross the date out and write a new one if the notary insists) and the notary stamp is still usually good. Sign and mail it in when you need, and do a dozen or so at once.

Transcripts are a guaranteed part of every application process. Save yourself some money and do not send official transcripts until the school requests them from you. You should have a scanned version of your transcripts available on your computer so you can upload them into job application systems or email them to HR or deans, to give the school an early look at your qualifications. To hasten the process of getting transcripts, you should visit the website for every college you graduated from and download their transcript request forms or note the link to do it online.

This way you can just open the files on your computer, fill them in, print them, and send them to the colleges with the correct dollar amounts. Make sure you find out exactly where to have the transcripts sent, and they must be sent directly to your target school to be counted as official, not to you and then on to the university. If your alma mater doesn't offer forms or online systems, then have your form letter typed up based on the registrar's requirements, fill in the blanks for the school it needs to be sent to, and enclose your check. Usually the target school will receive them in 10 to 14 days, which is expected.

When it comes to your references, you can expect a request either for a list of your references or for actual letters of recommendation. You should already have prepared a list and letters in PDF format, and be sure to let these people know when you use them as references so they are not surprised and they commit to supporting you. If you're in a particular profession, let your references know you're trying to get a teaching job so they don't talk about how great you are in the boardroom, but instead how well you trained the teams and what a great teacher you'd make. If you are asked for a letter of reference, that can be quite a demand for anyone; one option is to write a letter for each person to sign, allowing them to edit to suit their tastes, or ask the same individuals so they may use the same letter but address it to a new school.

Make sure the wording on each letter is quite different and speaks from the perspective of that person's knowledge of you. Use words like "I have known Jake since 2001" instead of "for 13 years" so that the letter does not become outdated. If they email you their letter, you can save it for future use and just change the date and name of the school each time you use it, if the person recommending you allows; if the school expects the letter to be mailed (which is rare these days), then you must ask your friends to print, sign, and mail the letters. Once you get a core set of references with letters written, this part of the process becomes smooth, albeit time-consuming.

If you are asked to complete a faculty qualification form, you are merely going to peruse the school's catalog and find courses you are qualified to teach. Then you must extract related work experience from your resume, add graduate course work from your transcripts, and list any related courses you have taught or developed. It doesn't hurt to list any articles you've had published or any professional organizations of which you are a member (e.g., Academy of Management, Decision Sciences Institute, American Society for Quality, American Statistical Association, etc.).

Typically, you must complete a separate form for each course, but once you fill out the first one, you can merely save it and edit it for the next course. Choose the courses that will most likely get you hired quickly; this means picking core courses that are offered every term versus an elective that is rarely offered. It also means picking courses for which you have the most graduate credits and teaching experience, which truly count more than work experience when the final decisions are made. You may say something to the dean like "there are a lot of courses I am academically qualified to teach, is there a specific area with greater need that would be useful to you if I list?"

One of the more annoying requests is to fill out the school's online application. You are so tempted to just put "see CV" in the application, but that won't work. This is similar in nature to the faculty new hire packet you'll receive; you will likely receive both – and yes, it is redundant information! They want to enter your data into their database and they don't have the manpower to extract this data from your CV unless it is done automatically. The good news is that you don't have to worry about getting past the clerical staff for approval; you are just filling this out as a requirement. You still need to invest the hour to do it correctly and to ensure that you included all educational information accurately, as that is what the accrediting body will look at if you ever are at risk of being terminated. Be sure to make a copy of any paper forms and a printout of any online forms you complete. You may find similarities across different schools and you wouldn't want to have to rethink your answers. Plus, in the unlikely event the mail gets lost or your online form doesn't load properly, you can redo it in just a few minutes.

In 2006, we noted "one of the less common requests is for a statement of your teaching philosophy. This is merely a paragraph or two of your personal philosophy with regard to adult learners, online teaching, and education in general." Not so in 2015! The teaching philosophy statement is vital. It should be included in your CV and it should also be a standalone document that can be sent when requested.

A teaching philosophy statement plays a bigger role than ever in getting an online teaching job. A teaching philosophy statement, whether standalone or integrated into your CV, is essentially a statement indicating your theory of education, what model you follow, why education is important to you, and then how this is put into practice in your course room.

There are two types of teaching philosophy statements. The first is the longer philosophy statement that is often a full page. I recommend starting the first paragraph with an introduction to your philosophy and beliefs about education. You can integrate theory about instruction into this initial paragraph if you like. In the second paragraph, you can elaborate more on your teaching style, how education has influenced you and why you find it valuable to others. A good thing to ask yourself is, "if someone came to me asking if they should pursue an education, how would I answer and why?"

Remember, you should be writing this in first person and do not feel as though you have to leave emotion out of it. Showing passion for education is good, in my opinion, and I have seen it positively correlated with getting teaching jobs.

Next, if you are comfortable, I suggest explaining a bit about why and how education has played a role in your own life. Personal stories and examples can help convey the meaning and value of education to you. You should also elaborate about what you find most important to students. Is it engagement? Is it retention? Is it leading by example? Feel free to explain as many of these elements with which you feel comfortable. Finally, you should wrap it up with a paragraph identifying how a dean, should he or she visit your online classroom, would see evidence of your philosophy carried out into the class. Essentially the first element is theory, the second is practice, and the third is application.

This is, of course, the longer version of the philosophy, which is often uploaded as a separate document into human resources job application systems. However, I highly recommend also integrating the teaching philosophy statement into your CV, as the very first thing after your contact information. Not only does this show that you "get" education and the requirements today, but it will help you convey a message to deans or human resources professionals as soon as they review your CV. It will also bump up the keywords for searching, which is important, particularly so when there is a job pool where thousands of candidates may apply and you want to stand out among them.

The version on your CV will be a shorter, more concise version of the longer teaching philosophy statement. When I write teaching statements during the CV-writing process for clients (which can also be used as the entire comprehensive philosophy statement - they do not need to be different), I write two paragraphs.

The first paragraph is theory and practice (why the client wants to teach, his or her methodology or theory of education, and if the client is comfortable with this – a little bit of personal information that explains the value the client places on education. I am sure to use accurate keywords that describe my client, such as "retention focused" or "highly engaged with learners" or "strong communicator in the classroom."

The second paragraph is all about evidence! How would the boss/dean/manager who is logged into my client's course see evidence of the theoretical components taking place in class? Would the dean see my client highly engaged in discussions? Sharing experience? Providing thorough feedback and suggesting ways to improve career skills through application of content knowledge?

The teaching philosophy statement should convey your passion and dedication to the profession, and thoughtfully identify ways in which others will see evidence of your beliefs in the classroom. Do you believe everyone is entitled to an education? Do you believe students should be have the opportunity to resubmit work until they earn an A? Whom do you see as the customer? What is your teaching style? These are some of the questions you should ask yourself in this unscripted document. Be sure that it reflects you, your personality and teaching style, and what you truly believe. You need to be genuine and make sure there is a good fit here.

In the unusual case that you receive an interview form to complete, treat it like an exam that is being graded. Do it quickly and do it well. Be prepared to speak from it during your phone interview, as you will likely be asked questions about your responses. This topic was addressed earlier in this chapter, but it is definitely something to be aware of and prepared for, because although it is uncommon, it is usually an excellent sign that you will get a phone interview if your answers are acceptable to the school.

Whatever request you get, the most important rules of thumb are that you respond quickly and accurately, write professionally, and be true to yourself and your style. It wouldn't be surprising to see more schools devise uncommon requests to separate truly interested applicants from the rest, and we expect to see this as schools juggle more and more online teachers with heavily increasing demands from students.

Chapter 8 - Sealing the Deal. Training. Your First Class

"The mediocre teacher tells.
The good teacher explains.
The superior teacher demonstrates.
The great teacher inspires."
— William Arthur Ward
(Author, Editor, Pastor, and Teacher)

In the previous chapter, I focused on what to do when you obtain an interview for a school that you want to teach for, how to integrate your teaching philosophy, and even how you can mess up an interview. In this chapter, I will focus on what to do when you are offered a position, subject usually to training. What happens next? What should you expect?

What Next?

First, congratulations on a big step in the process. Not many people make it this far, and to be considered for a position is an honor. Usually at this point, you're invited to join the faculty through a formal offer, usually by email or phone (but almost always followed up in writing). If you want to work for the school, then you accept. At this point official transcripts will most likely be requested if they haven't been already, and you will be sent a human resources packet with all kinds of goodies to sign and the aforementioned I9 to have notarized.

Fill out the paperwork and return it as soon as possible. Send out any remaining transcript request items and begin to prepare for training. If this is your first (or even your tenth) training course, expect to spend an hour or two per day on it. If you're an old pro, you will probably need less time and hopefully you have kept answers to common questions to avoid reinventing the wheel. Training courses will have requirements for participation, as you'll see in the training section of the chapter, so you need to work the next steps into your schedule.

You'll most likely be introduced by email to several key players at the university, but don't expect to be introduced to anyone higher up than the dean. This is normal. Unfortunately, you will be offered a particular set amount per class or per student and you won't have any negotiation room, particularly if this is one of your first schools.

Salary or Contract Negotiation

The school will tell you what it pays adjuncts or what the salary is for the position, and you have to decide if you want to accept. For full-time or part-time faculty positions you may be able to counter, to some degree. In most adjunct positions this is not an option. Some factors that should weigh into your decision include how many courses you expect to teach, what potential the school has for you, its reputation among faculty, and of course how you feel about the university. If the pay is insanely low, as it is at some schools, don't be reluctant to say no and politely explain why. If you need experience, though, take the job regardless of pay rate. You can change jobs later.

If you decline and explain about the low pay, sometimes there will be a counter-offer, but this is rare and usually happens only if the school really needs you and has no one waiting in the queue with a class pending. This is a good situation for the adjunct, but you also don't want to start off on a bad foot with your new boss. It might be best if you're new to online teaching to take what you are given and begin building your online reputation and adding some experience to the CV.

This is for you to decide based on your goals, where you are in your career, and how badly you want to work for the school. In the past two years, some schools have gotten particularly bad reputations, and in some ways are considered negative to be associated with. If you are offered a position, I recommend reading what others have said about the school in the forums before answering. It should only take you a few minutes to search and you will have a better idea of what others say. Also, know what the expectations are. Be aware that a really high offer may not be so high when you consider the extra, unpaid work you'll have to do.

After you decide whether to accept or reject the offer, consider this a done deal. Unless the entire university raises pay, often due to low retention rates and faculty surveys complaining about pay, your salary or contract amount will remain constant. Since we are either part-time employees or contractors, in all but the rarest of cases we are not given cost-of-living adjustments or random raises. If you need more money next year, you need to teach another class or two at the schools you work for or add more schools.

Some areas of your contract may be negotiable. Read through them but beware – deans and chairs expect you will not complain or even ask about any portion of the contract. Ask what you really need to know and truly need clarification on, and then make a decision either way quickly. A lot of emails flying back and forth make you appear ungrateful and will just upset people (see the prior chapter on ways to lose a job!). Asking intelligent questions (and collecting them all for one, short, bullet-point email) is appropriate and most administrators at schools will be thankful you asked up front rather than accepting and being upset later.

What to Expect

Now what should you expect? Prepare to wait. You will not usually be able to teach a course without training except in rare circumstances in which a course is beginning right away and there is a desperate need for you. In that case, you may ask to waive training altogether, depending on your experience with the platform the school uses.

The Training Program

After waiting some time, usually a coordinator will email you with a login ID, password, and link to your training course, along with the start and end dates. Log in as early as the course will allow so you can get a jump-start on training, particularly in noting the workload, which varies greatly by program and university, and introducing yourself to the course facilitator and peers. You also want to be certain that you can access the course before the start date rather than bringing up technical issues when it is too late. Don't expect the facilitator to arrive in the classroom until training actually starts, though, and we caution you against sending emails out about an absent trainer if the course hasn't officially started yet. Many trainers are also teachers (sometimes adjuncts like yourself), and some have multiple training classes at one time. They expect you to be self-directed, so be that way.

Types of Training

There are several types of training that you will most likely be subject to, as well as multiple types of checks and balances to be sure you are learning what the university intended. It's critical to note that every move you make, every email you write, and every post you make is being graded and judged, with reports usually given to the chair and/or dean. Treat this as you would any important training course for a job; you haven't gotten it yet! You must usually pass training before actually being given a class to teach.

There are a few key points that most universities have in common with regard to goals for training. First, they want you to be intimately familiar with their processes. This sounds simple enough until you start teaching for several schools! It's easy to confuse which date attendance must be turned in with another school's policy, or the grading scales, for instance, or which days you must maintain office hours if required. This is where your organization and technology will come in; you must be prepared to organize yourself and the requirements placed on you. So, intimate familiarity with their process is important. You'll cover ground like "what to do with a tardy student" and "how much flexibility you have granting assignment submissions after their due date." You will go through numerous policies, and some schools will also require that you are familiar with accreditation body rules or some higher authority rules. You will likely be tested and graded on this. Sometimes you'll need the material later on after you've begun teaching, so save the documents you get from training.

Another goal of training is for you to learn the school's platform. Even if two schools use Blackboard, they may have different features installed or be running entirely different versions. The training for the platform, while having some similarities, will be quite different. Don't simply tell your boss, "I already know Blackboard" and try to get out of training. They are assessing more than your Blackboard skills. They are also assessing your adherence to their way of doing things. If you like having students post assignments in the Assignments section, but a school likes to use the Digital Drop Box, learn to like it; the students will be doing it that way and you shouldn't try to make them adapt to your style.

Finally, most universities use training to try to gauge your responsiveness and your writing capabilities. Reports are frequently sent, and documentation is made in your HR file (yes. you will have one even though you aren't an employee). They will judge your attentiveness, your listening skills (there actually is such a thing online), how you use humor in the classroom, the appropriateness of your responses, and so forth. Treat this as you would any class and take it seriously.

Remember that someone is always watching you; even if they aren't watching at the time you are on. Whatever you post online is there for eternity, so they can watch whenever they like. A favorite metaphor is the dreaded driver's license photo—you can hold that smile for only so long, and then when you begin to sneeze, the photo is taken and you are stuck with it for a few years. Well, until you get the notice that you passed your training, keep holding that smile and behave!

Expect two training courses: a practice classroom and a training or sandbox classroom. The training classroom will have discussions you must participate in (with participation requirements, the most time-consuming part of training); lectures you must read (with rules, processes, and best practices); Q&A; as well as homework, quizzes, and usually a group assignment (by far the most frustrating, just as it is for most of our students!). I went through a training program in 2014 that had hours of collaborative wiki sessions with colleagues. Some schools will let you self-direct your pace and hammer out the entire program in two days if you can. Others will force you through a rigorous and very time-consuming directed process in which you follow a typical class pattern. Either is okay, but obviously one is less demanding because you can get it done all at once.

In addition to facilitator training forum or classes, you will have a practice or sandbox class in almost every school. The practice classroom is one where you will complete assignments, like "add a drop box item to unit 4" or "add an announcement." This is done with instructor-level privileges only, which you do not have in your training classroom. In the training class, you are a student, seeing what the students see and experiencing what they experience. In your practice classroom, you will have facilitator-level access, which means you can add, delete, and change items in the course. Your assignments will usually require you to perform various tasks, and the syllabus should tell you what portions of the practice class you are graded on.

Try to go overboard in your postings (but keep them substantive in nature – just like we tell our students: quality not quantity); respond to everyone's introductions with a warm, personalized welcome, and respond to every posting that is not directed at another student. While there is a qualitative side to this process in how you do the job, there is an easier-to-assess quantitative side in which your postings are counted and your time in the course room is tracked. Post early, post often, and be professional.

Communicating with Your Trainer

Communicate frequently with your trainer. I suggest not bugging your trainer about grades missing unless you are nearing the end of your training and have no feedback. Expect to be trained, then retrained, and then retrained again every time the system or a major process changes. It's a part of the job we don't necessarily like and is usually unpaid, but it's part of the deal. Don't complain about it and just do what you need to do.

Sometimes universities (typically the not-so-good ones) will keep you on their list of faculty to make their faculty seem stronger (more PhDs for instance). You won't hear from them for a while, except when it is time to update your online profile for accreditation purposes. In 2014, I had to send an email to the president of a college in California to ask them to take me off of their website. I hadn't taught for them in months and didn't intend to, and still, it required a follow-up with specific links and they listed me in their graduation program, although I hadn't taught there in some time! This is a red flag – either someone in marketing isn't paying attention or, worst case scenario, they did it intentionally because having your name and credentials on their website helped them. This is especially true if they are going through an accreditation process, which this particular school was.

You do not want your name listed on schools where you won't be working! Other deans likely will search for you online – in fact, it was a Provost of another university who told me about the school using my name. It is okay to leave it up there if you think you may get a class and it isn't impacting other possible opportunities; however, if you haven't for some time, it's entirely appropriate either to have them give you a class or officially resign, and force them to take your name off of their faculty list. Don't let them benefit from your credentials while you earn nothing.

Other universities that you apply to can easily

find you at these places via a search engine. You may keep a school off your CV, but you cannot hide yourself from the Web as easily. (An important note: make sure LinkedIn is also updated to match your CV – and more on that in the chapter on social media).

Associating yourself with an unscrupulous institution can come back to haunt you if you're not careful. Keep on top of your past and present schools as you would your credit report, because essentially your online teaching history is relatively public. You might even do a Google search on your name to see what others can see; it's actually interesting to see how many hits you have.

Length of Training Process

Training can be anywhere from a self-directed two-hour PowerPoint presentation and an email acknowledgement of understanding to a six-week training class. Some even have additional internships where you must work under an experienced faculty member and respond to his or her concerns about your course. These are the two extremes, with most falling in between, requiring four to six weeks of your time in a directed environment. Sometimes you can work ahead, but often trainers ask that you don't.

If you are asked to participate in an internship, as some colleges will have you do, note that although it is frustrating to an experienced faculty member, they are doing it because of either quality concerns, accreditation issues, wanting to guide instructors, or all three. Just try to work through it, listen to the trainer, and respond to his or her concerns the same day you receive emails. Often they will ask how you would "fix this problem" in a real course and explain to you the gap between policy and what you have done in the internship. It is frustrating to have someone look over your shoulder, but remember that most schools have someone check in to all classes once in a while anyway to make sure that faculty are doing their jobs. It's something you'll just need to get used to and it is better to learn the ropes in the "trial class" than it is in the classes you will be evaluated on each year.

If there is any chance you may not be able to complete the training per the school's requirements because of a planned trip or because of poor Internet connectivity where you are during that time, let the school know up front – or suck it up and do it anyway. There is no shame in asking for a later training date (though deans have told me they view it unfavorably – if you can't train, will you have the same issue when you are in class?); you have already been selected and likely won't be tossed aside because you need to delay the training.

First impressions are everything, so be honest rather than perform poorly and then make excuses afterward. If they really need you desperately, they'll tell you to do the training as scheduled, but will pay less attention to your number of postings and treat it more as a formality. If you were to fail the training course, you would essentially be banned from teaching there, so either give it your all or say up front why you cannot do so.

Proving Yourself to the Trainers and Your Chairperson

After you have proven yourself to the trainer,

who usually sends a report to the chairperson, it's appropriate to ask when you might expect a course to teach. Don't expect the trainer to know the answer unless the trainer is also the scheduler, which does happen on occasion.

If you don't have a class within a month, set an appointment in your calendar reminding yourself to email your boss, asking again about potential scheduling and reminding him or her that you completed training. Include your grade if you got one for the course. If you want to feel less intrusive, ask if there is anything else you need to do to move forward to teaching, while expressing your continued interest in teaching for the institution.

Prepping for Your First Class

After completing training, you'll need to prepare for your first class. If this is your very first time teaching, it might be a little intimidating. Here are some things almost every university will want you to do. Be sure to pay close attention to the checklists given during training or in the offer to teach (or even in the follow up email after accepting a class).

Most will include:

- Post 'welcome note' in the announcements.
- Post bio in the instructor portion of the class.
- Post bio and welcome note in the area students must post theirs.
- Set up the entire grade book such that the point total equals 100%, if not already done.
- Set up discussion boards for at least the first

week.
- Order the textbook and any required software if you don't have them already.

Some not-so-common requests:

- Configure assignment submission settings.
- Update syllabus or post syllabus.
- Send individual emails to every student welcoming them (which is a nice touch anyway even if it isn't required).
- Check all Web links to make sure the websites are still there.

It's important that until you have a school's checklist memorized, you go through it every time you receive it. Most will send it at the beginning of each term as a reminder and schools often change the list. Some schools even use auditors that log in to make sure you've done everything. Don't let your class be flagged, especially before you have a good reputation. Just follow the rules and eventually you will build rapport. Remember, most of the time classes are replicated so a lot of the data, like lectures and course assignments, remain the same time and time again. Customization to make your class unique to you is often all that is required to set up a new class.

If this is the first time you have taught a particular class, become very familiar with it so you can answer student questions efficiently. You will need to learn the school's processes and way of doing things and also respond to many requests when the responses are not familiar territory. You'll be learning the system, culture, students, grading policy, and how involved Big Brother is in the process. If permitted, ask if you can peek at another section of the course you will be teaching. You can often contact that instructor and even obtain some excellent ideas for discussion questions and course setup. The other instructor may share some exams and solutions with you, too.

One thing to remember is that you are human and prone to error. There will be mistakes in the course room that you overlooked, such as the wrong due date for an assignment, poorly worded instructions, the wrong point value for an exam. If you make a mistake, own up to it and fix it. You can even let the students know that, while you are not new to teaching, this is your first semester with Whatsamatta U. so you are just getting used to the platform, and for them to let you know if they find any errors.

Even if you're not new, there are bound to be mistakes made; perhaps you forgot to record an assignment or give a student credit for something. This is no big deal; just be honest and fix it. If the course has some areas for improvement with the design, keep an electronic notebook of the problems so you can fix them the next time you teach the course; the objective is to make it better. After about the third or fourth time, you will find it almost effortless, since you will have a bank of standard responses to common questions, few errors, and solutions files already set up.

Finally, and this is very important, come out of the starting gate as very strict but fair. Students may complain about you being tough or demanding, but in the end, they fall in line with your requirements and ultimately do well. If you try to be popular, you will find yourself working much harder to please everyone, and you will be dealing with a lot of strange excuses.

With a strict grading policy and a little forgiveness, as long as everything is clearly stated in the syllabus or faculty expectations message, you will have essentially created a binding contract that the school will support should a student protest your practices as unfair. Giving one student a lot of flexibility may not be fair to other students unless there is a major issue that caused the student to be late.

The rule of thumb is to manage by exception (such as for military deployment or storms), be firm but fair, put everything in writing, apply standards consistently, and be a teacher now and a friend later. Students will respect you first and like you later. If you want to see how you're doing in your students' eyes, review your student feedback or ask the learners for comments.

First Impressions, Making Connections, Communication, and Assessment

Leslie Bowman has 25+ years of teaching experience, both online and on-campus, and has written several books about online teaching methods and strategies for providing substantive personal attention to each student in the class while, at the same time, keeping daily and weekly work hours at manageable levels. In this section, she has shared some ideas about creating positive first impressions, building rapport, establishing a community of learners through interactive discussions, and finally, a few thoughts about formative and summative assessments. You can find Leslie's books and conference presentations on her website (www.profbowman.com). The advice from here through the rest of this chapter is all her! She wanted to share what she feels is vital to instructors.

First Impressions: Tone and Atmosphere

The tone and atmosphere in your class can make or break your students' success, and also actually has a huge effect on your own success. One of your most important responsibilities is making your students feel they are part of a community of learners and not just names on a screen. Online students often feel isolated and our job is to alleviate, and prevent if possible, this lonely feeling by creating a warm and welcoming atmosphere the very first day of class. If you don't make a connection with each student personally, in a timely manner, the end result can be decreased student satisfaction and motivation, which can lead to students dropping out of your class.

Making a good first impression on your students will go a long way toward establishing the tone of the class. You start from Day One in the introductions and continue right on through to the end of the course. You should provide lots of opportunities for students to get to know each other and you. Tell them about yourself, your work experience, your background related to the content of the course you are teaching, and make it all relevant to what they are learning. I have no qualms about telling "funny now, but not when it happened" stories from personal experience. Those types of interactions project our personalities as "real" people behind the names on the screen. The concern, though, is that doing all this takes far more effort and time than it does in face-to-face, on-campus courses.

In on-campus classes, we greet each student individually and build connections between learners and faculty. It doesn't take a lot of time; however, this is quite different in an online learning environment and all faculty, at some time or another, feel the burden of increased workload in online classes as opposed to on-campus classes. You need to be prepared for this huge difference in time requirements, especially the first week of class, because it affects not only your ability to get things done in a timely manner, but also affects your students' first impression of you. Let's take a closer look at the first class greetings at the beginning of a semester in an online class.

In a face-to-face course, a professor generally spends about 30-60 minutes during the first class meeting doing icebreakers and introductions, but it takes hours and hours to greet students individually in an online class. Responding individually in a timely manner means writing something substantive and personal, based on each student's greeting information, the very same day they post an introduction.

One school where I teach encourages faculty to check the course introductions at least twice a day so that students will see a welcoming personal message right away after posting. Some people say this is too much to expect of faculty; I disagree. I believe setting the right tone the first week is vital to ensuring your success as an online instructor. Why is that? Because when students feel welcome and part of a community, it's more likely they will stay in the class. If two days go by without an acknowledgement of an introduction, some students give up just that fast and disappear, never to return to your class. Not only does that reflect poorly on you, but you've also lost an opportunity to reach out and make a difference in someone's life. It's such a simple thing to do – just type a response to every student's introduction.

How you respond and what you write are just as important as when you respond. Sometimes online instructors do not respond to each student's introduction individually because it takes so much time. As lead faculty for several graduate courses, I've had the opportunity to observe in many online classes.

I am amazed at how many times introductions are shrugged off as not being important. I've seen instructors either post the same generic "welcome to class – nice to meet you" for each student because they were required to respond individually to the introductions, or, if not required to do that, just post a general "glad you're here" message at the end of the introduction week.

This is one area, though, where you simply cannot skimp; you must take the time to interact personally with each student during the first week of class. During the introductions, I look for something in common with each student and then make that connection in my response to his or her introduction.

Discussion Boards and Peer Mentoring/Review

Another way to establish connections and build

rapport is through the discussion boards, where learning takes place through interactive communication about course content. Learning doesn't happen in a vacuum and the best discussions are those in which students learn from and teach each other. All too often online course discussions are set up as "one post/two responses and done." Best practice, however, involves a student-centered, active learning classroom and, when done properly, discussions often take on a life and direction of their own. Good discussions are totally unpredictable because students tend to talk about what interests them about the lesson content and often they will go in directions that might never have occurred to us.

Each class and group of students will be different in how they interpret and apply the course content. This is because they are making the content and concepts important by relating the information to their real life experiences. All teachers know this is what happens when you get a bunch of diverse people talking about any issue. Everyone knows something about it and they all want to share what they know. And it all begins actually before the students' discussion, with framing the questions and setting up a peer mentoring/review procedure.

Questions should be open-ended so that students are not merely stating facts or opinions but are, instead, critically evaluating their own and their classmates' responses. The peer mentoring and review process promotes engagement in both teaching and learning from peers. And best of all, using peer mentoring and review throughout the week means that you won't have to spend hours and hours grading discussions at the end of each week. Here are some tips for facilitating your discussions.

- Set expectations up front about participation guidelines and acceptable behavior.
- Be flexible and let the students take the lead once they begin interacting.
- Ask students to post summaries periodically throughout the discussions.
- Ask them to expand upon their original comments to promote reflective thinking.
- Ask student volunteers to moderate discussions and pose new questions for the topics/issues.
- Show them how to cite, quote, and paraphrase others' comments in their summaries.

Don't let them get sidetracked into arguments (stating their opinions over and over in different words). Students should develop critical thinking skills and provide evidence to support their comments.

Assessment

Another essential element of online teaching is assessing mastery of the course content. This happens through formative and summative feedback and grades. Formative assessment (informal – may or may not be graded) happens throughout the week in the discussion board. In addition to weekly engagement in discussion course content, I set up review forums for students to post their assignments early as drafts so peers can review and offer suggestions. I also provide feedback in both those areas. Best practice is to always give prompt feedback and do it often; these two areas are perfect ways to provide continued interaction with your students, individually and as a whole group.

If you have promoted a welcoming atmosphere in your class, students will feel comfortable taking risks with their learning. People naturally want to help each other, teach each other, and learn from each other. Think about when you were a student. Don't you remember situations when you just could not understand what the professor was explaining to you, and yet when one of your classmates explained it, voila! Everything became clear as a bell?

Think of your students – many times they will understand a classmate's explanation when they didn't quite "get" yours. That doesn't mean you're a bad teacher. It means that ongoing peer mentoring is an excellent learning strategy that you should use throughout every week in your course. Here's how to do that through formative feedback. And then I'll say a few final words about summative feedback and why, although it's required and necessary at most schools, you can minimize the detrimental effects on learning, as well as on your grading time.

Formative Feedback: Using peer mentoring and reviews can significantly cut the amount of time you would normally spend grading. I have been teaching this way for well over two decades and it works at every grade level, age level, and subject area. This peer mentor/review process is relatively simple to set up. No single teacher can accomplish anything near what a mentoring and review group can as they plan, brainstorm, revise plans, draw up new plans, explore and expand all the possibilities, and finally start creating the presentations, group projects, writing assignments, science labs, marketing projections, the projects that involve math, physics, engineering, mechanical production projects, and the list is endless. Please note that this is NOT group work; students are assessed individually on the quality of their feedback and critiques to others, as well as their own revisions based on peers' critiques. I use peer mentoring and reviews during every discussion and before all assignments that are to be submitted for grading.

Overseeing the peer review process does not take a lot of time and the final product is always high quality work, which means less grading time for you at the end of the week. Sometimes grading is a chore (just read the topics and threads in the Facebook group about grading), but I actually enjoy commenting on drafts and prototypes during peer reviews. I'm not rushed because I have all week to make my own assessments and present individuals with feedback and suggestions. When the due date rolls around, I don't have to spend a lot of time on grading because I have already provided feedback throughout the week. For final grading, I do a simple quick comparison to see what was revised as a result of my feedback and their classmates' suggestions.

At that point, I have given feedback every day at every stage of the project – that is formative assessment. When it's time for the end-of-week summative assessment (grades in the grade book), like magic the final product (be it a paper, science lab or engineering problem, could be literally anything), is almost always worthy of an A. That makes my grading Mondays only about 2-3 hours instead of all day long or more.

Summative Assessments: And so we come to summative assessments, which are, in essence, the grades that you enter into the grade book. Without formative assessment, summative grades and comments don't help students learn. Again, read the FB group postings about instructors' frustration when students don't read feedback on assignments. The reasons is that summative feedback isn't going to help them learn from they've already done and it's a bit late to be helpful in the next assignment. When you do have to provide feedback only through summative assessments, here is a generally accepted formula:

- Be sure to include a relevant positive comment at the end of each paragraph in a short paper and after each section in a longer paper.
- At the end of the paper, write a short paragraph with your immediate impressions of the assignment.
- Copy the rubric at the end of your comments and tally the points.

Another note – if you have used the peer mentoring and review strategies prior to the summative grading, this grading process can be completed in 10 minutes or less for any kind of assignment. No more missing dinner and staying up all night with adult beverages to keep you sane through 200-300 papers you need to grade (and once you're done with those, then you get to start all over again next week).

These are just a few of the important issues

online instructors need to know: set the tone of the classroom; welcome every student and find a connection upon which to build rapport; interact and connect in weekly discussions; and perhaps most important of all – show your students how to learn together and how to teach other.

To read more about setting up learning communities, grading, and other online teaching strategies, along with step-by-step guidelines, visit my website (www.profbowman.com)

Chapter 9 - Working as an Online Faculty Member

"Better than a thousand days of diligent study
is one day with a great teacher."
— Japanese Proverb

Working as an online faculty member, course facilitator, online instructor, online professor, course mentor (our titles definitely vary) is quite different from working within other organizations, even on-ground universities. On-ground universities tend to be somewhat bureaucratic and are slow to change; they also focus on assignment and direction by committees of full-time faculty and administrators, and usually are not for-profit institutions. Online organizations, by contrast, particularly if they are purely online, like Walden University or Capella University, tend to embrace change and operate more like a business in terms of their flexibility and adaptability. Institutions that offer both an on-ground program and an online program can often be found operating much like a traditional university. State schools or public universities also tend to operate like traditional universities. Knowing how each works and the structure within is important.

Working as online adjunct faculty has its pros

and cons, as we detailed in the previous chapters. Each university will adopt a system to teach its courses online, and some are easier, while others are more time-consuming or, honestly, just more annoying.

In this chapter, you will read about several important pieces of information. First will be the different types of systems that the universities you work for may choose to adopt. Whatever system the school uses is what you will have to use as the professor. Although each university will offer a training program, it is important to know ahead of time what you may be asked, learn some of the terminology, and understand some of the basic pros and cons of each of the systems.

Second, you will see a pay versus workload matrix that may help you decide where to spend your time and invest your training as you begin to work for various schools. Once you have enough assignments to pay your mortgage, you can use this matrix to help you determine which schools you want to continue working for and which you want to abandon for better opportunities.

Third, we will address communication in the classroom and what you can do to make yourself visible to the learners, advisement teams, quality review teams, and department chairs who will probably periodically review your course rooms. This will include a review of feedback, postings, announcements, additional instructor resources, and several other ways you can make your presence in the classroom known. Remember this is a key to doing your job and for the university to know you're doing it. Unlike in the traditional classroom where you speak once or twice a week and what is said is between you and the students, in an online classroom Big Brother is watching.

In the book, I address learning what you're good at, documenting it, and doing it really well. This will be the basis for building your reputation and making you an invaluable part of university life at online schools. Everyone will have a specific niche – you need to identify it early, build on it, and become known for it.

This chapter wraps up with a review of using email – not the phone – for communicating, unless of course the university you work for specifically requires it. There are several reasons for this, and I will help you look into those in detail. The chapter concludes with yet another discussion about life as an adjunct, this time based on all of the new information you have gathered from the first several chapters, and how to balance your work and home life.

Types of Learning Management Systems – Knowing the Difference

Every university you work for will use one of several learning management systems (LMS); after all, like most technologies, there are only so many options. In this section, we run through those systems with which we are most familiar. Since I am only exposed to those I work with, I have surveyed the fine professors in our forum and have gotten their feedback to integrate into this chapter as well.

Blackboard

Blackboard has been around for a very long time. It consists today of enterprise software applications and services as well as the learning management software. Blackboard Learn, with over 37000 clients, is what you will most likely work with in the classroom. In 2005, Blackboard announced plans to merge with WebCT (a competing company at the time), which increased its market share to 75%. The new company remains under the Blackboard brand.

This tool set allows you to run your courses, collaborate, message, have discussions, submit assignments, and so on. The newest version is integrated with numerous assessment and live collaborative tools, wikis, and centralized design to give the instructor greater visibility into their classroom. Although each version of Blackboard can be highly customized, the core basics tend to work the same way, making it easy to adapt your skillset with one version at one school to another version at another school. Since they have such a large share of the market, it is likely after you work for four schools, three of them will be using Blackboard.

Blackboard was a publicly traded company under the symbol BBBB until 2011 and become private again. In 2012, Blackboard also acquired two companies based on Moodle's open source software, Moodlerooms, Inc. and NetSpot of Adelaide, Australia. In 2014, Blackboard purchased MyEdu, which has career-planning tools for students. Blackboard supports mobile devices under its Blackboard Mobile product and offers Blackboard Collaborate to replace the Elluminate product.

From the perspective of the online teacher, Blackboard is easy to use, simple to become familiar with, and nicely scalable with a lot of solutions. The newer versions offer some enhancements that allow for some auto-grading procedures to go a little more smoothly than in many of the other systems available out there today.

Blackboard has an easy-to-use message board system that allows you to run discussion threads and sort various posts. Its "collect posts" feature helps instructors manage large volumes of discussions at one time, and the message threading is seamless across different browsers. Blackboard has done a better job recently than in the past to provide facilitators tools to assess student discussion board performance, a welcome change for instructors (no one wants to print out and count posts!). Schools often deploy clickable rubrics into the courses, making it very fast and efficient to grade.

Moodle

Moodle is built on open sourced software, which means it is very customizable and it is not very costly. Often schools host their own Moodle courses, and when I had a training center, I built it on Moodle. Moodlerooms claims that Moodle is the number one most popular LMS, which given how many companies, small businesses, training centers and universities use it, makes sense. The 75% market share that is associated with Blackboard is at the University level, which of course is what is most relevant to us for this book.

In the old days, Moodle used to be what

schools ran when they wanted a cheap solution. Now, it is what schools run when they want a highly customizable solution that happens to be inexpensive. Moodle won a Best of Breed award for their LMS in Sept. 2014, which you can read more about here: http://c4lpt.co.uk/top100tools/best-of-breed/

If you are working at a university running Moodle, you can expect to see a lot of tiny icons, have a reasonable sized learning curve, and then absolutely love the flexibility once you get going. The ability to customize most every element (even as an instructor) is superb. The system is straightforward and easy to navigate, although making modifications to the course will take a while for newbies. It is not highly intuitive, but once you work with it, it's efficient.

eCollege

Pearson eCollege has been around since 1996 and provides an integrated approach for distance education programs from an administrative viewpoint, and is simple to access and manage courses from an instructor viewpoint. It is a hosted solution and some of its clients are Ashford, DeVry, University of Colorado at Denver, and many others. According to its website at www.ecollege.com, eCollege claims to be the only e-learning outsource provider that provides a single point of contact with assurance that the system will be up and running. It was named on *Forbes'* list of the top 25 fastest-growing technology companies in 2004 and 2005, and was recognized on the 2005 Red Herring Small Cap 100 list based on its innovation and smart business model. It was named Technology Company of the Year by the Colorado

Software and Internet Association Apex Awards in 2004, and won numerous other awards presented by respected organizations.

From an instructor perspective, eCollege is streamlined, fast, and efficient. There are separate tabs for the facilitator for authoring a course and actually participating in one, which can feel a bit clumsy, but makes changes quick and you can see the student view easily. When you select a particular area in the classroom you want to modify, you then click on the author tool that will allow you to modify the content there. For instance, if you click on Course Home, you will see announcements. If you then click Author, you can add an announcement. Some argue there are many added steps that don't make sense and really could be streamlined for the facilitators. It does have some nice features, such as the ability to set up a drop box that allows you to enter grades into the grade book with ease, much like WebCT used to.

If you're going to work for a university using this system, be prepared for a slow first few weeks while you get the hang of it, compared to a system like Blackboard. If you're asked to develop a course in this platform, you might want to consider asking for a bonus.

Sakai

Sakai is used by over 350 colleges and universities, according to their own data. (https://sakaiproject.org/) I personally find it cumbersome and slow running, even on decent systems and networks. Gradebook row highlighting can help instructors with more efficient grading, and mobile device support is decent. Lessons are built through a system called LessonBuilder. Forums are a bit slow and difficult to navigate from my experience. If you are going to work for a school using Sakai, be prepared for a sizeable learning curve and for it to take you a little longer to do your work than if the school is running eCollege or Blackboard. By the way, try Googling "Sakai sucks" and you will see about 470,000 results, as noted by a professor in our forum. Not everyone like it, that's for sure. It's known by professors to freeze up and not load discussion boards properly.

Vcamp360

Vcamp360, from Savant Learning Systems, Inc., has traditionally partnered with small, faith-based institutions that are new to online programs, but they are growing and expanding. Many of us who have used this platform prefer it over other learning management systems. It's easy to use and it is based on an instructional model using Read, Attend, Complete and Discuss. I have found that it provides a consistent learning experience for students and it is intuitive to use as a designer and instructor. Schools pay as they grow with scalable costs, and students have live 24x7 technical support through chat, phone, and email relieving instructors of some of that burden.

Some features are still in development though and are currently unavailable (though I anticipate perhaps by the time this book hits the shelves some of these may be ready), including a mobile application, an integrated video recorder and synchronous web or text chats. It also does not support some third party courseware applications. Instructors and administrators who want to try out the system can use a free trial from www.vcamp360.com or phone for a free trial (888-544-1207).

Other Systems

The university you work for may choose a proprietary method of serving up courses. Axia and the University of Phoenix used newsgroups for some time, which was a serious pain. Some schools are using Canvas or Desire2Learn and you may find yourself with more experience with those as time goes on. I have found that the core principles of design are relatively similar to other platforms, but the learning curve and details can vary widely.

Some universities still use Web-based proprietary systems and are either already migrating to something else or have no intention of doing so. As prices change for hosted solutions, some schools change LMSs often and I have found that this practice occurring often predicts instability in a school.

System Pros and Cons:

Here is a pros and cons list of each of the platforms above as noted by the online instructor forum folks!

Blackboard Pros: First post feature, requiring students make their initial post before they can read other student posts (cuts down on plagiarism and "taking ideas" from classmates). Features that can be turned on to disallow editing of posts after reading others' posts. Ability to add more features as needed. Announcements can be pushed by email to all students. Retention center feature that allows instructors to monitor student progress is useful. It has a superior math editor feature.

Blackboard Cons: So many versions running that you do not have the same economics of scale advantage as you may with other platforms as you become familiar with them. Replying to posts can require a lot of "right scrolls." Uploading files and course materials can be cumbersome. Data collection on students is inefficient; not very user friendly.

Sakai Pros: There were absolutely zero positive remarks posted for Sakai. I'm not kidding.

Sakai Cons: Inefficient. Discussion boards have to be reloaded often. Discussion threads disappear. Very slow.

Moodle Pros: Very customizable and efficient. Easy to use.

Moodle Cons: Gradebook features are not efficient to use.

eCollege Pros: Allows instructors to get creative. User friendly. Fast and efficient. Not too many versions so when you "know eCollege" at one school, you know it at the others.

eCollege Cons: Announcements must be recreated to be emailed rather than pushed out through the announcement feature. Limited "copy to another course" feature. Native HTML editor or format tool is not very good. ClassLivePro, the built in communication tool, requires Java and was "developed by Satan himself."

Vcamp360 Pros: Flexible, adaptable, easy to develop in, simple for students to use with four main functions for a course, built-in capability for scenario based learning and videos, support for students and instructors.

Vcamp360 Cons: Low exposure in the market means faculty may not have used it and may have a higher learning curve, mobile version is not yet available, no synchronous capabilities built in.

Time Matrix – Pay versus Workload

Most adjunct faculty members or course facilitators are essentially entrepreneurs who run a business that serves students. They work for numerous clients – the universities – and their goal is to maximize their pay for their workload while providing the best service possible. The same business strategies apply to acquiring and keeping a roster of good online schools as just about any other small business, with a few key modifications. We call this being adjunctpreneurs, as mentioned earlier in the book.

We have already identified many hidden efforts that can exhaust your time and resources. It's important to find out about as many of these as possible before beginning work with a school, and to also consistently monitor and assess them as you begin working. You might not have the luxury of turning down a teaching job while you're new to the adjunct world and in need of experience, but eventually you will want to balance your life and workload with your pay.

As a refresher, some of the key areas that will eat up much of your time may include: committee meetings, faculty meetings, quarterly meetings on updates, mandatory chats in some online courses, synchronous sessions, attending residencies or colloquia (although you may be paid for these), attending additional (often redundant) faculty development courses, and serving as a mentor for a learner (again you are usually compensated for this, but some schools require more work than others and some schools expect learners to be more self-directed than others).

Eventually you will develop your own time matrix, and you will be able to determine where your efforts are best spent. Keep in mind that this is only a picture of time and money, not a picture of satisfaction. Adding the satisfaction and enjoyment you get from teaching can make these pay versus workload considerations irrelevant. Nothing is more enjoyable than being supported by your bosses and having the academic freedom to teach your best. When you are treated like a valued faculty member, as long as you don't feel exploited and the pay is reasonable, you are not likely to evaluate whether it is worth leaving that university for higher pay elsewhere. After all, the biggest reason we teach is because we love it; the income potential just makes it an even better career.

Factors That May Affect Your Workload

Here is a list of things to look out for that may increase your workload dramatically or cut into your critical teaching or free time (although some of these can be time well spent). Let's look at some of the major ones to beware of, and then you can begin to utilize the matrix we have provided to help evaluate each school critically and determine whether you want to stay.

- *Micromanagement.* Some universities may micromanage, checking your time in the classroom, monitoring exactly how many posts you make, and asking you to make numerous administrative changes that don't have an apparent goal. The more they micromanage, the more time you waste, and this cuts into your earnings potential and increases anxiety and stress level.
- *Excess training.* It's normal to require training. When rules change or systems change, you need to be retrained. This will help you in the long run; however, if a school requires retraining or new training more than twice per year, consider this abnormal. It will increase your workload unnecessarily.
- *Attendance tracking.* Some schools have online attendance tracking by email or some other online tool where you are required to fill out a weekly form for each course you teach, which can be very time-consuming. Other schools ask only that you report students who are absent (which is a small percentage); this is a reasonable request that takes little time and can ultimately save you trouble, since the advisers intervene immediately with regard to those absent students.
- *Retention.* Yes it is our job to help students stick with a course, which means motivating a learner

when he or she may not feel like staying around. If we believe higher education has value, then this comes second nature to us – we want to encourage and nurture students to commit and continue with their education. However, at some point, schools can take this too far. There are schools that will hold you to a specific retention number, despite their poor quality students. They may encourage you to give a C- instead of a D+. They may ask you to email and/or call every underperforming student every week. In a class of 30 students with a 20% failure rate, you can quickly see what the schools' motives are here. I do not recommend working for these schools; though I also know sometimes we have no choice if we need to pay the bills.

- *Mentee tracking*. At the master's and doctoral level, you may be required to report periodically on the status of those you mentor. While this can add to your time spent, chances are that you won't have more than a few to report on and doing so won't be a real drain on you. Also, this may help to nudge some of you to keep in contact with those you mentor more regularly. It can also be a lot of fun.
- *Self-directed learner mentoring*. Mentoring learners can be extremely satisfying, and may even be a requirement at some universities. However, if possible, only do this for schools that require the learner to be self-directed so that you aren't answering process questions, but instead are working with the learner to actually learn. If you have to be a hand-holder, you will find yourself investing a lot of time for very small gains

318

(and often you don't get paid unless the learner actually graduates).

- *Conference calls.* Requiring more than a quarterly conference call may be considered excessive by some faculty, though many schools are moving to a monthly mandatory meeting. It all depends on your patience level and if the calls are productive. As long as you receive valuable information and get to network, consider them time well spent; otherwise, they are interfering with your work time.
- *Unpaid conferences.* In an effort to update faculty on policies and procedures, create a sense of community, and gain feedback, universities sometimes hold unpaid conferences. Your travel may be covered, but your time isn't compensated in most cases. Usually these are not mandatory, but if they are, expect them to be a drain on your time and your wallet. Some can feel like family reunions though, with the same folks there year after year. Many of us look forward to these occasional meetings, just beware that they are costly.
- *Faculty lead.* Being a faculty lead can be an honor that pays fairly or a drain on your time with no additional compensation. Find out the rules and the pay before you agree to be a faculty lead. Often it requires numerous extra duties for limited pay; however, the trade-off is that you typically get the first section of the course, which can ultimately increase your earnings potential with greater job security.
- *Heavy discussion boards.* Mandated heavy discussion board entries can often be the largest drain on your time. Moderating a discussion by

posting comments, facilitating, and expanding on the discussion is great – that is teaching! But some schools require you to comment on everyone's responses as well as to comment on everyone's comment on a classmate's response, and the thread grows exponentially as the weeks go by. If students' grades are affected by the number of postings, and they must post three times per week, just do the math: 15 learners, each posting a response, and each posting three comments to other learners, and you must comment to each of these as well as to all replies to your own postings. To make it worse, you may have to grade their responses individually by going to the grade book and assigning individual scores with comments on why they got the grades they did. The focus should be on teaching. Discussions are often the lifeblood of an online course. It is vital you participate thoroughly and are highly engaged, but schools that have a specific ratio usually have that ratio for various reasons (and I haven't found that they are very good ones).

- *Modification.* Some universities let you have free rein to modify courses as you see fit. You can modify them so students are happier and you are less overworked on menial tasks and can focus on what's important – learner interaction and engagement. Universities that allow this level of freedom are a good thing; though rare these days. At first, it may seem like more work, but this freedom, used wisely, is great in the long run and will ultimately save you time. You can make vast improvements to your course. On the flip side, some schools force adjuncts to teach from master course templates (often without allowing for any modification whatsoever). If this design is good for you and works with your style, then you are set; if the design is contrary to your style, you will find it more challenging to teach the course, and a waste of time when you have to readjust the course each semester. Find out if the school will replicate your particular course, not the master, as it may save you time. Note that if you are offered the opportunity to develop a course, you get to do it your way (within the development guidelines of the school, which will be considerably different university to university) and then there is no need to worry about which template is used; additionally, you can often ask for the right of first refusal. Even if the pay for course development isn't great, the perks can be, so check it all out before you accept such a contract. The best deal you can get is to develop a course you have already developed at another school; it takes little time to create a similar one, and if you use the same book and same general layout, you can teach the same course at multiple schools.

- *Chats.* A few universities require adjuncts to host one or more chats each week, usually via a webinar; Adobe, Collaborate, and Elluminate are all popular. This can be largely inconvenient for both students and instructors. Some schools allow you to pick the days and times, and others mandate it. If you enjoy face-to-face facilitation, this is a way to integrate that type of model online and can be a lot of fun. Just know it will also restrict your time and flexibility. You may have to assign grades for participation based on these chats, which further intensifies the workload. In some cases, a chat can be a time-saver, though, so don't judge too quickly. I would rather do a one-hour chat each week to explain a concept than answer 80 emails about tests.

- *Group Work.* If a course requires group work, you may find yourself assigning students to teams and then spending your time as referee. Sometimes, like for large papers, group work is a blessing that results in less typing, less grading, and often better products. Other times, though, you have to set up additional discussion forums and moderate them separately, which can increase your workload incredibly. If you must use groups, try to limit them to teams of two or three and you will eliminate the need for creating group areas since they can just email each other easily. You may find that students despise group work. It can be tough to get together at a specific time, and clashing personalities and skillsets can make things difficult. This has a trickle-up effect, impacting you as the instructor significantly.
- *Automated grading.* Many schools use automated assessments, such as quizzes or tests. If your course has objective exams, your only responsibility may be to create them the first time and monitor them for troublesome or unfair questions or for students who get locked out for various reasons. The other added benefit is that learners get immediate feedback on objective exams, and it takes the pressure off you to grade quickly. Essays are not automatically graded, so expect that they will take more work.
- *Submitting grades.* Some schools use grading

forms you have to mail in. This means (1) you have to actually be at your home office to send in grades (or have carried the paperwork with you), and (2) it's slower. Online grading is more efficient and will make you feel as though you've truly closed a class when it's over. Some schools automatically pull grades on a specific day and time from your classroom and there is nothing to submit. Others have a separate system to post grades to, or an email to send off to the boss. Having to mail in grading forms is not a reason to turn away a teaching opportunity, but it is something to take into account. You may find this occurs more at traditional or state schools offering online classes. I personally don't find it to be a big deal, but many instructors who travel a lot do.

- *Multiple Courses.* Teaching multiple courses at the same school will naturally earn you more money, but if you teach multiple sections of the same course, it will feel less stressful. Two identical sections do not take double the time since you are grading the same papers and posting the same questions and assignments; the only difference may be in the flow of the discussions, but you can often use some comments from one discussion to seed the other if needed. Note, depending on how a school pays, you should consider this carefully. If a school pays by the student, a class of 20 is better than two classes of 10, but if the school pays by the class, then you want as many small sections as you can get. We don't have much control over this as instructors though. The key is to balance time with earnings.

Once you have evaluated the workload factors at your chosen school and considered the pay you will be earning, put the school into your own pay matrix if you want to document it. This comes in handy as you decide if you can and want to take on more work, and if you do, which schools you may want to leave. As you begin to work for universities, categorize them to help you in initially determining where to focus your efforts. You may choose to construct your own matrix that also takes into account how satisfied you are working for that particular school as well. I think we all work at a place that pays less and has a lot of demands, but we like the team so much it's okay. Sometimes having a great boss but receiving low pay can keep good faculty at a school for years.

Time Matrix – Pay versus Workload

	Heavy Workload	Light Workload
High Pay	*Not a bad position, but you can handle only so many of these.*	*Ideal position.*
Low Pay	*Try to avoid these schools.*	*Not a bad position, but you can handle only so many of these, too.*

There is another component here: how happy you are with the school. As I mentioned before, there are schools that will phone and ask you to pass more students (yes, it has happened to me and just about everyone else I know who has been doing this for a while). There are schools that will hold you accountable for how many students pass (what do you think this makes instructors likely to do?) There are schools that do not care that their material is outdated as long as students enroll. Try to imagine a school asking you to give out a lot of F's so students have to take your course again, thereby generating more money for the school and more teaching opportunities for yourself. Could you really work there even if it is easy money?

You may not learn about the schools questionable ethics until grades are in, so don't be surprised if you find yourself teaching only one course at a school and not returning. When you find one that works with your conscience, you can stay there for a long time. The initial semester is a trial period with much time invested in application, training, course setup, and teaching, and one hopes it is a good fit so you can maximize the return on your investment. The more homework you do up front by networking and asking others about different schools, the less likely you will regret your decision.

Three University Situations

In the first edition of this book, we created three situations for you to look at. One is the "Absolute Ideal Situation," one is the "Tolerable and Acceptable Situation," and one is the "Cut and Run Situation." We will name these schools Great to Work for You U, I Can Live with You U, and Not on Your

Life U.

In Great to Work for You U, your position and your work are highly respected. The chairs and management believe that learner expectations and learner reviews are critical to your success and put some weight in them, but also understand once in a while a few bad reviews will pop up due to someone receiving a deserved low grade. The pay is good or high, the workload is average, many of the systems (like attendance tracking) are automated, and the system the school uses to manage its online courses is exceptional. Communication is somewhat frequent but by email primarily, and you are paid for anything you do that's above and beyond teaching. You have an opportunity to take on more, like faculty lead or mentoring, but you're fairly compensated for it and you are relatively in charge of the process. The school will get your input before changing course design or even textbooks on a class you routinely teach. You regularly get work and new contracts because your hard work and dedication are rewarded. Great to Work for You U is ethically sound, responsible to the community, and overall a pleasure to work for. Since turnover at these schools is incredibly low, as you might expect, you should hang on to these places for dear life if you find yourself in their faculty rotations. Even if they go through some unpleasant transitions, deal with them professionally and you won't be sorry.

I Can Live with You U respects your position and may value your contribution a number of ways, which includes student reviews, but may also be concerned with how well you play politically. Playing politically online is really tough (remember, you don't get to see these people, and your actions online are permanently stored and viewed by people you might not trust). There are some automated processes, the classroom software is all right, and you're decently compensated for work you do above and beyond. Contracts may be spotty, receiving one during one term but nothing for a while. Communication may be often and by phone, taking up a lot of your valuable time. Some administrators may be pleasant to work with, and others make you cringe when their email pops up. This school may routinely increase course size, but not compensate you additionally for it. I Can Live with You U is usually ethically sound, they care about the students and the community, and overall you enjoy what you do for the school. It isn't quite a Great to Work for You U, but is a good staple school to help increase your income and maintain stability. These schools are where you will find yourself most of the time if you follow our leads. They are common, and if you do your job well enough and become the go-to person in your department, the environment can almost seem like Great to Work for You U from your perspective.

Not on Your Life U may have some of the following characteristics: They may phone you the night before a class starts, asking you to build the class that night and teach it in the morning (not bad if they are paying you for it or you don't mind last minute). You may even be compensated well (they will have to when they ask you to do this!) but it isn't because they want to or because they value you; it's because they procrastinated. They routinely change textbooks one or two days before a course begins, leaving the learner and the faculty frantically updating and ordering new texts. They update or change their

LMS when one becomes too expensive. They become upset if your students are not passing at a number determined by the owner of the school. They do not allow you to update badly outdated courses, and the site of the administrators' names in your email inbox makes your heart race. They may sometimes be ethically sound, but appear more interested in tuition than learners' success. Their contracts may be spotty at best, or they may routinely ask you to work for them. Their system of accountability is awful and often you will be accountable to someone who is hired to do nothing but check in on classrooms. You may have an opportunity to develop courses but often for little pay and with tremendous rigidity. They may not even use a real course room system. They check their community awareness and desire to do good at the door when they come to work in the morning, and they treat adjuncts as mere contractors who add no value and are easily replaceable. While they may not fit the definition of a diploma mill, they will almost feel like one. Staying at one of these schools is like hanging on to a technology stock after the dot-com/dot-bomb crash of 2000; it will take a lot to make up for what you have already lost in time and opportunity.

Communication Is Key

Regardless of what school you teach for, what platform it is running, or how well (or poorly) it pays, chances are you are being measured and evaluated on your communication. Many of these schools do not have a formal review process.

There are several keys to good

communication. First and foremost, it must be fast. Chapter 10, the technology chapter, addresses ways in which you can accomplish that. You need to be quick on the draw and not let an email sit in the in-box for days before responding. Sometimes you literally have a day to respond to a contract offer. If you don't like the phone, be really, really good at email. If you don't like email, don't teach online! In all seriousness, most of the business you will conduct when teaching as an online facilitator will take place by email. Often no news is good news; you won't hear from your chair or dean for months. This is usually a good thing, but it's a good idea to remind them you exist.

Second, do not ever, ever take part in a group gripe. This is occurring at a university right now regarding lowering of pay for some faculty and increasing pay for others, or the Affordable Care Act. The gripers are copying everyone (faculty and dean included), and making themselves look really bad. This is *not* the way to remind your bosses you exist. Use the "reply all" option with caution or only when directed. If you don't like how things are going, either deal with it, discuss it privately with your boss, or leave.

Next, always respond promptly, the same day is usually not only expected but required. Even if your bosses take weeks to respond back, you shouldn't and you really mustn't. Waiting too long to respond may cause your manager to assume you also take weeks to respond to learners, which is not a good impression for your bosses to have. Plus, you need to be in the habit of immediate responses. Your students will demand it; and if you don't respond right away they will be calling you at home or on your cell phone because they are anxious. It's part of your job to reduce their anxiety and to avoid phone calls whenever possible.

It's also important to note here that in many instances academic records require written documentation, and phone calls don't count. If you do phone a student, keep a log. This is imperative in case of any discrepancy or dispute later. Simply put, use your email. Respond immediately, and keep your in-box clear so you know what's new and what needs a response.

If you are lucky enough to work for a boss who rarely pings you for anything, you will need to find creative ways to let your existence be known somewhat frequently. This will help ensure you are assigned courses and that your name is fresh in their minds when they are looking for course developers or course revisers. Some ways to send emails to your management without looking like you're vying for attention might be:

- Tell them of a new accomplishment, and ask them to add it to your faculty profile. Add a quick note explaining the benefit this brings to your learners.
- Update your profile, name, address, and so on.
- Create a website for your teaching material and update your profile with that information as well. This will show your dedication to the teaching profession and serve as a great resource for your students.
- Send an interesting article about an online teaching strategy that your boss may wish to share with other faculty. Keep these emails brief, and use attachments for the articles in PDF or

RTF format so most individuals can read them.
- Create an email indicating how well your course is going (assuming it is—don't be dishonest), and that you'd like to suggest some revisions for the future. Bullet-point these revisions. Ask the department chairperson in a nonaggressive tone to be sure the faculty lead is aware of these. If you are lucky, the faculty lead isn't doing his or her job, and you'll take over. The best way to gain status is to earn it; if you do a great job and your department chair or dean finds you highly reliable, you will be positioned for success.
- Discuss an idea for a new course. Perhaps you work in IT, and IT for Homeland Security is a hot topic. Write up a quick description and note that you feel the program would benefit from such a course. You may add that you have the expertise to assist in development should management wish to undertake the endeavor. If you develop the course, you typically get to teach the first section each semester, and will get paid whenever the course needs updating. What a way to generate income doing what you love!

You will find other creative ways to remind your bosses that you exist, and you need to do so at least quarterly. Again, think of them as your client base and yourself as an entrepreneur. How would you remind your clients that you're out there and willing and ready to serve?

Continuously Do What Comes Easily and What You're Good At

A key to being a really good online adjunct faculty is continuously doing what you're good at. This means you need to look inside yourself and figure out what aspect of online teaching suits you best. For example, you may be good at organizing your class schedule, super-fast communication, course development, or you may have strong attention to detail or be exceptionally friendly. Whatever you have "in you" already, do it well and do it often. You will be counted on and valued for that intrinsic trait. My bosses know that if they want a very fast reply, they can count on me. One of my bosses calls me the "fastest gun in the west." I smile every time I see him write that! I do not like waiting days for others to respond to me, so I give my colleagues and friends the same courtesy when I reply. It is nice to be recognized for what you do well. When a boss knows you are particularly good at something, he or she will call you first when that character trait is highly needed for a project.

Once you figure out what you are good at, stay good at it. Even when you are tired and don't feel like answering your email, do it. This will help guarantee your place in line to teach classes when the time comes. You will be known as the person the schools can count on. With many things on their plates, deans and chairpersons don't like worrying about whether tasks are being accomplished and even the lowest person on the totem pole reports up to the higher powers when things aren't getting done. You can get a bad rap or a good rap very quickly in the world of online teaching.

Using Email – Not the Phone!

This point may be driven home here more than in most books, because it is extremely important. No one wants to send an email to someone only to receive a return phone call back. It's annoying; usually there is a reason an email was sent in the first place. Some of us online professors are actually closet introverts! Perhaps it's their organizational method or perhaps they are using it to track what has been done and what hasn't. Perhaps they are evaluating your responsiveness. Use email, not the phone, unless your boss phones you and asks you to call him or her back or unless you need to discuss matters that you wouldn't want accidentally forwarded. When my bosses want out of their job, they don't put it in an email, they pick up the phone and call me. You will quickly learn the preference of each of your bosses, and then you should follow suit; in general, though, use email and be prompt about it.

If you are a frequent traveler and don't like being tied to your phone, this preference for email will come as a pleasant though life-altering surprise. Your students may phone you, and it's wise to return their phone calls; however, you should always encourage them in the syllabus and in your contact information to use email and not the phone. There are plenty of books telling you how to teach, so we will save that for our colleagues, but do be mindful of others' time and be respectful by honoring the online methodology.

Life as an Adjunct – Balancing Work and Home

Balancing life as an adjunct is easier said than done. As with most home-based businesses, the line can easily be blurred between home and work, and at times, it can be frustrating and feel overwhelming. When your office is upstairs, it's easy to let family or personal time suddenly be work time; the benefit is that the opposite also holds true.

There are many keys to making this work/life balance work. Some tips are:

- *Create a workspace that is just that—a work space.* This should not be your child's playroom or your kitchen unless that's truly how you work best (I recently moved from my home office into my kitchen to see my little girl more often); it needs to be a quiet space for you to type, work, write, and address questions. It should have a conference phone and all of your equipment close by.
- Schedule your time. I use my smartphone to schedule in time when I will do things. My schedule might say, "10 to 11 School X, 12 to 1 School Y" and so forth. If I finish early, great. If not, I have allocated adequate time to handle tasks, including submitting attendance, entering grades, and so forth. Be sure to track everything that has to be submitted and when. As you juggle multiple schools, you'll also be juggling multiple deadlines and universities that have various start and end dates. Without serious organization, it can quickly become a nightmare. You will need a calendar, and preferably one that syncs to every other device you own.

- *Remember that work time is work time, and personal time is personal time.* It might be tempting to check your email again at midnight, but one key to successfully working as an adjunct is creating office hours and sticking to them. (I freely admit I am terrible at this, and if I am awake I am also on my email). It is easy to feel as though teaching is your life, and it can quite literally take over your world. Since you'll be self-employed, you'll have to set your own boundaries and work schedule, which can be tough to adapt to, particularly if you're used to a rigid workplace.
- *Try to take at least one day off each week.* Many schools require six-day-per-week logins and/or seven-day-per-week availability, which means you work six or seven days every week without fail. You're lucky if you work for a school that gives you a holiday off; most don't. Kiss holidays and nonworking vacations good-bye. The good news is that you can be anywhere and still work; the bad news is that you must still work everywhere. Try to schedule your time so that you get one consistent day off per week.
- *Work the hours that suit you best.* If you have an infant at home, you may be working around his waking hours. If you have a school age child at home, your hours may be driven around when kids are in school. If you have insomnia like I do, you may not care what hours you work! If you are a sound sleeper, you may block off a full 7 hours (you lucky dog!) and then an hour for coffee and toast in the morning. You have to figure out what will make you happy and then work within those hours. The preferences may change over time,

too, as your life situations change. One of the great advantages of the asynchronous online world is that you can work any hours you choose. You can take trips at will, as long as you are willing to take your laptop. Dr. Tara Ross calls it the Laptop Lifestyle. What is important is that you decide what you value most and keep that in mind as you schedule your work and your time. Don't take on more classes than you can handle, and don't take on so many that you have no time for yourself or your family. I am all about integration of work and home life rather than trying to carve out specific time for the family. I brought my daughter to a fall faculty meeting in Nashville for example. Remember that you can make plenty of money and still have a life.

- *Above all else, have fun! If you are not having fun as an adjunct professor, then stop making yourself, your family, and your students miserable and go ahead and bail out. This is not a get-rich-quick scheme. It is a new career opportunity that has both intrinsic and extrinsic rewards, but it isn't for everyone. Some people love this job purely for the schedule, others for the freedom to work independently, some for the opportunity to put their education to fine use, and still others for the ability to make extra money during off hours. To make this your only source of income, it truly helps if you enjoy teaching and you are good at it.*

Chapter 10 – The Role of Social Media in the Online Teaching World

---

"A teacher affects eternity;
he can never tell where his influence stops."
— Henry Brooks Adams

Online teaching, as you will find out, if you haven't already, is a very highly networked world. At some point in your career you will likely report to former students, work side-by-side as colleagues with your manager at another school, or have a student who is also a boss. But there is another element to networking in online education as well: social media networking.

Social Media and Online Education

You don't have to tell an entrepreneur about the benefits of being online with a strong presence. So, to adjunctpreneurs, it might seem odd that faculty do not see the same benefit. But I can tell you from first-hand experience, both in my own career and helping others start theirs, that online visibility as a subject matter expert often plays a role in being hired.

There are at least three scenarios for you to

consider. The first is a dean or hiring manager finding you as a result of a web search, because you are visible and present in your area of expertise. The second is other colleagues finding you and developing rapport, and you help one another get jobs. The third is when a dean or hiring manager looks you up online before interviewing you and knows everything about you that you have made public. The goal is to be in control of this, and use the tools as networking advantages. We have developed social media profiles for clients and have had incredible networking success. At the very least, a LinkedIn profile using professor tools and a Facebook Professor page help make you visible while locking down what can be seen by others. An active Twitter account in your subject matter area is great, and Pinterest or Instagram accounts for your area of expertise are even better. Not to mention Google+ and the other tools that are having an impact on search results. I want you to come up in a result when someone enters a search engine query for "professor" and "area of expertise." So does Dr. Tara Ross, the social media expert and partner for our business.

In 2012, I started a group called ExclusiveEDU. You can learn more about it at thebabbgroup.com. It is a networking group for educators who want to be cited in publications using the media queries I post during the week. They want to learn about social media from experts like Dr. Ross, who helps professors create a brand, engage, network, and find unique job posts – all in a private and confidential place where privacy breaches are taken very seriously. In Jan. of 2013, Dr. Ross joined the group to develop networking contacts and learn how to work as an entrepreneur. She was active in building ExclusiveEDU, and built her own blog, EdJourneys, where she wrote about teaching and traveling, networking on social media, and learning the ins and outs of the online teaching world. She was mentored early on by Carissa Pelletier, who is also an expert and helps professors get published (you can check out her website at www.moderninstructor.com.)

Dr. Ross became a social media expert, learned how to develop websites and how to use blogging as a way to build and maintain an online reputation. In July 2013, I asked her to become the social media educator for the group; she graciously accepted and began writing and blogging about social media. She published *Social Media Mastery* in Nov. 2013. In Dec. 2013, we co-created a Teach Online Boot Camp and a teaching toolkit to help faculty learn about strategies for landing an online teaching position. Her background in social media, online teaching, and education administration was a great complement to mine and she has been our social media educator ever since. I asked Tara to share some advice in a chapter on social media with readers and she kindly accepted. She has helped a lot of clients and friends vastly improve their careers and chances of being hired, so I highly suggest taking her recommendations very seriously and trying out social media for your professional work, even if it's in baby steps. The rest of this chapter is Tara's!

Instructor as a Brand

As faculty members, it seems odd to think of ourselves as a brand, but we are a brand. Our research helps to define us; our writing, our publications, our credentials, and our presentations all help to create our brand. In this era of strong competition among applicants for online teaching jobs (Dani's research shows that it takes between 80-120 applications to land an interview; for each job advertised there is an average of 600 applicants), it helps to have a strong online brand.

How do you define your brand?

As an online instructor, your brand is likely your degree credentials combined with your publications, presentations, and web presence. Do not be limited by this, however. You may not have any of those things except for your degree credentials and are wondering how to define your brand from scratch. Regardless of your existing brand presence, consider how you can further define and differentiate yourself from others in the academic space. Defining yourself clearly will help you determine how best to promote yourself, and differentiation is crucial in the increasingly cluttered online academic world.

Consider the following elements as part of your brand:

- Degree credentials
- Academic publications
- Presentations
- Prior work experience
- Research specialty
- Specialization within your field

Further elements may be part of your brand; however, they may also be how you *differentiate* yourself from others with similar backgrounds. For example, the following items can be used to set you apart from others:

- Service work
- Trade publications
- Specialization within your field
- Systems you created to help students succeed
- Citations in printed media or appearances in television media

Alternatively, you may decide that a niche outside of your academic field should be your brand. The rationale for branding yourself both inside and outside of academia is that you multiply your areas of expertise. I have done this, as I find that I need to express myself beyond my degree field and pursue both academic and entrepreneurial goals. Therefore, my academic brand is in the social science and leadership field, and my trade brand is social media and travel. I teach in my academic field, but I write books and run online trainings within my trade field.

Find a need and fill it

If you despair of finding an online teaching job or increasing your online teaching opportunities, then take a step back and ask yourself what the needs are in the field in which you are credentialed. The key with building your opportunity is to help others. That may sound altruistic, and to some extent it is, but it is also hugely practical. Everyone has problems, fears, goals, and dreams. Identify those needs and determine how you can help others overcome problems and fears to achieve their goals.

The problem may be as simple as a school needing to hire an online mathematics instructor, and you have the credentials and experience for it. Alternatively, you may identify a tremendous need among incoming college students for help with math skills, so you create a service to tutor students in math. You might then decide that tutoring one-on-one is too time consuming, so you create an online series of videos that walk students through learning essential math skills.

Do not limit your opportunity

Do not limit yourself to working only for others. Ironically, academics are notorious for limiting their potential within their field of expertise. You have skills that can help others achieve their goals. People will pay to have their problems solved so they can achieve their goals. Why should you limit yourself to teaching an online class for a university when you have abilities that people will pay for so that they can succeed? The two are also not mutually exclusive: teach online *and* be entrepreneurial. You may eventually discover that the entrepreneurial work is far more rewarding and lucrative.

If you cannot conceive of what the problems might be within your area of expertise, approach the issue as if you were creating a research study. Conduct background research: identify your target audience, and interview members of that target audience to uncover their problems, fears, goals, and dreams. Further research can uncover how to monetize that niche or scale that niche so that you can make a living from it. Need a helpful formula?

At the intersection of others' problems and your expertise is your niche.

For example, I have taught in my subject area since 1999. I enjoy teaching and that is not limited to teaching for my university. As I learned more about social media and applied what I learned, I began to help others learn how to use social media effectively for building their online presence and brand. The content I created eventually was developed into my book, *Social Media Mastery*, which became a bestseller on Amazon. I followed that up with *Social Networking Success.* I discovered a need and also discovered that I enjoyed helping others understand social media.

Building your brand

Marketing experts will tell you that in order to build your brand you need to dominate your niche. We have all been on the receiving end of online marketers, however, and thus it is important to ensure that you are solving problems rather than annoying your audience. You must also differentiate yourself as a means of dominating your niche. Known as your Unique Selling Point or Unique Selling Proposition (USP), this differentiation is crucial for motivating hiring managers to contact you over the competition, for readers to buy your book over the competition, and for customers to buy your product or service over the competition. What makes your brand unique in a way that moves others to action? Note, too, that some types of USPs are not always good; therefore, you must be professional in your differentiation.

For example, you may be credentialed to teach English Composition. How will you gain the attention of universities in order to receive online teaching offers? First, examine the problem: a university needs English Comp instructors who are credentialed, experienced, and available to teach for the pay they are offering. You have the credentials, some experience, and are available. Great! So are the other 2,000 applicants. Thus, the next question is: How will you differentiate yourself from them? This is where your branding comes in.

Distinguish yourself with the quality of your CV, your experience, your publications, your social media presence (especially on LinkedIn), your online presence, and your trade publications. There is no magic pill to help you gain these things. Building your brand takes time, persistence, and expertise. Yet it's not rocket science, either. If you are that English Composition applicant mentioned above, you build your brand by creating content that fills a need that you push out on the web, in conferences, and in trade publications. Perhaps you do the following:

- Develop articles for your blog about writing tips for students
- Create a short, daily podcast where you answer one grammar question a day
- Offer a creative writing course via Udemy or your website
- Develop a "how-to" book on technical writing or grant writing
- Offer webinars using Google Hangouts on Air (a

free resource and indexed by Google) about how to use APA format.
- Design a course that helps corporate executives in other countries learn English writing skills
- Start an editing service for student research papers

As you create content and design services, you begin to see new opportunities. You also solve the problem of "how do I get an online teaching job if I don't have any online teaching experience?" by creating your own experience. As I started developing content for social media, I began connecting with people who needed help with social media or who wanted me to write for their publications, which furthered my web presence and enhanced my brand. Likewise, developing content in your niche will expose you to people who need your services, and will differentiate your CV from the others in the pile when you are applying for online teaching jobs.

Finally, remember that none of this assumes a "one and done" approach. Building a brand takes time and effort. Then again, anything worthwhile that you do takes time and effort. Do not assume that a career as an academic in higher education is easy, fair, or relaxing. However, it does not have to be poverty inducing, and it can be quite rewarding. Gain attention with your brand, build your expertise, and seek opportunities that pay well and are worthwhile.

Promotion

Now that we have discussed building your brand, we shift to exploring how to use social media to promote it. Think of social media as the amplifier of your brand as well as a means to build relationships with people in your niche. Think social media isn't crucial to finding an online teaching job? Think again. As this chapter will show, social job seekers are wealthier than those who do not use social media to search for jobs. Using social media isn't just a good idea; it's an essential tool in your kit to finding the job you want.

Amplify your brand

Social media can help you increase your brand exposure, demonstrate your authority, and generate awareness of an upcoming event (such as a book launch or a presentation). Social media can be overwhelming, however. Where should you start? If you try to be on too many platforms, you likely will present a watered down version of yourself while finding social media to be stressful and time consuming.

Goals. I suggest starting with your goals. What do you want social media to do for you? What are your career and online presence goals? What is your niche? Knowing the answers to these things can help you design your strategy.

The online instructor. For example, if you want to teach online science courses, you may decide that your career goals are to have 3-5 schools where you work as an adjunct while at the same time you want to have a strong presence online in order to attract an audience to your blog about alternative health options. You have written content on your blog about the science of ancient alternative health treatments. You are considering writing an ebook for Amazon to further your brand and potentially increase your income. Your hope is that you will increase your online teaching opportunities and your entrepreneurial income by building and amplifying your brand.

Once you have established your goals, match them to the appropriate social media channels. While Facebook, YouTube, and iTunes dominate the scene in terms of millions of users per platform, don't discount some of the smaller social media platforms that may be more useful for your brand. Pinterest, LinkedIn (especially for academics), and Google+ (for ranking highly in Google search engines) are worth exploring. Understanding the different platforms and what they offer can help you prioritize. Read *Social Media Mastery* to learn more about the specific platforms, and watch my Social Media How To videos to understand how to use them. Go to http://edjourneys.com/howto for help.

What do hiring managers do?

JobVite is a recruiting software company that conducts annual surveys on how job seekers find jobs and how recruiters find candidates. The findings are always fascinating and always instructive. The 2014 survey held some interesting nuggets about the social job seekers (i.e., the job seekers who wisely use social media to increase their potential for finding jobs).

One of the most fascinating findings of the survey was that those who earn over $100,000 used social media more than any other income bracket to find their job. Social media may not be the way you prefer to job hunt, but it is superior as a means for finding high paying jobs.

According to JobVite, 93% of job recruiters *are* looking at your social profiles, with 42% of them influenced to make a hiring decision (both positive and negative) by your social profiles. Use social media as a way to differentiate your brand from the hundreds or thousands of other applicants.

LinkedIn. Another finding of the JobVite survey was that LinkedIn is the main social media tool used by job recruiters, with 94% of hiring managers active on LinkedIn. By contrast, Facebook is the second most used tool, with only 65% active on that platform. As a potential faculty member, you cannot afford to ignore LinkedIn as a hiring tool. Make sure that your LinkedIn profile is completely filled out, that you have a professional picture, and that you include keywords that identify your brand in your title and top sections. A free LinkedIn account permits you to embed your content, so take advantage of this feature. Embed important publications and presentations on your LinkedIn profile to demonstrate your authority. In addition, LinkedIn enables you to embed images, videos, and audio clips.

The JobVite survey also indicated that the quality of social media posts made by job applicants matters. Grammar teachers can rejoice that poor grammar skills demonstrated on social media posts can kill a job candidate's chances for getting hired. Likewise, profanity on social media is a major detractor when it comes to what hiring managers think of you. In fact, grammar and profanity are far more likely to get your CV put in the trash than are the posts about drinking, unless updating your Facebook status while drunk results in poor grammar or profanity. Unfair? Perhaps, but who said this process was fair? Your goal is to establish a professional online persona. Avoid posting content where you come across as immature, unprofessional, or uneducated.

Leslie Bowman, former private investigator and current online professor, author, and editor, suggests keeping private information private and public information professional. You may decide that deleting your account or using a nickname that will not identify you as the job applicant is a good option. Alternatively, if you do not want your students finding you on Facebook, a family nickname may be a good strategy to consider.

Provide quality content on LinkedIn by using the LinkedIn Publisher feature. If you do not have a blog, publishing quality posts on LinkedIn Publisher can help you demonstrate expertise, and your connections may then decide to share it with their connections.

Google. Use Google platforms to enhance your online search engine discoverability. If you are the science and alternative medicine potential faculty member who wants to demonstrate your expertise, consider holding webinars about alternative health options using Google Hangouts on Air. A free service, Google Hangouts on Air can be viewed by anyone, can be saved on your YouTube account to be shared later, and are heavily indexed by Google. You can embed Google Hangouts on Air on your website, send invitees the link to the page with the embedded window on it, and tell them to refresh the page at the start time to watch you live from your website.

YouTube and Google+. Google owns YouTube, so creating videos related to your niche can also enhance your search engine optimization. While Google+ may seem like Google's less popular version of Facebook, it should not be ignored. Very often, I tell my social media clients to pick two platforms and Google+ to demonstrate their authority. Why? Because what you type into Google+ on a public post (meaning that the post is set so that anyone, not just your connections, can see it) is indexed by Google, comes up on Google search engines for the appropriate keywords, and enhances your visibility.

Google uses something called a social search, which means that who you are connected to on Google+ will determine what results you see when you Google something on the search engine. My Google search results are different from your Google search results for the same search term. Therefore, if you use Google+ to connect with people in the higher education sphere, as well as people related to your field, your content will appear on their search results when they search using keywords related to your niche. Nice!

Networking. Beyond increasing your exposure, use social media to network for jobs. Join networking groups on LinkedIn where you can interact and build relationships. While there are dozens of adjunct faculty LinkedIn groups, I recommend you fish in a different pond where there is less competition. Research the schools where you are interested in teaching, and join groups where their administrators and hiring managers belong. Engage in those groups purposefully by offering valuable content, contributing ideas without dominating discussions, and demonstrating your online professional personality. Use Google Alerts to curate web content related to topics that you can then share and discuss in a LinkedIn group. I talk about this strategy in-depth in *Social Networking Success*.

Twitter. Twitter is also a worthwhile platform to use to expand your reach and to network. Twitter enables you to connect directly with anyone, tag anyone, and participate in tweet chats to build your network. Twitter chats for higher education can be a valuable way to connect with those in the higher education landscape. Likewise, using relevant hashtags related to specific content within higher education can help you gain the attention of those with similar interests. Tweeting with hashtags can be especially effective if you are attending academic conferences where the organizers have established a conference hashtag. Follow that hashtag before, during, and after the conference to connect with highly engaged twitter users in your field. Even if you cannot attend the conference, it is still worthwhile to follow the hashtag and reply to tweets where appropriate. For more information on the best hashtags, twitter chats, and strategies for higher education faculty on Twitter, go to http://edjourneys.com/twitter.

Build a blog. Remember that social media is rented

space. What you write there may be your content, but it will be managed and delivered by a social media company that is not working for you. Therefore, consider developing a blog where you can write your original content, share tips, sell your products and services, and create your image exactly the way you want. From there, you can promote your blog posts via social media. You can also include the first few paragraphs of a blog post on Google+ with a hyperlink to your blog so viewers can read the rest of your post. This strategy increases your Google search engine optimization while also getting readers to your blog.

While free blog services are available, I recommend that you purchase your own domain name and use an inexpensive hosting service. Free blogging services limit your ability to customize and sell on your site. Including banner ads (if you choose to do that) is typically prohibited.

I use BlueHost for my hosting service as I find it easy to set up a blog with them, and find their customer service very helpful via both phone and chat. They give you the first domain for free. I also use Wordpress.org (not to be confused with the free blogging service Wordpress.com) as the web software for the professor websites that I build as it is free, open-source, has wide support on the web via Wordpress communities, has hundreds of themes, and also has premium themes for even greater customization.

Ultimately, your goal is to deliver your content to an audience eager to learn more about you. After you have perfected your CV and created a strategy for submitting your online teaching job applications, it's time to set up your social media accounts and promote what you are doing online.

For all of my latest books and blog posts about social media, please go to edjourneys.com.

~Tara Ross, PhD

Chapter 11 – Must-Have Technologies

"Education is not preparation for life;
education is life itself."
— John Dewey

Teaching online is exactly what it sounds like: an online, remote job. As with many online jobs, there are essentials and nonessentials, and one of the essentials is technology—lots of it! Technology not only is required to actually do the job, but much of it is required to keep your hectic life organized while meeting many demanding deadlines, scheduling conference calls, and reminding yourself of important to-do items.

The payoff for implementing some of these ideas is immeasurable, but the most important task is first to get hired; so get what you need to do the job, then get the job, and then get what you need to do the job better so you can maximize your earnings! Let's begin with what you absolutely must have to do your job. That, after all, is most important.

Internet Access

When it comes to Internet access, speed isn't

everything; it's the only thing. Don't even think about using a dial-up phone modem (I am not sure anyone even has that anymore anyway) if you expect to be an online faculty member. You cannot afford to waste time uploading files, downloading files, and opening websites when that time could be put to more practical use. The extra cost of high-speed Internet access in your home will easily pay for itself if you teach just one online course per year. Long ago, some schools would reimburse you for it; not so anymore, unless you are a full time employee – then it may be an option. Also, the cost of having high-speed Internet access is tax-deductible if you are earning income as an online professor (but ask your tax guy or gal to confirm)! Obviously connecting your Internet access (Wide Area Network: WAN) to a WiFi (wireless fidelity) router is useful. I have personally found ASUS routers to last the longest and have the best built-in firewall and proxy options, but most any high-speed router will do.

Computers

Of all the equipment in your home office, the most critical is the computer, and it needs to be a fast one. This means your computer must be able to take full advantage of the high-speed Internet access and must be capable of multitasking well enough that you aren't frustrated, nor are you waiting for your machine to catch up while you have 10 web browsers open and your email up constantly, recording videos and doing live chats. This is one case where the speed of your computer truly will make an impact on how fast you are capable of doing your work.

There many components in a computer, as you know if you've ever opened one. Every one of them contributes to speed in some way. The speed of the computer's central processing unit (CPU) is measured in gigahertz (GHz) unless your computer is really old – then it's MHz – with higher numbers indicating higher speed. If you buy one of the slowest on the market just to save money, you are buying trouble; you will find that it is incapable of keeping up with the programs you install. You will need plenty of memory and decent hard drive space; anything less than 2TB (terabytes) is not going to last long in my view. If you intend to have multiple windows and applications open, you'll find memory is used up quickly, and your computer begins using what is known as virtual memory. Virtual memory is hard disk space that is used as temporary memory, so it's extremely slow. Memory has speed, too, so get fast memory.

Some of you may choose to work off a laptop computer (I do most of the time), while others may prefer a desktop. Be sure you have a reliable machine. You cannot afford to have your computer crash or be bogged down with software you don't need, and I highly recommend a redundant computer in case you lose a drive and need to wait for Amazon to deliver another one. If you are not computer savvy, you might want to invest in a service where you get 24/7 technical support. My personal preference is to steer clear from name-brand computers and have a clone built at a local computer store, unless you know how to do it yourself, which is cheaper and often as reliable as or more reliable than name brands. Think of it like the generic products in the grocery store for which you pay less because their packaging and marketing costs are less. Also, it won't come with a bunch of software installed that slows down your computer.

If you are like most people and don't have a lot of computer knowledge, then buy a brand name, but format the hard drive when you get it and start over, reinstalling the operating system and the software you need. I know that it sounds like a lot of trouble – and in fact it is. But you can easily speed a machine up by starting from scratch and installing only the software you want or need versus the junk software that manufacturers typically install.

To help maintain reliability, there are certain programs every computer needs, which will be addressed later in the chapter. You must also try to implement certain practices to minimize problems. If possible, download and test potentially unusable or unneeded software on another machine, not the one you teach on. Consider your teaching personal computer (PC) your production server for business; no testing is ever done in a production server in a reputable IT shop. It's done in the test environment, or what we call the "sand box," before it is transferred to production. It's amazing what using a download site can do to your PC when you install a free tool that tracks your every move as part of its free use agreement. You may not have the luxury of a second computer, but if you plan to teach online more than just as a hobby, it is worth the investment in a second machine, which doesn't have to be new or even top-of-the-line.

You should also consider having a laptop even if you prefer to work off a desktop. Even with the best computer equipment, you cannot control how often the Internet may go down in your home. Short of a hurricane that wipes out power in your city, there is no reason you cannot take your laptop to the nearest coffee shop and continue to do your work. Moreover, there is the added benefit of being able to take a trip while working on your laptop to keep up with your classes. Name brands are fine here, but get something fast. Don't skimp on the processor or memory to save a few hundred bucks.

Backups

Backups are the second most critical item, next to Internet access, that you will need for your computer. You absolutely must have backups. Some online systems store student grades on their systems; others don't and you must keep spreadsheets and records. Certainly you will build a database of discussion responses and videos. I like Norton Ghost for backups (and I use version 15). I can make a mirror image of a drive, and I keep the recovery CD with me on the road. If the drive dies (or worse), I can rebuild my computer in 12 hours by having a friend send me the backup drive. You can back up files to cloud services like Dropbox, Google Drive or the myriad of others out there, but it will still require you to reinstall your applications and reconfigure your computer – which is why I like ghost. Pop it in and the mirror is restored.

Other solutions include backing up to a remote server (there are many services you can buy to do this) or simply moving data perhaps from a desktop to a laptop weekly. I cannot emphasize enough how absolutely terrible solutions like Carbonite are for online professors. We have a lot of data! I recently tried to use it and after 2 months it had moved 2% of my data up to the server. I have a 130mbps download and 50mbps upload connection (very fast). The servers that do the automated backups are horribly slow. Trying to restore or backup from these types of services, from my experience, has been a joke.

The key with backups is consistency and making certain you have at least one copy off-site in case someone steals your computers. Make sure your backups are working and make sure you do them often. This will save you tremendous headaches should something become corrupted, you get hit with a virus, have hard-drive failure, or worse.

Also, if your PC is down, you won't have time to get it up and running before teaching again. Students will be waiting; you'll need to take your laptop to a local coffee shop and get working, then come home and fix up your machine. If you have off-site backups, you can pull data from anywhere you have Internet access. Ideally, if you set your PC to automatically back up to the Internet nightly, your risk of losing files is minimized.

Organization Systems and PDAs

It doesn't matter whether you use Outlook, your iPhone calendar, Google calendar, or some off-the-wall product you got free online, but use something to remind yourself when to submit attendance at certain schools, when various programs start, when to set up new classes, when to email your bosses, and various other recurring tasks. Make sure you can schedule recurring appointments, and if you can categorize, it will make doing so even easier.

Now, this brings up yet another requirement. Whatever you choose, it *must* synchronize to a smart phone. If you teach for more than seven schools, watch out for Android limitations on the number of email addresses you can add. I was (am) a big Android fan, but had to move to Apple because they do not limit how many email addresses you can have. With 10 personal accounts alone, a Droid wasn't an option for me and it may not be for some of you, either. With mobile applications of some of the LMSs, you can login and work from your smartphone, too. I personally like adding every email address at every school into my phone as it allows me to check them under the "all mail" option at one time, and reply to students and bosses as items come in. Some schools do not allow for mobile access, but I have found 90% do.

Voice Over Internet Protocol (VoIPs)

VoIP was a "nice to have" in the old days when we had to pay for every long distance phone call, but since most home landline providers offer free long distance now, it is less of an issue. I recommend a VoIP service (like Google) and also a landline in case Internet is out. With my students and bosses, I Skype, FaceTime and Google Chat.

Unified Messaging

Unified messaging is a system that sends voice mail into your email. Many cable providers that also sell home phone service have this built into their service. This allows you several advantages: (1) if you are traveling out of the country, you can forward your cell phone to the unified messaging system and still check your voice mail and not miss messages; (2) you can retain your privacy and not give out your cell number unless for emergencies; (3) it's nice to have everything in one system. I like K7.net (online at www.k7.net) and Google Voice, which will follow you if you want it to. I recommend asking callers to leave their email address so you can respond to them by email if you prefer. This saves headaches if you're out of the country. The system automatically records the number the caller is calling from and puts it in the subject of the message (unless it's a blocked number) so if you do need to call back, you will know the number without having to listen to the entire message.

Comfortable and Ergonomic Workstation Setups

You will be on your computer a lot. Have a comfortable, ergonomic workstation environment and save your wrists and hands. Dr. Babb recommends natural keyboards; you can even purchase a natural mouse depending on the size of your hand. Check out the numerous ergonomic sites and be sure you are comfortable. The Microsoft 5000 quite literally saved my wrists from surgery.

Instant Messaging

One option to consider for allowing your students to get hold of you is instant messaging (IM). You can use any of several systems, including America Online (AOL) (does anyone still use this?),

Microsoft MSN or Google Chat, among many others. Having one of these or another of your choosing will help you keep people from phoning on your cell. Some find the instant messaging more annoying than phone calls, though, so this is your call.

Fax – Electronic and Traditional

Electronic faxes will allow you to send and receive faxes by email and via a Web interface. This is incredibly convenient, especially when traveling. In addition, moving is a breeze; your numbers don't change! Traditional fax machines act as copiers and also let you send out quickly, another consideration. I use both; a traditional fax machine for sending and receiving large files or contracts unrelated to teaching, and a MyFax account for smaller teaching-related faxes. Either way, you'll need to fax contracts to schools and even sometimes copies of textbook pages to students who might find that a page is missing from their text. Add this capability to your home office.

PDF Converters

Adobe's Portable Document Format (PDF) has become the de facto standard for sharing documents and information. Even official documents are being sent online this way. PDFs are less difficult to tamper with than Word or Excel documents, for instance, and most people are able to view them on their equipment. PDF readers are free online, and most universities will share information this way. A PDF converter lets you take, for instance, a Word file and save it as a PDF file, and vice versa. This lets you manipulate PDF files to sign contracts and easily send them back; it also lets you save, for instance, a Word test file into a PDF that students can't copy and paste from. This software has a multitude of uses and is relatively inexpensive. I like PDF Converter Professional as it allows me to compile PDFs from multiple files into one (many schools require uploading your documents like this into their job application systems). CutePDF Writer is also very good.

Printers

Even though you're teaching online, you'll find yourself printing student files or contracts. I would recommend asking around on the forum to find out what other professors use that are efficient. I like multifunction printers for their efficiency.

Backup Internet Providers

It might not be a bad idea to have a backup Internet provider, or to have hotspot capability on your smartphone in case your Internet goes out.

Uninterruptible Power Supply (UPS)

Don't run your PCs and laptops without an uninterruptible power supply (UPS). Not only will a UPS protect your equipment from power surges and lightning, but your system will continue running even in a power outage. I connect my modem and router to it, and can continue running without power as long as the cable provider keeps their equipment up.

Virus Protection

This is a must-have on any machine. Virus writers write destructive forces faster than we can keep up. Get a good one, pay for it, and have it auto-update its definition files daily while you're not using your computer. Let it auto-scan every morning sometime before you start work. Everyone has different opinions about each one. The two I use are Spybot Search and Destroy and McAfee. Check with your Internet provider (and universities) as many times they offer it free or highly discounted. I leave my computers running all of the time and let them scan and back up at nighttime.

Email Accounts with In-Box High Limits

Some of your learners will send you enormously large files; some of your bosses will, too. However, many schools still limit the size of attachments to very small sizes, or limit mailboxes in general to a low disk space threshold. At the minimum, you should be able to receive a 25 megabyte email. I recommend using one of the big companies like Yahoo, Hotmail, or Gmail to store and tag files. If you use Gmail, you can turn Google Labs on and get some really cool features, like canned responses ("Have you read the syllabus?") and multiple color flag identifiers, along with subfolders. Some schools will allow you Post Office Protocol (POP) or Internet Message Access Protocol (IMAP) access into their email, and if that is the case you may be able to have it load into your major mail provider account. Just make sure the school allows you to reply from there; some schools ask you reply only from the school system. You can also have all your email come into Outlook or Outlook Express to avoid checking each school's Web mail system. However, we must caution you that schools usually require you to use their servers. This means you need to have both the Post Office Protocol, (POP3, incoming) and Simple Mail Transfer Protocol (SMTP, outgoing) mail addresses for their servers, if possible, or use your own local ISP for the SMTP address; however, you must be sure to send out through the account the mail came in on. This way the university has the email coming from their school, yet you're using your own system.

Professional Websites

A web presence gives you credibility and allows you to expand your reach. It gives you a platform by which you can give resources to students, show your bio to potential universities you want to work for, and demonstrate that you take the job seriously. This helps make you real to your online world, something that is tough to do sometimes. The more you can make yourself a real person behind a keyboard, the better off you'll be. Dr. Tara Ross, as the social media expert for our company and guru to thousands of professors, will be expanding on this in the book chapter on Social Media.

Office Suites

By office suite, we don't mean renting an office, although sometimes with the noise of children that would be a nice thing! I mean acquiring software including a word processor, spreadsheet program, and presentation package. I love that we can access work from Google, but – unfortunately, it is highly inconvenient and inefficient compared with downloading student files, particularly for systems that require that we upload the marked up version. Some newer LMSs allow us to read the entire file and even comment online, but there comes a time we will have to save and open a file. I know ... I know ... We all know that Microsoft Office dominates in this area, and most schools will use these. Be able to at least support them.

Password Storage

You will be asked to remember more passwords than you ever thought imaginable in your life! This means you need a password and site storage utility. I personally like LastPass. In 2014 when the Heartbleed bug was made public, LastPass identified the sites where I had used the same password and recommended I change them. Combined with its ability to randomize passwords and then store them encrypted on their server and synchronize to all of your devices, including mobile devices, it is a dream come true for efficiency. Storing passwords in your browser is insecure, and while many argue having any single point of failure with all passwords is also insecure, I find their encryption technology and methods to be safe and sound (and my background is in IT). That said, nothing is foolproof. I have colleagues who also store passwords in their safe deposit boxes. Whatever you feel most comfortable with is what you should do.

Video Capability

There is no way around this. No matter how many hours we spend in our pajamas working (yeah, you!) you will have a day when you have to throw a professional looking jacket over the PJs, put on a headband and comb your eyebrows to do a video. Whether it's a welcome video, a meeting with a boss, a synchronous session, or an interview, someone at some point will want to see your face. Get a decent quality camera and microphone and make sure it works every now and again.

Other Technology Recommendations from the Forums

Our forum members have some other great technology suggestions for efficiency and sanity! If you would like to read every comment, you can find it at www.facebook.com/groups/onlineprofessors.

Docusign account is used for contracts at more schools today than ever.
Evernote is for storing account information and remembering notes.
The website www.toggl.com is good for timing your work and seeing what universities are paying you.

Khan Academy website is a good reference on many topics, especially math.

Boingo is an as-you-go data plan.

Use SlideShare to upload lecture notes or slide presentations and embed them into Blackboard.

Office 365 enables you to access your data from any device.

TypeItIn is a great tool for repeating comments by clicking a button on your desktop.

High quality, noise canceling headphones are a necessity to block noise and keep the energy up.

Many online professors use multiple computer screens (this can come in very handy and save your neck from pain).

SoundCloud is used for integration of audio into lectures.

Dragon Naturally Speaking is another way to save valuable body parts from stress and, for some, is faster than typing.

Standing desks or treadmill desks are useful if you want to keep moving and maintain ergonomics.

Ergonomic mouse or newer style replacement is helpful for hands and wrists.

Private Internet access, or a virtual private network, comes in handy to surf safely and securely while away.

Livescribe pen is for marking up papers, taking notes or converting handwriting into text.

Synchronized queues for integration with Google, such as GQueues, which also was recommended in the forums.

Camtasia is a screen recording software tool that records what you're doing on your screen including audio, video, narration and description of slides you are developing or reviewing. This is a relatively painless way to create more engaging course content and share it with others.

Making Your Life Easier and the Students Happier

Most of the technologies mentioned thus far are designed for you to support your students, keep your life more organized, and make your business easier to manage. Some also help you look good to your bosses and make you more accessible. I recommend giving students many ways to contact you, while keeping it simple enough that you'll actually use them.

Here is what I offer to my own students. I am a tech nerd and I work on social media all of the time, so many of these are no big deal to me but understandably not for everyone:

Twitter direct message questions to: @danibabb
Email (school and personal for emergencies)
My k7 number for non-emergencies
Cell phone
Facebook page messages
Whatsapp support
iMessaging
Skype
Google Hangouts

I selected the tools I am "on" most of the time so that it isn't an extra step each time I sit down to work. Also, these tools work on my smartphone, so they notify me when a text or Skype request comes in and I get a badge when a notification comes in on

Facebook. Everyone will choose tools that are easiest and best for them. My goal, particularly teaching technology courses, is to be streamlined, efficient, and to be where the students already are – which usually means online browsing social media.

Setting Up a System to Support Flexibility and Travel

When you begin life as an adjunct, you may not be traveling much for work. As time goes on, you will find that this schedule picks up much more dramatically, particularly if you teach in doctoral programs that have residencies that you participate in. You'll want to set up a system that supports flexibility and travel. This means several things:

- Data that's easily transferable between laptop and desktop or automatically syncs (Dropbox, GDrive, SkyDrive, etc.).
- An organization method for your calendar that keeps you consistent and working well (I use Google Calendar and sync it to my smartphone).
- Smartphone with fast Internet access.
- A laptop with wireless capability.
- A straightforward, reliable laptop configured just like your desktop. This includes software you will use for only one class, but may need while traveling. Better to always install on both PCs than be traveling and realize you don't have what you need.

The key here is to understand how you do things, your lifestyle, what's important to you, and how you work. Then mimic this in your technology. You will find traveling a joy and far less stressful.

I would encourage you to share new technology tips in our forum and tell others what you find useful and productive. I learn of the best tools from my colleagues and many professors in our group are gurus with efficiency tools!

Chapter 12 – Maintaining Relationships and Growing Your Business

---

"None of us got where we are solely by pulling
ourselves up by our bootstraps.
We got here because somebody – a parent, a
teacher, an Ivy League crony, or a few nuns – bent
down and helped us pick up our boots."
— Thurgood Marshall

Either you've begun teaching for at least one
university, or are being trained to do so, and you're on
your way to a successful life as an adjunct, or you've
made the life-changing decision to earn your degree
and pursue this incredible life. Whether this is a
transition period for you or your intended future
career, you will find many rewards and opportunities
in the virtual world.

As you begin your new adventure and freedom
working online, and have quite possibly taught or at
least trained in your first course, maybe it was
everything you dreamed of and more, maybe it was
just an okay experience, or maybe it was more painful
than a root canal. Before you either pack it in because
it's not what you expected or go to the opposite
extreme and quit your full-time job because you struck

pay dirt, you need to reflect on your goals.

Personal Motivation

Why are you doing this? Are you teaching online so you can share the wisdom that you have gathered over the years with those who might benefit from it? Do you enjoy facilitating adult learners (this is by far your largest audience) who bring their own knowledge and expertise to the table? Are you just hoping to have stimulating discussions on your favorite subjects because you cannot do so at work or at home? Are you trying to make contacts for your full-time career in consulting or some other profession? Are you trying to repay a debt that a former teacher of yours told you that you owed for what he/she did for you? Are you in pursuit of a full-time teaching position? Are you just looking to supplement your income? Take some time to reflect on why you are doing what you're doing.

Whatever your needs and goals, ask yourself if online teaching is going to meet them. Perhaps you've tried it but it doesn't really stimulate you or let you earn enough money for the time invested, or it doesn't give you the fulfillment you expected. Or maybe it does all of this and more. This is not a fly-by-night opportunity; it is real work, and often hard work at that, but it has incredible upsides and is one of the most fulfilling jobs imaginable. The commitment involved to make this a success is huge, for it takes a lot of effort not only to get the job, but to keep the job, too, and you cannot even think about joining this profession in a full-time capacity without first earning an accredited graduate degree.

You must have an unselfish attitude and genuinely care that others learn. The respect you get from being a faculty member is unprecedented. Besides making some excellent income, the biggest thing you can make is a difference. How many jobs are there where you can feel good about what you do while actually making a living from home or while traveling? How many jobs are there where you touch so many lives at once, and people will talk of you for years to come? How many jobs are there where you are treated as an expert because of your title and where the respect is yours to lose? How many jobs are there where you will have had dozens of good and bad role models to observe firsthand for several years?

Keys to Successful Relationships in a Virtual World

Just as with any job or career you undertake, you must maintain relationships to be successful in the online world. It can be even more difficult and demanding because, unlike a more traditional workplace, you don't actually see your boss very often, if ever. Social media has surely changed this process as well. Despite this difficulty, you must make yourself known and be considered present. Your bosses must know you by name and think of you when they think of various positive qualities (like responsive, student centered, a great writer, etc.), and it is your job to maintain these virtual relationships.

With the growth of online education, deans sometimes spend more time recruiting and training new faculty than they do maintaining the current ones, so it is easy to be forgotten if you are not the go-to faculty member. This is not always intentional, but it does happen. Sometimes you will learn that you were deselected but never told, or that your course has been dropped from the catalog but no one bothered to find a different course for you. You may find yourself creating a canned email asking if you still have a job, which is not a very good feeling. It's very much like asking a customer if they would like to continue with your services, which is why entrepreneurial skills are valuable as an adjunct.

So how do you maintain relationships when you never see your manager? You could just do your job and chances are your contracts will be renewed, but your workload probably won't increase. You probably won't be considered a subject matter expert or be at the top on the list for well-paying speaking engagements. Most likely, you won't be considered for development work, either. You need to be on top of your game and proactive with your work. In IT, we use the word *ping*. To ping means to hit or tap another server. According to SearchNetworking.com, "Ping is a basic Internet program that allows a user to verify that a particular IP address exists and can accept requests. Loosely, ping means 'to get the attention of' or 'to check for the presence of' another party online." Ping is the best word we can find to describe what you need to do with your online managers. But first, you need to know who they are – something that is often unique to our profession and causes concern for newbies in the workplace. At some point, you won't worry about such things anymore! It's probably hard to imagine if you are just considering this as a career choice and haven't begun working yet.

In the real world, you need to ping your managers on a regular basis. This is true in the virtual world too. If you use a smartphone for scheduling, you might consider scheduling a recurring event in which you find an article of interest and send it to your managers. Don't do a mass "to" email! Be sure to email each person privately and indicate how you thought it might pertain to that person's school, if in fact you do. Otherwise a simple "I found this article interesting and thought I'd pass it on" is fine. In some cases, a general email inquiry might just get forwarded to another department chair who is looking for faculty. It's far easier to give additional classes to existing faculty than to hire a new one.

Some other examples of emails you might want to send are:

Last year, I updated XYZ course. It might be time to consider another quick glance at the course because several technologies have changed. Last year when we discussed convergence in the course, we did not have the ability to segment traffic like we do today. This is one example of areas that may need updating. FYI.

Or:

Thanks for forwarding my evaluations. It's very motivating to hear of student satisfaction, and I wanted you to know how much I enjoy working for you!

I have a boss in Tennessee who backs her faculty so much that when I see bosses do the opposite, it reminds me to send her a thank you email. If it crosses your mind and it's a kind thing to do, my recommendation is to just do it.

Quick emails are often best, because they don't ask for anything but they do show your desire to work there and subtly reinforce the impression that students think you're doing well. "Thanks for your confidence in me. I won't let you down" is a nice reply to an email from your boss letting you know your contract has been renewed. Sincerity is definitely a key here. It's okay to toot your own horn; just be sure you're also being honest and genuine in your approach.

Find your own style, but remind your bosses that you exist. Remind them of your capabilities. Remind them of other areas of interest that you have. Sometimes it doesn't pay off because you're filling a need for them in the area where you already teach, but sometimes it does. At the very least, they are reminded of your existence! Sending greeting cards for holidays or boss's day is entirely appropriate, though I have run into cases where bosses donated items and asked me not to send anything in the future because they are state or government supported, so be careful of that. Most of the time I have found a small gesture over the holidays is appropriate and appreciated. Remember the administrative assistants, too. They help us with a lot of tasks and often with contracts. Think of them as gatekeepers; they often are. Just a simple, "Thank you," email to these gatekeepers will go a long way.

Fit in before you stick out! And once you do fit

in, you can speak up about changes you recommend. But be careful; if you speak too soon, you may be seen as a complainer or misfit with the organizational culture; if you speak too late after everyone sees the problems, you may be seen as a blamer who looks for reasons why things aren't working well but won't accept personal responsibility; and if you time it right, you are a team player and a trusted adviser. The object is to join the team, become a vital part of the team, become a superstar, and then seek to become a team leader if you so choose.

Varying Demands by University

Every university that you work for will have different demands of you, as addressed in chapter nine. Some require weekly attendance reporting and some don't require it at all. Some require that you hold regular and posted office hours, and some don't require office hours. When you go through training, the requirements of you as a faculty member will be clearly laid out. Ask any questions you have then, because you will want to be clear when each item is due. Note it somewhere, and then if you get to teach a class with that college, find an organizational method that works for you and stick with it.

Remember to keep your own time demands in check, and realize that one downside to this career is that most likely schools won't take breaks at the same time. This means very little, if any, vacation for you; the last thing you want is to be burned out before you even start, and it can happen. Find ways to manage your time and create personal boundaries, such as not working past a certain time of night or not giving out a cell phone number that is only for family. You will learn with time what works for you and what doesn't. In my case, being very available all of the time and integrating home and work rather than creating boundaries is less stressful for me, and I hope (time will tell!) I am developing a strongly modeled work ethic for my daughter where she does not feel she has to choose between family and a career.

The important thing is that you identify the demands placed on you, clearly note them, find an organizational method that works for you, and begin to effectively manage your time and the demands placed on you.

Keeping Everyone Happy

Every university and each school within it will have particular demands. Remember that often an accreditation body governs these demands, or the university's interpretation of the rules, and without this accreditation, enrollment drops and so do your teaching opportunities. You do not want to work for diploma mills and you don't want to work for universities that don't respect your position.

So, while juggling multiple positions at multiple universities, how do you keep everyone happy? For starters, tell people what to expect, or at a minimum meet the guidelines set by the school. When I am hired, I always send every boss, if I know who he or she is, my cell number and an emergency email address. I know, having managed faculty, that there is nothing worse than sending an email on Friday evening to a faculty who hasn't set up their course starting Monday, and not knowing if they have read it, if the course will be set up on time, and not having a backup phone number to reach them. Try to put yourself in your boss's shoes.

Everything you commit to must always be followed through in its entirety. This means your commitments need to be realistic and not forgotten! It sounds simple enough, but when your course development manager is emailing you daily with course updates that need to be done, three bosses are asking questions, and you have classes at five different schools, this can be quite a feat. Failure to meet student commitments will quickly be noticed by the department chairpersons, and this is not the kind of attention that you want. Once you make a commitment, find a way to schedule it and remind yourself of it so you can work on it and beat your own deadline. Sometimes your needs and the school's needs won't mesh and you have to make concessions.

Of course, work must be completed within the established time frame; if grades are due in seven days, you can't email your boss and tell him or her to expect them in 10 days! The deadlines are not negotiable. Just pace yourself and schedule accordingly. Be very organized and diligent, and meet your commitments. Should you fail at a commitment, own up to it, take your bumps and bruises, and move on. You will be respected more than if you try to create a lame excuse. You know when your students use one, and teachers are finely tuned to notice such things. More often than not, a slipup will be overlooked if it is infrequent. If you find that meeting commitments is becoming challenging, then cut back on the commitments until you have more time or can perhaps reorganize yourself. You will be respected more for declining an opportunity than failing at one.

Next, stay in touch. One thing department chairpersons have noted they like is feedback on a course – what students complain about or like. Some schools do a good job of trying to get the faculty community established and maintained, but others do not. So reach out first and provide valuable information.

It is important to build rapport with your management. Once you have it, you will be free to express yourself and your thoughts professionally to your manager, within reason. Stay away, at all costs, from public venting sessions that often occur on faculty newsgroups or with the dreaded reply-all function. I have read many of those reply-all emails thinking, "sucks to be him right now." I am often surprised if those faculty members have jobs next term. This is a death sentence in online teaching. Claiming academic freedom will get you only so far! All in all, be responsive to your managers and your students, even if only to say that you'll be responding to a request "Thursday morning." Follow through with that commitment, which will require scheduling and organization on your part.

Getting Organized

Getting, being, and staying organized are critical factors for successfully managing your bosses and their requests, keeping everyone happy, and making your mark in your online teaching career. You may choose to use a technological method of organization, as discussed in the technology chapter (chapter 10), or you may choose to use the more traditional approach of sticky notes and agenda books. Either way, record even the most mundane things, unless you have the memory of a superhero. Whatever your approaches to scheduling, find something that works for you and stick with it.

Additional Work Opportunities within the Schools You Work For

Once you have a job at a university, you will want to expand your workload if you like working for it, or reduce it if not. After you have an established positive rapport with management, you can look for additional opportunities within the school you work for. Sometimes the best way is to simply send an email to your boss indicating that you enjoy working for XYZ School. Indicate why your schedule has opened, maybe you dropped some schools you don't feel have credible programs, for instance, and then explain that you are pursuing further opportunities at schools you enjoy and with managers you respect. Use your own words here; this needs to reflect your true thoughts and feelings. Then simply ask for additional opportunities. You may suggest course revision, development work, or even courses you saw on the schedule of classes that you feel qualified to teach and are interested in. Either way, your candor will prove effective in showing your interest and also perhaps finding additional opportunities. You may ask your boss what that university requires of someone to be a subject matter expert, and then clearly state what you're an expert in.

Some areas in which you may be able to pick up additional work include new course development, minor and major course revision, book evaluation, additional courses in the same or new programs, as well as becoming a lead faculty member, dissertation committee member, comprehensive exam committee member, committee chair, or mentor. You may also pick up an additional workload at residencies or school colloquia, which are usually required for doctoral and some master's learners.

You may be asked to serve as a quality auditor for new faculty, wherein you evaluate how well a new instructor is meeting the school standards in delivering a course. You may also be asked to serve as a quality coach and spend several weeks working one-on-one with an instructor who failed his/her quality audit. As you might surmise, if you are asked to be either a quality coach or a quality auditor, it is indeed a compliment; it means they see you as a role model, and you should take these jobs when offered.

Lessons Learned

I didn't want to wrap up this book without offering some personal lessons learned from my own experiences and from clients in the last decade.

Keep yourself well networked in the online world. You will be amazed at who will show up in a training class that you already know, like your boss at another school who assumes and expects your anonymity, or who will be made a dean at a college where you work. You won't know when your former students suddenly become your managers and yes, this has happened to me, three times in fact!

Likewise, you never know who from your doctoral committee you might end up working *with* as peers later! Don't burn bridges. Make your reasons for doing things clear and logical. Keep your sense of humor.

Read documentation that the university sends out. As cumbersome as it might be sometimes – particularly if you work with students in a doctoral setting – understanding what you're doing and why will keep you out of hot water and make you look good to those who count. In the last three years in particular, the for-profit sector has created completely new methods for managing dissertations and dissertation mentees. It can be exhausting to figure out what forms to send in, what to send to whom, etc. I recommend finding a method to track such changes and processes, and updating your notes every time something is modified.

Get contracts in place for work up front. If you teach a class, you should have a contract before the course begins, but you will sometimes find that a contract won't come your way until the course has already begun. This is okay if you trust the school. Be sure to keep a copy for your files and let the university know if you haven't been paid.

You may also be asked to develop a course; it isn't unusual that you might ask for right of first refusal in teaching it. You should also know exactly how much you are being paid and what the conditions of the contract are. In the online world, administration can change frequently and sometimes promises are left unfulfilled, or you don't know who your new manager is or who to ask for courses when you are forgotten in the scheduling. This is one reason why networking is so vital. I cannot tell you how many times I have sent an email to a boss asking for my status and to be assigned a course, only to have it bounce back and no other contact information available. I have gone to networking forums and asked others for the current contact person.

Have a backup plan for light teaching loads. This is a particular problem in the summertime when enrollments drop. In the past eight years, my income has dropped in half (or more) every year come June. Every time this occurs, your paycheck drops with it. This might be an opportunity for a mini-vacation, but you need to plan for it. You might want to consult or do paid research on the side for extra income, particularly in these situations. When you don't have classes, remember to remind your bosses that you do in fact exist and are eager to work hard for them. I know how anxiety producing it can be to not know your status and not be on schedule.

Don't lower standards for your students just to gain popularity points. If a boss asks you to do this, take note and get out as soon as you can. Education is precious, and for some reason it seems to be the only commodity in which customers want less than what they paid for. If you spell out your standards to your students on day one, you can hold them to these standards without fear.

During the last week of a course, don't be surprised to see several of your students with family emergencies, some of which are obviously fabricated. It becomes impossible to decipher the real excuses from the made-up ones, so the best advice is to stick to your stated policies unless the student provides documentation of the excuse or you are directed by your boss to make an exception. If you find yourself being questioned for failing students who deserve to fail and lectured on how the school is a business first and cannot afford to lose these students (or their money), then you have found yourself in the midst of a diploma mill wannabe. It may be accredited and legal, but is willing to sacrifice academic standards for the sake of money; if this makes you cringe, then leave. Remember that there are many places to teach and you don't need to sell your soul for this lifestyle.

Adding Opportunities at New Universities

Having experience as an adjunct at various schools, even at some of the less-than-prestigious colleges, will help you find jobs elsewhere and will open doors to other positions. You need to stay networked, help your managers, help your colleagues, and maintain your social media profiles. If you have a master's degree, you should seriously consider working on a doctorate. If you are already terminally degreed, consider improving your professional skills, attending seminars regularly, and reading and taking courses on being a more effective teacher. When you complete something of significance, send an email to your boss to update your profile.

One way to add new universities is to network with people in your training course. Adjuncts often discuss what happens at other schools that they work for in a different school's training session. This is done to find best practices, share personal examples, and so forth. If you notice Joe Smith works for XYZ College and you'd like to work there, perhaps send him an email introducing yourself and asking him how he applied and began working for XYZ. You might want to have some online conversations in the discussion boards first to make your name is more familiar to Joe before you send a message. It's important to offer something in return!

If someone refers you to a university, offer to do the same. Once you make online friends and contacts, you should create a list of people you send new opportunities or referrals to regularly, and ask that they do the same for you. You will find an incredibly networked environment in the online teaching world. Some people are better at networking than others, but in an online environment you need to do it and you need to do it well. You will quickly make friends, and possibly enemies, so be careful what you say. Chances are the person you offend knows someone or works for someone where you work or where you apply.

Remember, a bad referral has your name written all over it! I once referred someone for course development work who flaked on the Vice President. I was the first person she phoned and she was very angry. While I explained that my experience with this candidate had been strong in the past, she was still very upset and frustrated. It took some time for me to regain her trust.

It isn't unusual or unexpected to work for and inquire at many universities at the same time. You may choose to list only some of them on your CV once you work for many. Just be sure you can manage your workload effectively.

Managing Your Cash Flow: The Ups and Downs of Contract Work

As an adjunct, in particular, you'll find very quickly that you have a rather peculiar cash flow situation; for some months, you may have none! Every school has its own pay schedule. Some are monthly, some biweekly, some quarterly – you name it.

You will need to budget yourself well, and find a way to keep track of which schools owe you and what they owe you for, as well as when the amount was payable to you and when you should receive it. If you aren't paid within a week or so of the expected time frame, send a tactful email to your boss and/or the administrative assistant inquiring after the status. In other words, don't count on being paid promptly, and do assume you will need to be your own accountant. Many schools aren't good at tracking adjunct pay—in particular, the items that you may be paid hourly or all at once for.

I recommend not counting on anything by any particular date, unless a university has a decent payroll system. Some schools send out a pay schedule in advance, and even send you a new one when your course load is modified. These are great schools and they often pay every two weeks, leaving you less stressed.

Some universities will make you a W-2 employee, meaning they will withhold taxes. Other schools will send you a 1099 form for your work at the end of the year as an independent contractor. It is becoming far more common to be an employee due to Internal Revenue Service (IRS) requirements, making it easier for schools, and Affordable Care Act adherence. Many instructors set up businesses to manage their money and maximize their work-related expenses to be deductible for income tax purposes.

Talk with a tax professional and/or accountant if you aren't sure how to do this and you're beginning to make money teaching. The fee won't be worth it for income of $10,000 per year, but when you start making six figures and the tax man comes to collect his 35%, you won't be a happy camper if you haven't planned properly. In general, I recommend obtaining the advice of a tax expert.

There are various ways you can set up your business for a high workload, and there are various tasks you'll need to do for each setup, like possibly having an Employee Identification Number (EIN) registered with the Internal Revenue Service (IRS), for instance. Incorporating or creating a sole proprietorship may open up tax advantages, along with some unexpected costs.

Also, be sure to check on the requirements of your county or city for business licenses. Some cities require that if you do business at all out of your home, you have to have a business license. This is a way for the city to generate revenue. Some states' franchise tax boards and state tax authorities report your business activity to the city, and you'll receive a lovely letter requiring you to register your business. You don't want to be scrambling or paying fines, so find out the rules ahead of time. I'm not a CPA, so find one and get solid advice.

Not All Teaching Opportunities Are Created Equal

By now, you have a good feel for what will take tremendous time with little financial gain, what will take time with a great feel-good factor, and what isn't worth doing, plain and simple. If you can find a way to quantify your time and to document what is most worth your effort, you can give good, positively spun, feedback to your bosses and also make decisions later when your workload is high and you need to weed out the bad stuff – or, if you're lucky, the not so hot stuff. Start noting which universities require more of your free time and don't pay for substantial efforts of work. These may be on your hit list when you have one.

Referring Others

Once you're in a university and you've earned respect (you may even be a subject matter expert), it's perfectly acceptable, and universities appreciate it, if you refer qualified candidates. "Qualified" doesn't necessarily mean they are your friends! They might also be your friends, but they must be people you're willing to put your reputation on the line for. If you're highly respected at a university, your selected candidates may skip through much of the interview process. You may have been hired at some schools this way. Networking is very strong and an intense requirement in this online world.

Remember everything you write in public can be seen by potential employers. Screen your referrals as you would if you were doing the hiring. One mistake can damage your reputation, and it isn't worth it. Many of us are asked hundreds of times in a year for a referral, and unless we really know you and your work, we just can't do it.

Remember to be kind to those who help you. If you are not comfortable actively referring a person, you can still direct that person to the website, as there is a difference between giving directions for getting hired and personally sending in someone's resume with a recommendation for hiring.

Go For It!

Working as an adjunct will give you tremendous flexibility to do all sorts of things, like writing books, for instance. Remember that there are many ways to boost your career, and try not to look at your newfound free time as vacation time. You need to publish, you need to research, and you need to put yourself out there to truly make it in a market that has gotten very competitive. Make yourself invaluable to students and to your bosses; this will only appreciate your value to universities and add to your influence.

The better networked you are and the more you are liked, the more doors will open. Stay focused; stay tuned into yourself, your managers, and, more important, your students. As more people realize what a terrific career this is, expect the demand to continue to rise. With state schools and private colleges creating online programs, there is plenty of work for all of us.

Above all else, have fun. A Chinese proverb says, "There are two kinds of jobs a man can do – the one he loves and the one he does best. If they're both the same, he's truly blessed." It is my hope and desire that you are truly blessed.

Should you have questions or comments, suggestions on future material, or tips, feel free to email Dani at DBabb@thebabbgroup.com or visit our website at www.thebabbgroup.com. We offer numerous community forums, places to share job search tips, job openings, and advice from the authors! We offer seminars, supplemental materials, and newsletters on our website too!

INDEX